Eva Marsal, Barbara Weber,
Susan T. Gardner (Eds.)

Respect:
How Do We Get There?

Philosophie in der Schule
Philosophy in Schools
Philosophie à l'École

herausgegeben von/edited by/sous la direction de

Band / Volume 19

LIT

Respect: How Do We Get There?

A Philosophical Inquiry

edited by

Eva Marsal, Barbara Weber, Susan T. Gardner

LIT

Front Cover by Kirk Madison, Vancouver

Printed with the kind and generous support
of the University of Education Karlsruhe

This book is printed on acid-free paper.

Bibliographic information published by the Deutsche Nationalbibliothek
The Deutsche Nationalbibliothek lists this publication in the Deutsche Nationalbibliografie; detailed bibliographic data are available in the Internet at http://dnb.d-nb.de.

ISBN 978-3-643-90406-5

A catalogue record for this book is available from the British Library

Klosbachstr. 107
CH-8032 Zürich
Tel. +41 (0) 44-251 75 05
Fax +41 (0) 44-251 75 06
E-Mail: zuerich@lit-verlag.ch
http://www.lit-verlag.ch

LIT VERLAG Dr. W. Hopf
Berlin 2013
Fresnostr. 2
D-48159 Münster
Tel. +49 (0) 2 51-62 03 20
Fax +49 (0) 2 51-23 19 72
E-Mail: lit@lit-verlag.de
http://www.lit-verlag.de

Distribution:
In Germany: LIT Verlag Fresnostr. 2, D-48159 Münster
Tel. +49 (0) 2 51-620 32 22, Fax +49 (0) 2 51-922 60 99, E-mail: vertrieb@lit-verlag.de

In Austria: Medienlogistik Pichler-ÖBZ, e-mail: mlo@medien-logistik.at
In the UK: Global Book Marketing, e-mail: mo@centralbooks.com
In North America: International Specialized Book Services, e-mail: orders@isbs.com
e-books are available at www.litwebshop.de

Dedicated to Dr. Richard (Mort) Morehouse,
Professor Emeritus at Viterbo University (Wisconsin, USA)

Richard (Mort) Morehouse is Professor Emeritus at Viterbo University (Wisconsin, USA) and Visiting Professor at Glyndwr University Wrexham (Wales, UK). He is the author of *Beginning Interpretative Inquiry: a step-by-step guide to research and evaluation* (2012) and co-author of *Beginning Qualitative Inquiry: a philosophical and practical guide* (1994). He was a Co-Editor, *Analytic Teaching*, (1990 to 1996) and editor of *Analytic Teaching: The Community of Inquiry Journal* (1996 – 2008) and past president of the North American Association for Community of Inquiry (1994 – 2010). His work in education, psychology, and philosophy for children has been published in the United States, the United Kingdom, Finland, and Denmark.

Forward

Most of the papers contained herein were presented at the North American Association of the Community of Inquiry (NAACI) conference in Vancouver, Canada, in June 2012. The suggested topic for the conference was: **RESPECT (for self, for others, for animals, for cultures or cultural practises, for the environment, etc).** *What precisely do we mean (or ought we to mean) by respect, how ought we to adjudicate between conflicting demands of respect, (e.g., respect for self and respect for others, or respect for others who have conflicting demands, or respect for humans versus respect for the environment, etc.), and what obstacles stand in the way of respect.*

The first paper presented in this anthology is an attempt to synthesize the various positions presented at the conference, as well as the various issues that arose during the conference itself, e.g., how the inequity of respect built into gender roles played out in the conference discussions, and so on.

Not all papers presented at the conference are included in this anthology, and one is not presented at the conference at all (Gardner's synthesis). As well, some of the content (even some titles) of the papers have changed since their initial presentation. Nonetheless, an in-depth, exacting, and exciting analysis of the notion of respect awaits the reader—an analysis that we believe has the potential to have lasting and extensive practical consequences.

We say this because we believe that a "viralized," robust "respect for persons" would fundamentally transform the world into a better place. Likewise, we believe that *a* (perhaps *the*) major obstacle that stands in the way of that ideal is a pervasive lack of understanding of what respect requires of us. And clearly, if we (who are presumably "in the know") do not understand what respect requires of us, we cannot teach this *to* our children, let alone even know what respect requires of us in interacting *with* our children.

Our hope is that this anthology will help to annihilate the obstacle of conceptual confusion and, in so doing, guide us toward a future saturated with respect. The title of this book is *Respect: How Do We Get There? A Philosophical Inquiry.* We offer this anthology, in other words, in the hope that this philosophical inquiry is precisely what we need to get there from here.

Eva Marsal, Barbara Weber, Susan T. Gardner

Contents

Susan T. Gardner
(Canada)

The Complexity of Respecting together: From the Point of view of one Participant of the 2012 Vancouver NAACI Conference[1]

Dedication: I would like to dedicate this essay to ***Mort Morehouse,*** *whose intelligence, warmth, and good humour sustains NAACI to this day. I would like, too, to dedicate this essay to* ***Nadia Kennedy*** *who, in her paper* ***"****Respecting the Complexity of CI," suggests that respect for the rich non-reductive emergent memories and understandings that evolve out of participating in the sort of complex communicative interactions that we experienced at the 2012 NAACI conference requires "a turning around and looking back so that we might understand it better." Thus, though "we cannot grasp the essence of the system in some determinate way, since each description provides a limited view, and portrays some aspect of the system from a specific position inside or outside it, and at a specific point in time," nonetheless respect requires that we try "to take different 'snapshots' of such systems and attempt to make sense of them." It is as a result of this urging that the following snapshot was attempted. My thanks to Nadia for being such an inspiration, and to all the participants for making this conference such a memorable occasion.*

Note: All references are to papers presented at the Vancouver 2012 June/July NAACI conference unless otherwise noted. Since none are published as of yet (August 2012), referencing will be informal (see reference list). My apologies for any misrepresentation or under-representation. My apologies, too, for non-representation of the fruitful contributions of non-presenters.

Does respect require unconditional regard?

The notion of respect seems inherently confused. Children are taught that they ought to respect their parents, their teachers, indeed, all their classmates. Adults are lectured about the need for respecting all persons—a touchstone that some argue anchors human rights. But what precisely does this notion of respect mean?

Many believe that respect, as used in the above edicts, requires that one avoid acting or speaking in ways that the other, whether present or not, might find unpleasant or offensive (extreme cases being the exception). Interestingly, this subliminal understanding became evident at the 2012 Vancouver NAACI conference when a number of those present expressed discomfort at "the way the conversation was going" following a presentation on the issue of "Respect and the Veil" (Susan Gardner). The central argument of Gardner's paper was that since face covering (as in the burka or the niqab) appears to those outside the practice as being potentially oppressive, and since those who wear the face covering know this (an analogy of crying

[1] This paper was also published in *Analytic Teaching and Philosophical Praxis*. Vol. 13, 2012. 1-12.

fire in a theater), and since the face covering tends to preclude the possibility of genuine communicative interaction so that the presence or absence of oppression cannot be estimated (leaving those who are concerned about the oppression women in an impossible bind), and since loyalty to the Muslim tradition can be visibly upheld by wearing the hijab (head scarf), the paper concluded that "the practice of face covering and respect for that practice are . . . incompatible."

Many who joined the Communal Inquiry following the paper suggested that the argument, in and of itself, was insulting to those women who "voluntarily" wear the face covering—an insult that was doubly egregious as it smacked of imperialist arrogance, i.e., that those outside the practice have no business judging those inside the practice. Many expressed discomfort in subjecting this sensitive issue to overt critical inquiry at all—thus, at least subliminally, supporting the intuition that speaking in a way that the other, whether present or not, might find unpleasant or offensive was somehow disrespectful.

This reluctance to get into the judging game (does respect not require that we avoid it?) was one of the central issues that was the focus on the 2012 NAACI conference, so it is ironic that the distaste for judging emerged surreptitiously in a conference whose focus was to analyze this very issue. Such reticence, interestingly, also underscored the point made by Dale Cannon in his paper "P4C, Community of Inquiry, and Methodological Faith" in which he noted the important role that *faith* plays in process of critical inquiry, i.e., that participants in Communal Inquiry must have *faith* that something of value will come from the process of *doubt* (hence the claim that the role of doubt is subordinate to and serves *faith* in reasoned inquiry). As Cannon notes: "To give oneself over to reasoned inquiry clearly involves a sort of venture that is fraught with uncertainty and risk."

In this particular instance, faith in the method seemed weak. However, happily, it blossomed through most of the ensuing tangles over many equally contentious issues, a central one of which was the general topic of the degree to which respect required unconditional regard.

Respect does not require unconditional regard?

The first paper of the conference, by its very title, i.e., "To Tolerate Means to Insult," took issue with the suggestion that a bland hands-off non-judgmental "tolerant" attitude is a form of respect. In it, Barbara Weber quoted Marcuse as warning that "tolerance gives the aloof and uncaring majority of people a 'legitimate reason' (in form of an accepted value) to stand back, even when they are direct witnesses of social injustice or violence; and the ruling class welcomes this 'cultivated indifference' in the form of tolerance, because they can proceed with their practices and sustain the system of power" (95f). Gardner, in an article published elsewhere (2009), makes a similar point, though with a tangential focus, when she warns the *Philosophy for Children* community against adopting "caring thinking" as one of its primary educational goals, as the very name tends to anesthetize both students and teachers against the frequent need not only to judge, but to stand up against injustice and individuals perpetrating harm. Lena Green referred to this point in her paper, entitled "Philosophical Inquiry as a Means of Teaching Respect in South African Classrooms," in which she notes that "though teachers in South African schools are aware of the need to respect diversity, it is far from clear at what point diversity becomes unacceptable and is no longer a right." Green refers to Gardner (2009) as arguing that "there are circumstances (e.g. bullying) in which approval and respect is not appropriate" (3, 4).

The argument that respect does not require unconditional regard also threaded its way through Gardner's paper "Gifting Freedom, Not Favour," in which she argues not only that unconditional regard is not required, but that such an attitude can be ethically contemptible. This is so because selves and their corresponding sense of agency develop as a function of intersubjective *practical* reasoning, i.e., we become aware of (and hence gain control over) our actions as a result of the changing evaluative responses of others toward our own actions. A bland "'I'm okay, you're okay, and it's okay', within which nobody really cares what other people are doing or whether or not their cultural practices are acceptable" (Weber), would quite literally obliterate the intersubjective mirror which keeps an agent's freedom alive.

Jason Howard, in his paper "Claims of Conscience and the Space of Reasons," echoes a similar position with the argument that an individual's sense of agency emerges in interpersonal *judgemental* interaction. Howard quotes Ricoeur as defining imputability as "the ascription of action to [an] agent, *under the condition of ethical and moral predicates* which characterize the action as good, just, conforming to duty, done out of duty, and finally, as being the wisest in the case of conflictual situations" (292). Howard defines this awakening of our capacity for accountability as "conscience," and he argues that its specific function is best understood when seen in reference to the core moral emotions of guilt, shame and pride. "More specifically," he says, "conscience mediates the inherent volatility, disruptiveness and alienating effects of these moral emotions, empowering agents to see themselves as the author and proponent of these emotions rather than their victim." I take Howard to be arguing here that it is in response to the changing and potentially threatening judgments of others (hence shame and guilt), that conscience and its integrating power of reason emerges. Thus, Howard says that "we come to the world of reasons as a way of appropriating the hold that values have on us," and that "we come to care about rationality and the power of reasons not primarily because of a desire to be correct or consistent, as much as from the ability of reasons to disclose and amplify our capacities and concerns." "One's sense of self-worth," in other words, "is always in negotiation with others, for better or worse."

Mort Morehouse, in his paper "Thinking about 'Gifting Freedom, Not Favour' and Our Future," also underscores the importance of intersubjective negotiation for self-maintenance by warning us about the potential deleterious impact of distorted communication on those who are immersed in social media in general, and who interact with robots in particular. Morehouse refers to Sherry Turkle's research (2011) on robots (e.g., companions for senior citizens, pets for children), as well as the use of texting and other electronic ways of connecting with others. With regard to robots, Turkle's research indicates that we seek uncomplicated affection from robots as well as uncomplicated affection toward these objects. Morehouse notes that what is of concern to Turkle is that, in these situations, the robots can become more real and often more consistent than "real" people, hence alerting us to the fact that such "unconditional regard" (of and to robots) can become so addicting that it can blind us to the freedom-diminishing impact of a responsibility vacuum. And Morehouse also notes Turkle's concern about the safety and superficiality of connecting through social media, which tends to bring with it a diminished propensity to take the deep risks of uncertain connections in "lived" interactions. Thus, Morehouse quotes Turkle as noting that many people "nurture friendships on social-networking sites and then wonder if they are among friends. They are connected all day but are not sure they have communicated. They become confused about companionship" (17).

Respect requires *value*-communicative-interaction

The arguments presented by Weber, Gardner, Howard and Morehouse harmonize toward the message that due to our intersubjective dependency, respect requires that we attempt to engage in authentic dialogue with others—the authenticity of which would inevitably require honesty with regard to one's evaluative stance. The approaches, however, slip slightly from each other with regard to the optimism for success of convergence. Thus Howard ends his paper with the comment that "Nothing can or should undermine the imperative of finding common moral ground with others, least of all our conscience." And Weber ends her paper saying "in our movement towards the other, in this continuous approach and dialogue, we gain a momentary understanding (of ourselves, of the world, of other people). Due to freedom and alterity, our understanding of the other will always remain fractal: he will forever elude our ultimate grasp. But this call will lead to the continuous return to his/her Otherness."

In contrast to these hopeful positions that dialogue with the other is always possible and always potentially positive, Gardner, since her investigation begins by focusing on the question of what kind of respect is owed a serial rapist/killer, is more obvious in recognizing that a meeting of minds may not be possible and, in many cases, should not be expected (e.g., the tragedy of the years of naïve American confidence that they would find common ground with the Nazis, despite years of shocking Jewish oppression long before the outbreak of the war, and even after the 1934 public declaration given by Goebbels, the Nazi propaganda minister, that Jews were "the syphilis of all European peoples" (Larson, 2011)). Gardner argues that respect in the sense of striving toward mutuality may, in certain circumstances, be inappropriate, but that nonetheless "recognition respect" demands that we view the other as a member of the moral community in the sense that the person is capable of controlling his/her actions and thus s/he is someone who is accountable. Thus, Gardner notes that "Though attitudes of disapprobation and indignation may short-circuit what Darwall calls 'appraisal respect' (122), they are not in the least disrespectful in the sense of suggesting that I view you as other than a member of the moral community. As Strawson points out 'The partial withdrawal of goodwill . . . is, rather, the consequence of continuing to view (the other) as a member of the moral community; only as one who has offended against it'" (16).

Value-communicative-interaction: A tripartite distinction

The slippage between the above points of view, along with the initial intuition that there are areas that are truly none of our business (it is not our place to judge), suggest that, with regard to the claim that "respect carries the imperative of value-communicative-interaction," there might ultimately be three positions: (1) the "intolerant," (2) the "engaged," and (3) the "tolerant."

Based on his paper "Taking Interreligious Dialogue to the M.A.T. (Martial Arts Technique): Toward a Rethinking of Respect and Dialogue with the Interreligious Other," Eugene Muhammad would, I think, only be prepared to recognize #2. I will therefore briefly comment on the potential disagreement with respect to #1 and #3 below.

THE INTOLERANT POSITION: An imperative to demonstrate a "stand up and be counted" intolerance of those positions that appear to have no merit whatsoever and which will result in great harm (e.g., a serial rapist/killer, Goebbels, bullies, etc). In such cases, one can be described as intolerant in the sense that, though one may enter communication with the other, *one does so knowing from the start that one will not be persuaded* (an initial position that would disqualify the claim of genuine dialogue), but knowing that communication ought to be attempted nonetheless in the hope that some kind of mutual understanding will lay the groundwork for effective accountability. Muhammad, by contrast, seems to suggest that it is not only possible, but desirable, to engage in every dialogue with the understanding that one might be "converted." He refers to terrorists to drive this point home. In contrast, one could argue that while there is huge merit to try, where possible, to bring oneself fully and authentically to the table, the result surely would simply be hypocrisy if one pretended to see the merits of a position that had no merit, e.g., someone who bayoneted children for fun.

THE ENGAGED POSITION: An imperative to engage in "personhood-maintaining practical-reasoning with others" (Gardner "Gifting"), i.e., being prepared to continuously reason with others to try and parse out what sort of rules ought to govern the behaviours and judgements of all reasonable people. Gardner reminds us that given that only genuine "second-personal reasoning" can contribute to the maintenance of our mutual freedom (as opposed to raw judgemental attitudes or the mental manipulation of 'faux reasoning' that can be destructive of our freedom), it is important that we make explicit the implicit assumptions that reasoners must make in order for this sort of reasoning to be efficacious. These assumptions are: (1) that we agree on a common *non-subjective position-guiding* reasoning process (i.e., you must be prepared to follow reason where they lead, including changing your mind); (2) that the goal is a common perspective *anchored by reason* (i.e., the goal is not just to persuade); (3) that our initial positions are different and that we are comfortable with that (i.e., something to be cherished); (4) that there is some common value-overlap (we know that a meeting of the minds is in principle possible); and (5) that we see one another as equal in this freedom-producing accountability relationship.

It is of note that virtually none of these conditions are present in the "intolerant position."

THE TOLERANT POSITION: An imperative to remain silent in the absence of invitation (despite what could be described as an imperative to *think it out* so as to understand one's own position). In light of the fact that genuinely "engaged" dialogue is hard and time-consuming work, it is clear that it can and should only be activated with regard to behaviours and judgments that matter. And while there is no doubt that there can be much disagreement with regard to what behaviours and judgments really matter (see discussion above with regard to the veil), nonetheless, it is vital that we prioritize our commitments with regard to what we believe are fundamental for maintaining the good life for us all. In other words, there is lots of "stuff" about which we can, without shame or guilt, remain "aloof." Since Muhammad is committed to the importance of pervasive deep authentic dialogue in general, and interreligious dialogue in particular, he would be concerned with the suggestion that I ought to simply "tolerant" your belief in the Big Pumpkin (or whatever). According to Muhammad, religious people ought to dialogue "to the death," i.e., enter the dialogue being prepared to convert. However, it is of note that for Muhammad "a religious person is neither a fanatic nor someone who already has all the answers." Since such a description does not fit any religious person I know, Muhammad's view on the need to enter dialogue with those who "know they already to have all the answers" needs further discussion.

Respect for the power of relationship

The crucial mechanism that fuels self-conscious agency is the ability of the emerging (expanding) agent to see the changing evaluation of her actions in the responses of those in her social circle. There are two things of note with regard to this process. The first is the notion of the *social circle*. Clearly the influence that any value judgement might have will vary as a function of the *quality* of the bond between the agent and the other. Young Johnny, for instance, will clearly care less about the negative evaluation of a grumpy neighbour than he will about the disapproval of his beloved mother. Speaking in tune with the notion, Eva Marsal, in her paper, "The Concept of Respect – a Philosophical Challenge," argues that the *affective* degree of respect *felt* or *not felt* is dependent on the relative proximity to the object," and that the closer we "zoom in" on the referent, the more concrete the web of conditions becomes which induces us to say "We respect X."

This fact, that "the quality of the bond affects the quality of the influence," while clearly having important pervasive *general* implications, has critical ramifications with regard to *education* in particular. That is, if we presume that agents live in a social world of concentric circles characterized by succeedingly weaker bonds, it follows that part of an educator's job is to ensure that she is perceived within the influential inner circles of her students if she hopes to be effective.

The second not-unrelated thing of note with regard to the process of perceiving the changing evaluation of one's actions from the viewpoints of others lies in the notion of *change.* That is, since it is *change* in the evaluative stance of the other that acts as a "somatic marker" (Gardner, "Gifting"), it is important to keep in mind that what is perceived as negative will be a function of the baseline quality of the relationship. Those who have had the privilege of swimming in a sea of highly positive regard can testify that even a hint of disappointment can have a life-changing impact. Thus, since *pervasive* (as opposed to "unconditional") positive regard helps to ensure a close-circle location thus increasing the potential for educative influence, and since *pervasive* positive regard also fuels the power to transmit a negative evaluation with minimal negativity (e.g., the raising of an eyebrow) which, in turn, helps preserve the inner location, it could be argued that *pervasive* positive regard, *at least insofar as it is not unwarranted (i.e., when intolerance is not more appropriate),* may be an important element in respecting others, at least in the sense of optimizing value-communicative interchange.

This claim that ***quality*** *relationship* underpins our interdependent self-consciousness calls to mind part of the message of Jessica Davis's paper entitled "Being Participation: The Ontology of the Socratic Method." Though her primary focus is on the use of the Socratic Method in educational settings, Davis's central message is that preserving/creating relationships is a basic good underived from other values. As Davis points out, "engaging as such is what it means to *be*. . . . We *are* participation." Thus, since I exist and grow as a function of our communicative interchange, and since you do as well, and since our responsibility for responsibilizing one another is, in the process, discharged, the inherent value of relationship *per se* becomes manifest. Dialogue against the background of pervasive positive regard is valuable because, in a slight variation of Davis's words, it best facilitates the means by which each person develops their practical identity and *engages in being*. We are inherently interconnected and, as such, dialogue is a method conducive to self knowledge and wisdom; we can't know anything – even ourselves – without recognizing our interdependent ontology. Thus Davis quotes Paulo Freire (89) as saying that "Love is at the same time the foundation of dialogue and dialogue itself." As a testament to this very principle, Claudia Ruitenberg and Parvaneh Ghazinezhad argue in their paper "Is Respecting Children's Rationality in Their Best Interest in an Authoritarian Society?" that the mere hope that youngsters might one day learn to own their own thinking is sufficient reward for attempting to engage them in transformative Communal Inquiry despite the dangers (both to students and teachers) of so doing in a highly authoritarian country. As a testament to the love of which Freire speaks, Parvaneh quite literally takes up this challenge.

Creating possibilities through respect

In his paper "Respect and Dignity in The Discourse Between The Private And The Public Space," Jan Kleine argues that with regard to respect, we ought to do away with "artificial" forms, i.e., the kind of "public" respect as in respect for an office, e.g., the presidency, or the general "respect for persons," and focus, instead on the respect deserved (concrete or private respect). Thus, according to Kleine, a misbehaving president ought not to be respected.

On the surface, this view seems to run counter to Gardner who argues in favor of the need for "recognition" (or *abstract*) respect in the sense of "being prepared to participate in the game of interpersonal practical reasoning." Gardner notes however that this abstract respect actually requires that one be prepared to engage in "appraisal" or *concrete* judgments of others. Gardner thus notes that "It is imperative to keep in mind . . . that participant reactive reasoning is inherently judgmental. I can send the message that I believe that you are *free* not to do what you are doing only through the message that you *ought* not to be doing what you are doing (or sending its mirror image of praise)."

Thus, where Kleine sees a collision between recognition (abstract) and appraisal (concrete) respect, Gardner does not. This may be because, from Kleine's point of view, public respect toward various offices or roles demands a kind of corresponding "submission," and that this allows occupants to misbehave in ways that would otherwise be found utterly unacceptable, i.e., abstract respect might warp concrete respect. And there is surely merit to this view, i.e., that *roles per se* garner respect. Thus, we expect, do we not, a kind of reverential attitude not only toward the obvious revered roles of heads of state or dignitaries, but also toward virtually anyone occupying publically recognized roles, e.g., doctors, lawyers, teachers, parents, etc. Indeed, it is hard to see how a society could function without such role-respect. Interestingly, Eva Marsal's account of how students at the University for Children in Bretten, Germany, reflect on the concept "respect" supports these very points. Marsal quotes 8-year old Laura as saying that she would have a whole lot of respect for the mayor who would soon be visiting her school, and 11-year-old Louisa as saying that "respect is important because …if nobody respected anyone else there would be total chaos."

Differences aside, however, Kleine's initial question as to why we should respect a misbehaving president lays bare a function of respect that often goes unnoticed, namely the importance of **creating possibilities through respect**. What I mean by this is that, in **respecting roles *per se*** (what most certainly would be classified as "abstract respect"), we create the possibility of an individual inhabiting that role. Thus, in respecting the role of the teacher by, e.g., inhabiting the role of the student, I create the possibility of an individual becoming a teacher. If I did not, if instead I argued with every suggestion that the teacher made, or, in the words of 11-year-old Marvin, if students just kept getting up and running around the classroom (Marsal), the teacher would be unable to teach. And similarly, if I did not respect the role of self-conscious personhood by holding the other accountable, I would not create the possibility of other becoming self-conscious and hence accountable.

What is particularly intriguing in the above cases is that, in neither of these instances, am I respecting an *actual* individual. I am, rather, respecting *the possibility of what an individual might become*. This is, in a sense, a forward looking, but presently vacant, respect. However, precisely because of its lack of concreteness, this sort of respect can be fragile since it is maintained solely as a result of mutual agreement. If we break ranks and start accusing the Emperor of wearing no clothes, the emperor will indeed be seen as naked. If we refuse to insist that our students respect the role of the teacher, we will have no teachers. Thus, Kleine seems right in maintaining that roles *per se* seem to call for submission, even if the individual occupying the role falls short of expectations. However, in contrast to Kleine, it could be argued that, at least for the roles that contribute positively to societal functioning, that is a small price to pay for role-maintenance; and that rather than losing respect for the role when an occupant falls drastically short of role-expectations, the appropriate response would be that that individual be dismissed from the role, precisely in order to maintain respect for the "possibility-creating" power of roles.

On the other hand, Kleine's challenge rings out an important warning, namely that we ought to be blind neither to "naked Emperors," nor to royalty in servants' garb. Reflecting back on the "veil issue," I have in mind here gender roles that persistently and stubbornly ensure that those occupying the male role are often saturated in unearned respect, while those who occupy the female role (particularly the mother role) often suffer from a pervasive lack of "abstract respect" along with the limited possibilities that such lack of respect entails. What is interesting about the later situation is that it suggests that abstract respect for roles may, in part, be a necessary condition at least for some sorts of concrete individual (appraisal) respect (e.g., since mothering *per se* is not respected, excellence in motherhood isn't either). What is interesting, too, about the latter situation is that, had the discussion with regard to "Respect and the Veil" been couched in terms of abstract respect (i.e., that the veil is worrying because of its impact on the "role of women" rather than women *per se*), it might have been seemed less potentially insulting to those actual women who wear the veil.

All in all, then, it turns out that the distinction (and potential connection) between recognition and appraisal respect, or between abstract respect for roles that create (or limit) possibilities, and evaluative judgments of actual concrete others, is clearly one that needs to be kept at the forefront of our understanding, if we are to gain a deeper appreciation of the multi-dimensional role (Marsal) that respect plays in our lives.

Silence as a sign of "respect deficit"

Picking up on the theme of gender roles in the conference itself, it came as a shock to participants when it was noted near the end of the conference by our Washington State colleagues (Jana Mohr Lone, Sara Goering, and David Shapiro), who gave an intriguing presentation entitled " The Connection between Respect, Inquiry and Philosophy for Children," that though the gender representation at the conference was equal (18 males to 18 females, including non-presenters), approximately 80% of voices in response to the various papers were male. When this was brought to our attention, it is of particular interest that 80% of the enthusiastic responses were again male—some saying they didn't believe it, some saying they found it unsurprising given the pervasive, often invisible, forces of the patriarchal society in which we live, some talked about feeling self-critical because they knew they frequently occupied an inordinate amount of talk-time but seemed unable to stop, and some said that even if it were true, it wasn't necessarily a bad thing since, after all, many females had not been aware of this inequity, thus echoing the second response that many of us have become habituated to the patriarchal status quo. The latter point, that the women in the room were unaware of and/or not upset by the male monopoly of talk-time, interestingly reflects a point made in Christine Ng's paper, entitled "The 'Problem' of Quiet Students," in which she says that silence isn't necessarily a bad thing, i.e., that silence on the part of participants in Communal Inquiry may be a function of the fact that they are so wrapped up in, and presumably benefiting from, the argument that they fail to notice the source of the comments, or even their own relative silence.

Nonetheless, though silence may not necessarily indicate a lack of inclusion or benefit, the bottom line of Ng's paper was that those who facilitate dialogue have a responsibility to create strategies that discourage monopoly and its co-variant, lack of overt participation, since, clearly, the greatest benefit of dialogical interchange accrues to those who are actively involved. Active engagement, after all, ensures that one can grow as a function of testing one's viewpoints against those of others, and it ensures that one gets practice in, and hence becomes more efficient at, quickly formulating one's own views coherently. And, as was previously noted, overt engagement is also the active ingredient out of which relational bonds are formed—all of which leads us to an interesting paradox. On the one hand, believing that one is well-placed in one's social relationships (e.g., the "respect-saturated male role") is a necessary condition for being comfortable in throwing oneself into genuine dialogue, and yet, on the other hand, genuine and engaged dialogue is a necessary condition for creating relationship. Thus, on the assumption that women (who occupy an under-respected gender role) tend to be more intimidated by bonded-dialoging, respect-saturated men than the other way around, and if the result is that men feel more comfortable than women in expressing their viewpoints, and, as a result, in fact do so, then this will create even stronger bonds between the men who are talking, who, in turn, will feel even more at ease to speak in the safe place in which they have already created bonds. It is thus a self-sustaining process, and it is to Christine's credit that she brings what's in the shadow of those who talk front and centre in her paper. In that regard, we ought to heed Ng's argument that teachers and facilitators have a serious responsibility to be alert to the quiet voices who may be under-confident due to the "respect deficit" of the roles that they occupy, while at the same time being weary of the monopolizing voices of those who may be innocently blind to the "respect deficit" of others.

And so, interestingly, we are back at the beginning. The first day of the conference brought an uncomfortable confrontation with the issue of women wearing literal veils (and how that may distort genuine participatory dialogue). In this discussion of talk-inequity, we found ourselves uncomfortably confronted with the issue of women wearing invisible veils (and how that may distort genuine participatory dialogue). In this regard, Gardner (Veil) quotes Susan Sherwin as noting that the capacity to at least recognize and possibly (*perhaps even easily*) resist structures that may be oppressive (40) is a necessary condition of gender equity. Sherwin also notes that it is the *society*, not just the agent, that ought to be the subject of critical scrutiny under the rubric of what Sherwin refers to as "*relational autonomy*" (42). This "scrutiny of society"—in this case our own interactions during the NAACI conference—brought to light the lamentable fact that invisible oppressive forces can creep into the interactions of even well-meaning, self-reflective, highly intelligent, non-patriarchal individuals gathered within a Community of Inquiry, one of whose goals was to examine this very issue. And it demonstrates in spades that, if respect and the practice of veiling (visible or otherwise) are indeed incompatible, and if pervasive respect is the sort of ideal toward which we all aspire, then we all have our work cut out for us.

Children and animals call out for "individuating respect"

Both David Kennedy and Wendy Turgeon made a strong plea for ramping up our respect for children. Though Kennedy argued for the need to "**listen** to children," it has noted that such an edict, as it stood, carries the danger of being misrepresented as a requirement even for helicopter parents to further intensify their tendencies to indulge (pamper, cosset) youngsters, some of whom are already be on the path of becoming whining, self-centred, spoiled, narcissistic brats (!). (That such a threat is real and has serious gender implication is the topic of Elisabeth Badinter's recent book *The Conflict: How Modern Motherhood Undermines the Status of Women.*) A further suggestion was that what was needed for the flourishing of children was not so much listening *per se*, but rather authentic communication—though this suggestion too remains opaque. The possibility of an answer to what sort of respect children might require floated through Wayne Henry's paper entitled "Respect for Non-Human Animals." Though Henry's defence of a "strong animal rights position" was met with some scepticism, the challenge that Henry's paper lays at our feet is daunting. Since children are, in many ways, more like non-human animals than human adults (we don't, for example, recognize the central adult human right/responsibility of self-determination in either), we are seriously lacking in theoretical framework that sets out guidelines as to what is required with regard to the ethical treatment of either.

This need to realign our view of *both* children and animal/nature is a message found throughout Kennedy's paper. Though the title of his paper is "Why Children Deserve To Be Listened To," his general message (it seems to me) would not be drastically dislocated if one transformed its title to "Why Animality (wherever one finds it, e.g., child or nature) Deserves To Be Listened To." I say this because of Kennedy's insistence that we become sensitive to neoteny, i.e., the child within that remains through adulthood. Since the new born child is, after all, a "mere animal," becoming sensitive to neoteny surely requires that we become sensitive to our enduring animal nature. In line with this view, Kennedy refers to Marcuse (Sensibility1969) in arguing for a new sensibility "which is marked most significantly by the way we experience nature and the lived world"; for an emergent paradigm which finds its primary narrative in a "new relation to nature," and that "liberation of nature is the recovery of the life-enhancing forces in nature."[2] It is for that reason, Kennedy argues, that we must transform education so that it is "grounded in an experience of nature as a totality of life to be protected and cultivated"—a suggestion that would support Henry's crusade to enhance respect for non-human animals.

Turgeon, too, speaks to this child/animal (nature) dyadic challenge. She notes that from the adult human standpoint, many believe that "nature (from rocks to plants to many animals) need not be honoured because as inert matter, as simply 'natural,' it has no moral standing. Since nature cannot function as a moral agent, the call to acknowledge its status as a moral patient is still suspect." She goes to note that "Children and animals do offer us pause for thought: children as future-persons and animals as metaphorical humans with faces," but that "too often it is simply a pause and we return to our common ways of treating them." And though the primary focus of Turgeon's paper is the child, much insight can be gleaned (as was done with Kenndy's paper) by substituting "animal" in many of Trugeon's references to the child. So when Turgeon makes the case that there is a connection between respecting the child without (Korczak) and respecting the child within (Bachelard), one can likewise make the case that there is a connection between respecting the animal without and respecting the animal within. Similarly, when Turgeon makes the case that it is important to relearn how to see the world through the eyes of a child, one can easily make the case for the need to relearn to see the world through the eyes of the animal. Intriguingly, Turgeon actually refers to Temple Grandin, in this regard. Grandin, an autistic, believes that she is able to see the world in a less conceptualized abstract manner than the way "normal" adult humans see it, i.e., that she believes that she sees the world more like animals do. In support of this point, Grandin claims that, like animals, she actually sees trees, i.e., specific individuated trees, rather than mere instantiations of the concept of tree. If all of this is true, i.e., that our actual perception of the world becomes progressively less concrete as our ability for abstraction is enhanced, this child/animal dyadic challenge suggests that, aside from "respect for persons," we ought to construct another basic category of respect, namely "respect for individuals." That is, since we are progressively less able or less inclined to see individuals, and we ought to relearn how to do that.

This edict, that we ought to "respect individuals," asks us to don the eyes of the artist—to attempt to see what is right before our eyes. What is particularly interesting about the imperative that we ought to "respect individuals" is that seeing individuals would seem to be a necessary condition of eliciting **emotive responses** for those *actual* individuals (rather than for categories, such as "persons")—something for which Turgeon, Kennedy, and Henry all seem to be making a case. As well, this

[2] Marcuse, Nature and Revolution, p. 235

view is concurrent with the behaviourist claim that emotional responses at their most primitive (and perhaps at their most sophisticated) are elicited through *perception*: it is the stimulus that produces the response. Marsal, too, notes the importance of what *we actually see* when she reminds us that the notion of respect is derived from the Latin *respicere*, which means "to look back at" or "to look again," i.e., that respect is a particular mode of apprehending the object: that the person who respects something pays attention to it and perceives it differently from someone who does not, and responds to it in light of that perception. Marsal goes on to say (referring to Dillon) that "The idea of paying heed or giving proper attention to the object which is central to respect often means trying to see the object clearly, as it really is in its own right, and not seeing it solely through the filter of one's own desires and fears or likes and dislikes. Thus, respecting something contrasts with being oblivious or indifferent to it, ignoring or quickly dismissing it, neglecting or disregarding it, or carelessly or intentionally misidentifying it" (4).

In summary, then, if we step back and adopt a phylogenetic/epigenetic perspective, this view suggests that as we animals morph into persons, we may become so preoccupied with managing our self-worth in negotiation with others (Howard) that we lose our ability to see any entity who is not a potential partner in this epic struggle, except in energy-saving ways as instantiations of abstract concepts. We can hypothesize that relearning to *see* other actual concrete individuals (outside of any reference to the struggle for self-worth) would bring with it emotive responses different in kind from those entangled in personhood: emotions such as wonder, amazement, and un-reflected appreciation, as opposed to the emotions of conscience, such as shame, guilt and pride (Howard). It may be, too, that in "becoming present" to actual concrete others, we ourselves concretize our own individuality, i.e., we become more than simply the reflection in other people's eyes. If such is the case, it behoves us to become more aware of the fact that we are "animomorphs" rather than merely being "pedomorphs" (Kennedy), and in so doing, we may relearn to see the world through the eyes of the animal within. And in so doing, hopefully, we will thereby honour Henry's plea to see and respect the animals without, and to honour Turgeon and Kennedy's plea to see and respect the ever-morphing animals that we refer to as children. If we insert the "animal tag" into the final words of Turgeon's paper, the argument looks as follows:

> We discover our being in the world through the animal/child gaze and unless we can keep that gaze below the surface as still vital, we lose our centre. This demands that we respect the animal/child-within, even as Korczak passionately argues for the animal/children without. Respecting my animal/child-self will open up my vision of the animals/children around me in ways that I can acknowledge and hold in dialogue with my adult self and respecting animal/children around us reminds us of our own animal/child-self. Both movements, within and without, require a relational openness to the other as familiar and sharing in the "astonishment of being." And that movement can open up a window to the larger challenge to respect Being in all its manifestations.

Respecting the Limits of Communities of Inquiry

Many who are loyal to the wonders of the learning experience imbedded in participating in Communities of Inquiry may leave conferences dedicated to that topic somewhat ill at ease due to its seeming absence (with notable exceptions, of course, such as the Communal Inquiry lovingly facilitated by Rosario Del Callado at the 2012 NAACI conference). This unease emerges because conferences on the topic of Communal Inquiry often tend to resemble the more traditional format of presentation, followed by questions. The 2012 NAACI conference was no different.

Reflection on this fact brings to light two related issues, both of which speak to the question brought up by "team Alberta" (Rob Wilson, John Simpson, Jason Taylor) who challenged us to articulate where we go from here. The two issues related to *lack* of Communal Inquiry in conferences dedicated to that topic are: (1) whether teaching others how to facilitate Communities of Inquiry ought to be done solely through the use of that method, and (2) whether teaching practical reasoning, or practical wisdom, ought to rely solely on the use of Communities of Inquiry.

Beth Dixon and Charles List in their paper "Breaking the Rules of Respect" seem inclined to accept suggestion 2. They argue, on the one hand, that conceptual analysis has limited use in guiding behavior in real world circumstances, and, on the other, they argue in favour of the educative merits of, for example, participants, having been given a stimulus (such as the tale of the dancing camel who thought she had become a splendid dancer), and thereafter communally exploring such questions as: Should we aim to *only* please ourselves? Should we always please ourselves? Who should we listen to when critical advice is offered? and so on. Dixon and List argue that, through such experiences, individuals gain the habit of taking into account the myriad of particular contexts in which they will be required to make nuanced judgements.

What is interesting about Dixon and List's paper is that it ends with a plea for advice as to how best to teach various ethical concepts in varying circumstances (teaching respectful hunting was also an area that they explored). Given that their paper demonstrated the efficacy of Communal Inquiry, one wonders why the unease as to how to proceed.

The answer may lie in a subliminal recognition of the limits of the Community of Inquiry, at least insofar as it is served up "plain vanilla," i.e., a short stimulus followed by facilitated discussion of the sort they describe. And it may be precisely the subliminal recognition of the limits of the Community of Inquiry that scaffolds the comfort that experts feel in abandoning the method in the very conference whose topic *is* the method.

In recognition of the fact that respect for Communal Inquiry need not be exclusive, Maughn Gregory, in his paper "The Teacher as Satyagrahi, or, the Necessary Inter-relationship among Socratic, Critical and Contemplative Pedagogies," explores the strengths and weaknesses of the different approaches named in his title. If we follow Gregory's line of reason, it would appear that, clearly, there are other ways of knowing/learning than through Communal Inquiry; why not apps, for example (Leask)? And with regard to the lack of Communal Inquiry at the conference itself, a second look reveals that its use would, in fact, have been inappropriate. That is, had we attempted to treat presented papers as mere stimuli that had no worth other than the capacity to prod thought (as in the dancing camel), this would have been blatantly *dis*respectful to presenters who were offering up products of the Communities of Inquiry that they had carried out in their own heads, at the cost of considerable time and energy. And though, as Graham McDonough reminded us, in his paper "High School Philosophy Teachers' Use of Texts: Dominated, Negotiated, or Oppositional?" there is considerable risk in straying from a genuine interchange, I would venture to say that the abandonment of the traditional rules of Communal Inquiry at the conference in no way diminished the value of the learning experience, even for (contra Dewey) facilitating future Communities of Inquiry. That is, to the degree that we came away with an enriched and more complex view of respect, we will not only be more adept at handling that specific issue should it arise, but more importantly, we will be better equipped to understand what is required of us in maintaining respect in future situations of Communal Inquiry.

Parting ways with orthodox COI rules in this instance thus generates the suggestion that though it is hard to see how the targeted benefits of Communal Inquiry such as thinking for oneself, learning to listen to opposing views, and so on, can be gleaned in any other way, there are a myriad of other knowledge gains (gains that can indeed enhance the communal experience) that cannot be so gained, e.g., understanding why Communal Inquiry enhances one's freedom, how to logically determine the strength of reasons, and so. To find our way forward, then, in response to Team Alberta's challenge, will require ever further clarification of this issue.

Concluding comments

From the point of view of one snapshot of the 2012 Vancouver NAACI conference, it seems that we learned, through a complex combination of didactic presentation and Communal Inquiry, that, aside from situations in which either intolerance or tolerance is required, we ought to heed the imperative to engage in the sort of authentic hard-nosed value-communicative-interaction that supports our interdependent self-consciousness and freedom. We also learned that, with regard to its context, pervasive (though not "unconditional") positive regard maximizes both the efficacy and worth of such interchange. We learned, too, that (abstract) respect for future possibilities may be as important as, or is at least connected to, the (concrete) respect of actual others, and that, in this regard, that we ought to be alert to the oppressive potential of respect-deficit for those who occupy roles of comparatively low worth. And we learned that "respect for persons," i.e., respect for autonomous rational self-conscious entities, ought not to so preoccupy us that we fail to see the value of, and hence respectfully respond to, individuals who are non- or merely-emerging-persons, and so, ourselves, be diminished in our failure to be "present." And finally, we have learned the importance of Nadia Kennedy's call to respect to the complexity of Communicative Interaction by "turning around and looking back so that we might understand it better." This snapshot, that is the result of such "turning around," is ultimately a product of the gifts we brought severally to, and through communal engagement in, the challenging project of trying to understand the complex notion of respect. It is in that spirit that this snapshot is submitted with a deep and abiding respect to all who so graciously contributed: presenters and non-presenters alike.

List of Presenters (and papers) at the 2012 Vancouver NAACI conference (last names in alphabetical order)

Rosario Del Callado	Community of Inquiry Demonstration.
Dale Cannon.	P4C, Community of Inquiry, and Methodological Faith
Jessica Davis.	Being Participation: The Ontology of the Socratic Method
Beth Dixon/Charles List.	Breaking the Rules of Respect: Character Education in School and Nature
Jason Howard.	Claims of Conscience and the Space of Reasons
Susan Gardner.	Respect and the Veil
Susan Gardner.	Gifting Freedom, Not Favour.
Lena Green.	Philosophical Inquiry as a Means of Teaching Respect In South African Classrooms
Maughn Gregory.	The Teacher as Satyagrahi, or, the Necessary Inter-relationship among Socratic, Critical and Contemplative Pedagogies
Wayne Henry.	Respect and Non-Human Animals.
David Kennedy.	Philosophies of Childhood and Children's Philosophies.
Nadia Kennedy.	Respecting the Complexity of CI
Jan Kleine.	Respect and Dignity in the Discourse between Private and Public Space
Amy Leask.	Tap, Swipe, and Think: Exploring the Use Interactive Technology in Introducing Philosophy to Children
Jana Mohr Lone; Sara Goering, David Shapiro.	The Connection between Respect, Inquiry and Philosophy For Children.
Eva Marsal.	Respect and the Philosophy of Education
Mort Morehouse.	Thinking about "Gifting Freedom, Not Favour" and our future
Eugene Muhammad.	Taking Inter-religious Dialogue to the M.A.T.T. (Martial Arts as a Teaching Tool): Rethinking Respect for the Other within Inter-religious Dialogue.
Graham McDonough, Laura Pinto, Dwight Boyd.	High School Philosophy Teachers' Use of Texts: Dominated, Negotiated, or Oppositional?
Chris Ng.	The "Problem" of Quiet Students
Claudia Ruitenberg and Parvaneh Ghazinezhad.	Is Respecting Children's Rationality in Their Best Interest in an Authoritarian Society?
Wendy Turgeon.	Bachelard and Korczak on Childhood: Constituting Respect for the Child
Barbara Weber.	'To Tolerate Means to Insult' (J. W. V. Goethe): Towards a Social Practice of Respect and Recognition
Rob Wilson, John Simpson, Jason Taylor.	Building Undergraduate Communities of Inquiry in Philosophy, Education, and Schools

Other works cited

Badinter, Elizabeth. *The Conflict: How Modern Motherhood Undermines the Status of Women.* Trans. Adriana Hunter. Toronto: HarperCollins, 2011.Print.

Darwall, Stephan. *The Second-Person Standpoint: Morality, Respect, and Accountability.* Cambridge, Mass.: Harvard University Press, 2006. Print.

Dillon, Robin S. 2010. "Respect". *In Stanford Encyclopedia of Philosophy.* http://plato.stanford.edu/entries/respect/ (2.1.2012). Web.

Freire, Paulo. *Pedagogy of the Oppressed.* New York: Continuum, 2000.

Gardner, S. 'Love thy neighbour? Maybe not, in E. Marsal, T. Dobashi & B. Weber (eds.). *Children Philosophize Worldwide*. Frankfurt: Peter Lang. 2009. Print.

Larson, Erik. *In the Garden of Beasts.* New York: Crown, 2011. Print.

Herbert Marcuse. "Repressive Tolerance." Ed. Robert Paul Wolff, Barrington Moore, jr., and Herbert Marcuse. *A Critique of Pure Tolerance.* Boston: Beacon Press, 1969. Print.

Marcuse, Herbert (1969). "The New Sensibility." In *An Essay on Liberation*, 23-48. Boston: Beacon Press. Print.

Marcuse, Herbert (1972). "Nature and Revolution." In *Counterrevolution and Revolt*, 59-78. Boston: Beacon Press. Print.

Sherwin, Susan. "A Relational Approach to Autonomy in Health Care." *Biomedical Ethics: A Canadian Focus.* Ed. Johanna Fisher. Toronto: OUP, 2009. 35-43. Print.

Strawson, Peter F., "Freedom and Resentment," *The Determinism and Freedom Philosophy Website,* (Spring 2005), Ed. Ted Honderich, *URL=* <http://www.ucl.ac.uk/~uctytho/dfwstrawson1.htm>. Web.

Paul Ricoeur. *Oneself as Another*. Trans. Kathleen Blamey. Chicago: University of Chicago Press, 1992. Print.

Sherry Turkle. *Alone Together: Why We Expect More From Technology And Less From Each.* New York: Basic books, 2011. Print.

Susan T. Gardner
(Canada)

Respect and the Veil

The ethical challenge of multiculturalism

In 2007, in Mississauga, Ontario, Canada, 16-year-old Aqsa Parvez was murdered by her father and brother for refusing to wear the hijab.[1] According to media reports, not one of the 12 people present in the house at the time would bear witness to this "honor killing."[2] Discussing this crime in a workshop for South Asian women three years later, Aruna Papp[3], a Toronto Family therapist, noted with alarm, *that the consensus among the 19 South Asian Mothers present was that Aqsa brought her death upon herself for being a disobedient daughter.*

In Canada there is an average of approximately 2 honor killings of girls and women every year[4] (though in 2011, 3 teenage girls and a superfluous wife in the Shafia family of Ontario were murdered all at the same time in a so-called honor killing). Papp's worry, however, is not primarily focused on the horror of culturally driven murder. Her worry, rather, is more general; namely that those of us brought up immersed in the values of the Western world, and who normally could be relied on to fight vigorously in defense of equality and freedom for all, have somehow been rendered mute to the creeping female oppression that is sneaking in through the back door of multiculturalist tolerance. Thus Papp writes:

> The ideology of multiculturalism, even among the most well-meaning advocates for female equality, tends to preclude any discussion of cultural values and traditions. Such advocates are afraid of being seen as "colonialists" and try to avoid a perceived "racialization" of an entire ethnic community.
> Such advocates of *multiculturalism run amok* are afraid to ever imply some cultures are better than others where treatment of women is concerned (emphasis added).
> Problematically, most advocates and activists for female victims of abuse shy away from challenging the immigrant communities to examine their

[1] http://en.wikipedia.org/wiki/Aqsa_Parvez.
[2] Papp 2010, p. A11.
[3] Ibid.
[4] Ibid.

> own traditions and cultural values in explaining the violence in their homes.[5]

In poignant emphasis of Papp's point, four days later in the same newspaper, the founders of *Free the Children,* (an organization whose mission is to eliminate the exploitation of children around the world), Craig and Marc Kielburger sang praises to the Designer House of Givenchy for sending models down catwalks with their faces covered in protest the French government's ban on *burkas*. The French law, which the Kielburgers refer to as "institutionalized racism" and one that "counteracts the gains we've made toward a more tolerant world,"[6] fines women $190 US if they are caught wearing a face-covering in public, while it fines men *who force their wives or daughters to wear such face coverings* $38,000 and up to a year in prison (emphasis added to underscore that the Kielburger thus apparently think that there is no problem with women being forced to wear face coverings). The Kielburgers' objections to such a law are that it further isolates such women and perpetuates stereotypes that Muslim women are submissive, and that it validates racism and Islamophobia in the West.

These opposing views create a dilemma for those of us outside the Muslim tradition who (a) wish to adopt the most ethical attitude possible but (b) believe that women covering their faces is, at least on the face of it (!), symbolic of oppression, subservience, and gender inequality. What would the notion of "respect for persons" have us do? Ought we to follow Papp's call to vigorously challenge "the immigrant communities to examine their own traditions and cultural values," or ought we, rather, to follow the lead of Kielburgers and vigorously defend cultural differences, at least those that are not obviously harmful? How might philosophy help us answer this question?

What does "respect for persons" require of us?

Kant famously argued that morality requires that we treat others never merely as "means to ends" but also always as "end-in-themselves." Kant argued that we ought to do so because to act morally was to act freely. If we take either part of Kant's dictum to be true, i.e., (1) that morality requires that we treat others as ends (which I take to be the Kantian definition of "respect for persons") and/or (2) that treating others as ends is actually a benefit to ourselves, we are nonetheless left with the problem of having an unclear guide as to what precisely treating others as ends requires that we do. What precisely does "respect for persons" demand of us?

The guideline that most easily emerges from this categorical imperative is that, since Kant took the paradigm characteristic of persons to be the capacity for self-conscious rational choice, respecting persons would appear to require of us that,

---

[5] Ibid.

[6] Kielburger 2010, p. B3.

at least as long as a choice does not hinder the choices of others, we ought to honor the choices that another makes.

Honoring choices

This "liberal" ideal of honoring the choices of others as a foundational value has wide-ranging repercussions. The medical establishment, for example, whose original compass was anchored in the value of paternal beneficence, now expects doctors to consult patients and to honor their choices, at least in so far as those choices are not illegal and/or unprofessional, and as long as they can be considered authentic, and not a result of pain and fear, or the pressure of manipulating relatives. But this is the elephant in the room, is it not? How can we know when a patient chooses to, for example, forego life-saving treatment that it is "her choice"? And returning to our original topic, how can we know when a Muslim woman chooses to wear a hijab, or a more pronounced face covering such as the niqaab, that that it is really "her choice"?

Supporting "real" choice requires challenging the chooser

Within the medical context, Buchanan and Brock argue, in their article *Standards of Competence,* that the degree to which one ought to *shoulder the responsibility of checking* to make sure that the patient's choice does indeed stem from her "own conception of her own good"[7] varies with the degree to which the potential outcome is substantially worse than other alternatives.[8] Buchanan and Brock stress that what is important in such scrutiny is that one focus on the *process* of the decision-making (rather than the actual decision made), which would include a check to make sure that all other options are clearly understood. With regard to the interesting question as to whether or not *we have a responsibility to check whether wearing the veil is an authentic choice,* since veiling one's face almost inevitably distorts and/or curtails communication with those outside one's reference group thus short-circuiting the kind of communicative rationality[9] necessary to underpin authentic choice, Buchanan and Brock's position suggests that we shirk our responsibility if we do not challenge this practice.

Drawing from a more feminist tradition, Susan Sherwin worries about Buchanan and Brock individualized method of evaluating autonomous choice as it fails to recognize the possibility of "internalized oppression."[10] Sherwin argues that we need to distinguish "agency" from "autonomy," where agency can be described as the capacity to merely exercise reasonable choice, while autonomy, i.e., self-governance, requires that one have the capacity to at least recognize and possibly

[7] Buchannan 2009, p.28.
[8] Ibid., p. 30.
[9] Of the sort described by Habermas in *The Theory of Communicative Action,* 1992.
[10] Sherwin 2009, pp. 41-2.

(*perhaps even easily*) resist structures that may be oppressive.[11] According to Sherwin, "*The condition of being oppressed can be so fundamentally restrictive that it is distorting to describe as autonomous some specific choices made under such condtions*"[12] (emphasis added). Interestingly, Sherwin focuses on Western women in this regard. She says, for example, that many Western women "believe they have no real choice but to seek expensive, risky cosmetic surgery because they accurately perceive that their opportunities for success in work or love depend on their more closely approximating some externally defined standard of beauty."[13] Sherwin's example thus brings some balance to the "veil argument" by pointing out that many Western women may be as blind to their own oppression as those they seek to liberate. Sherwin goes on to argue that if we are truly concerned that individuals have the opportunity to live autonomously by making real choices, then it is not enough to merely offer these individuals choices. "It also requires that the person have had the opportunity to develop the skills necessary for making the type of choice in question, the experience of being respected in her decisions, and encouragement to reflect on her own values."[14] And Sherwin goes on to say that it is the *society*, not just the agent, that ought to be the subject of critical scrutiny under the rubric of what she refers to as "*relational autonomy*"[15] (emphasis added). In so doing, her position supports Papp's call to vigorously challenge communities (immigrant or otherwise) to examine their traditions and cultural values that may, by their very nature, preclude genuinely autonomous choice.

Is wearing a veil a sign of internal oppression?

With regard to the question of whether wearing the veil can be accurately perceived as a sign of internal oppression, Ayaan Hirsi Ali, in her book *Nomad,* argues forcefully that the greatest slavery of Muslim women is indeed internal. She writes, for example, that in Muslim schools, both abroad and in the West, "girls learn all day long to be subservient and lower their eyes, to veil themselves to symbolize the suppression of their individual will. They are taught to internalize male superiority and walk very softly into the mosque by a back door. In weekend Quran schools, girls learn that God requires them to obey, that they are worth less than boys and have fewer rights before God."[16]

With regard to the veil, Ali writes that the "different sorts of masks and beaks and burkas are all gradations of mental slavery"—that

> The veil deliberately marks women as private and restricted property, non-persons—that the veil sets women apart from men and apart from the

[11] Ibid., p. 40.
[12] Ibid., p. 37.
[13] Ibid., p. 37.
[14] Ibid., p. 42.
[15] Ibid., p. 42.
[16] Ali 2010, p. 129.

> world; it restrains them, confines them, grooms them for docility. A mind can be cramped just as a body may be, and a Muslim veil blinkers both your vision and your destiny. It is the mark of a kind of apartheid, not the domination of a race but of a sex.[17]

Yet Ali is not surprised by the fact that "Many Muslim women in Western societies are demanding that they be allowed to wear the *hijab* (the head scarf)—some even the *niqaab* (the face covering with only the eyes showing)." "These women," according to Ali, "believe that their own bodies are so powerfully toxic that even making eye contact with other people is a sin. The extent of self-loathing that this expresses," Ali believes, "is impossible to exaggerate . . ."[18] And Ali goes on to say that though a veiled woman "may be downtrodden from an objective standpoint . . . she doesn't feel that way. . . she is protected from loneliness. She *belongs.* She has the certainty, the strength, the clear goals that stem from belief."[19] This is her opportunity "to be like a child again, protected, taken by the arm and told what is right and what is wrong, what to do and what not to do—to take a break from thinking."[20]

Unlike those of us outside the tradition, Ayaan Hirsi Ali has the credentials and knows whereof she speaks. She was brought up in the Muslim way during her childhood in Somali and later in Kenya. She was subjected to female genital mutilation (FGM) without anesthetic at the age of five. And for those of you who think that this abomination—this cutting off of the young girl's clitoris and the excision of the lips of her vagina so that they fuse together in wait for the virginity test of her wedding night—is just an aberration, it is important to note that roughly 130 million women around the world have had their genitals cut:[21] i.e., this amounts to approximately six thousand little girls being subjected to genital mutilation every day. A brief survey of various countries reveals that, for instance, 98% of Somali women have undergone FGM, 97% in Egypt, 95% in Mali, and 90% in Sudan.[22]

Ali goes on to note that since all but the most assimilated (of immigrant) parents want their children to marry within the community, and since they believe that an "impure" girl, i.e., one whose clitoris and vagina are intact, will not find a husband, it is not farfetched to assume that it is not an infrequent occurrence for little girls to have their genitals cut without anesthetic on kitchen tables in many parts of the West.[23]

In support of this assumption, Ruth Macklin, in her article *Ethical Relativism in a Multicultural Society*, reports that the medical community is indeed increasingly

---

[17] Ibid., p. 16.
[18] Ibid., p. 18.
[19] Ibid., p. 39.
[20] Ibid., p. 38.
[21] Ibid., p. 128.
[22] All figures come from *Integration of the Human Rights of Women and the Gender Perspective/Violence Against Women (2003), Report of the special Rapporteur on Violence against Women, Its Causes and Consequences, Radhika Coomaraswamy, submitted in accordance with Commission on Human Rights Resolution 2002/52/.*
[23] Ibid., p. 128.

experiencing requests for genital cutting, as well as increasingly having to deal with incidents of hemorrhage and/or infection following "at home" ritual female circumcision. Trying to walk a reasonable path through this treacherous multicultural territory, Macklin relates a talk given by a physician who conducted research with East African women living in Seattle, and who argued that "Western physicians must curb their tendency to judge cultural practices different from their own as 'rational' or 'irrational.'" This physician went on to say that "Ritual genital cutting is an 'inalienable' part of some cultures, and it does a disservice to people from those cultures to view it as a human rights violation." Furthermore, "in countries where female genital mutilation (FGM) is practiced, circumcised women are 'normal'."[24]--thus trying to make a case in support for the increasing number of requests for genital cutting by immigrants to the Western world.[25]

Arguing against this position that she characterizes as "overtolerance,"[26] Macklin notes that since cultures change over time, it makes little sense to consider any ritual as "inalienable" (let alone one that does harm—what in logic circles is known as an illegitimate appeal to tradition[27]), to say nothing of the fact that the statistical normality of FGM no more supports its legitimacy than the fact that malnutrition and malaria are "normal" in Africa supports the suggestion that it ought to be maintained.[28] Macklin goes on to point out that, in any case, there is an inherent contradiction in the very notion of "multiculturalism." If the basic premise of multiculturalism is that "all cultural groups be treated with respect and as equals," what does this imply, she asks, with regard to cultural groups that oppress or fail to respect other cultural groups? And even more problematic, what does this imply with regard to cultural groups that oppress or fail to respect sub-groups within their own cultures?[29]

Ali would reply that tolerance of oppression internal to a group is "racism of low expectations—that this Western attitude is based on the idea that people of color must be exempted from 'normal' standards of behavior."[30] She expresses anger that "this subjugation is silently tolerated, if not endorsed . . . by so many in Western societies where the equality of the sexes is legally enshrined."[31] And she is particularly aghast that "Even though their predecessors had once agitated for the rights of workers, the rights of women, and the rights of blacks, American liberals today are hesitant to speak out against the denial of rights (and the ill treatment of women) that is perpetrated in the name of Islam."[32]

Terry Glavin, in his book entitled *Come from the Shadows,* makes a similar point when he notes the disturbing tendency for human rights to be viewed as a peculiarly Western set of values. Glavin argues that this belief primarily benefits

[24] Macklin 2009, p. 53.
[25] Ibid., p. 52.
[26] Ibid., p. 49.
[27] Gardner 2009, p. 84.
[28] Macklin 2009, p. 53.
[29] Ibid., pp. 55-56.
[30] Ali 2010, p. xviii.
[31] Ibid., p. 16.
[32] Ibid., p. 106.

Western Liberals as it underscores a sense of superiority while simultaneously distancing themselves from the struggles of others in the name of respecting their cultural customs: "As if people in other societies somehow find oppression more agreeable."[33]

It could be argued, however, that such criticism of the apparent "overtolerance" of Western Liberals is unfairly harsh, as it fails to recognize the fact that differentiating *authentic choice* from *quasi-choice that emerges from internal oppression* is often difficult, and that it is this "masking" of authenticity, not condescension or lack of care, that is the major cause of a retreat behind tolerance.

Differentiating "authentic" from "quasi-"choices

In her book *A Quiet Revolution: The Veil's Resurgence from the Middle East to America,* Leila Ahmed, a professor of Divinity at Harvard Divinity School, attempts to explore the threads of authentic versus "forced" choice as they are woven through the modern resurgence of the veil. Ahmed notes that this resurgence is particularly perplexing in light of the fact that, in the 1950's, being unveiled and bareheaded was the norm in the cities in Egypt and other Muslim majority societies.[34] Ahmad discusses at length the growing strength of the Muslim Brotherhood[35] (who have affirmed the veil as a foundational Islamic requirement)[36] and Islamism's 'quintessentially political agenda' of Islamizing society.[37] She notes that even here in America, the Islamic Society of North America (ISNA) appears to embrace what the veil seems to imply: male dominance and gender hierarchy and separation.[38] Nonetheless, she notes that some Muslim women are reluctant to discard the veil as doing so may be perceived as a product of white men saving brown women from brown men.[39] Her exploration of the history of the veil resurgence supports this claim. Following Nasser's and the Arab world's devastating defeat by Israel in the war of 1967, a mood of religiosity swept across the Arab world.[40] The defeat was interpreted as a clear sign of God's punishment of Arabs for putting their faith in nationalism and secularism and turning away from Islam.[41] Women who now took up the veil reported undergoing an "internal transformation," or feeling "psychologically and intellectually separated from mainstream society."[42] And the dress enabled them to easily recognize each other.[43] The general goal of this movement was to bring forth

[33] Sajoo 2011, p. A11.
[34] Ahmed 2011, p. 10.
[35] Brotherhood members are typically welcome immigrants because they are typically well-educated: engineers, chemists, doctors, scientists, and teachers. Ibid., p. 57.
[36] Ibid., p. 8.
[37] Ibid., p. 9.
[38] Ibid., p. 7.
[39] Ibid., p. 24.
[40] Ibid., p. 66.
[41] Ibid., p. 66.
[42] Ibid., p. 79.
[43] Ibid., p. 79.

the ideal Islamic Society and to oppose such ideologies as Communism, Zionism, and Feminism.[44] The standardization of material and color visibly modeled the egalitarian principles of social equality and justice for all. Islamic dress provided a way to "sit in judgment of mainstream society,"[45] and it imbued women with a kind of moral and religious authority that might discourage sexual harassment (which, in Egyptian universities, was routine).[46] In Saudi Arabia, particularly following the soaring oil prices after the war of 1973, Islamic dress became a sign of wealth, chic, and prestige.[47] Nonetheless Ahmed notes that both religious and social pressures made it difficult for individual women to choose *not* to wear the veil.[48] She notes that researchers studying the Islamist movement more broadly suggest that veiling spread because *male* leaders conceived of veiling as strategically important to the movement,[49] as a sign of resistance to Western civilization and of the beginning of *iltizam* (pious commitment) toward Islam,[50] and as a pushback against the degradation heaped on Muslims as a result of the economic imperialism of the West.[51] The resurgence of the veil supported widespread optimism for an Islamist future, particularly as it accompanied what appeared to be a cultural decline of the West.[52] Ahmed notes, though, that this so-called optimistic view of the future includes a "biologization" (i.e., enslavement) of Muslim women—an ideological picture that was reinforced by the influential Islamist theorist and member of the Brotherhood in the 1950 and 60's, Sayyid Qutb, who was executed by Nasser in 1966. Sayyied Qutb stated unequivocally that a woman's responsibility to society is synonymous with her biological function in life. Being the caretakers of the family and children define women's identity, importance and dignity.[53]

We thus leave Ahmed's exploration with the sense that Muslim women have been caught in a double bind. If she covers her face, she will inevitably short-circuit her capacity to access alternative viewpoints and challenges which in turn will undermine her ability to make real "self-affirming" choices (even if she avoids the religious and cultural oppressive practices that often accompany the wearing of the veil). Yet if she refuses the face covering, she undermines the efforts of her men, her religion, and her culture to launch a visible public pushback against the oppression that they suffered at the hands of the imperialist West.

---

[44] Ibid., p. 79.
[45] Ibid., p. 86.
[46] Ibid., p. 87.
[47] Ibid., p. 101.
[48] Ibid., p. 124.
[49] Ibid., p. 131.
[50] Ibid., p. 134.
[51] Ibid., p. 139.
[52] Ibid., p. 154.
[53] Ibid., p. 108.

The Answer

Though on the face of it, it appears as if Muslim women are caught in a real dilemma, it is actually a false one, as there is **third option** already readily available whereby Muslim women can reaffirm her loyalty to the people and ideology that she cherishes, while not undermining the communicative rationality necessary to maintain her status as a person. The third option is that she can wear the hijab, i.e., the head covering. Thus, to the degree that criticism of full face covering is accompanied by a celebration of "the hijab option," charges of racism and promoting Islamaphobia[54] are defused. Indeed, if criticism of face covering is persistently paired with an honoring of the hijab, it will be become evident that condemnation of any sort of face covering has nothing whatsoever to do with Islamaphobia. It will become clear that those who denigrate the covering of one's face do so *not* because it is perceived as a sign of religious piety; it is deemed wrong because it threatens the communicative personhood of the woman who wears it (and hence, importantly, the personhood of her female offspring). Face covering also instills highly-charged preoccupying worries in countless Western Liberals who fear that to tolerate such practices is to tolerate rampant oppression (witness the energy imbued in the writing of this paper). Echoing this pervasive worry, Craig McInnes,[55] a noted member of the editorial board of the Vancouver Sun, writing in support of Canada's new restriction on veiling one's face while taking the oath of citizenship, notes that the practice of females covering their faces is troubling because it is associated with parts of the world where women have fewer rights than men and that therefore we ought to be legitimately worried that this unacceptable inequality is filtering into Canada. As well, echoing the communicative issue discussed above, McInnes says that what he finds even more troubling is that wearing the veil is "like hiding behind a one-way mirror; (that wearing) a mask allows a person to read the faces of others without themselves being read" –and that therefore "wearing a full face covering is just plain "rude."[56] He concludes that accommodation cannot be a one-way street.

Conclusion

The overall conclusion to which this foray into veil territory thus brings us is this. It is a mistake to perceive persons and their choices as "objects" in the sense of "things that ought to be revered as one finds them," and to do a "liberty dance" around them to the tune of the sort favored by John Stewart Mill. To do so, is to view a person, or a culture, as one might view a work of art, as if one has an obligation to preserve it as a finished product. In Buber's terms, this is to enter into an "I-It" relationship with the other, rather than one he poetically describes as "I-Thou."

[54] Kielburger 2010, p. B3.
[55] McInnes 2011, p. A1.
[56] Ibid., p. A9.

It brings us to the conclusion that respect, rather, requires the sort of communicative interchange that underscores one's recognition that one is *freedom* interacting with others who are *essentially free* (to borrow Sartre terms); it is to embody a deep understanding that we are *processes*[57] not *objects,* and that, as such, the foundational cognitive/moral attitude ought to be one of genuine, though challenging, curiosity with regard to the ever-changing social landscape and the wildly different ways in which persons, not wholly dissimilar to ourselves, attempt to carve out a good life.

It is absolutely imperative, however, that we keep in mind that "the other" may be unwilling and/or unable to meet us in the "in-between" of communicative rationality, and that even if such an interchange takes place, compatibility may not be possible. In such situations, personhood, nonetheless, requires of us that we vigorously don the mantle of active responsibility in the lifelong pursuit of constantly reconstructing our own best answers to the questions that life continuously asks of us.[58]

And so, with regard to the specific questions that address us here, the answers seem to be as follows.

With regard to harmful traditions, such a Female Genital Mutilation, precisely because they cause harm, the onus lies squarely with those who would continue such practices to articulate a reason-based defence of such traditions, which in turn needs to compete "objectively" against the very strong reasons that oppose them.

With regard to veiling, since the sort that hides the human face interferes with the communicative interchange that is necessary to maintain mutually dependent personhood, if the choice is forced, then clearly it ought not to be respected. If the wearer argues that the choice is hers, since the practice is indicative of a shirking of one's responsibility to do one's part in maintaining our common humanity (though she maintains a one-way read on others), it is a form of disrespect, and hence ought not to be respected. And since, to those outside the practice, a veiled face is symbolic of internal oppression that cries out for external assistance, to the degree that those who maintain this practice know this, this is similar to crying "Fire" when they themselves perceive no threat present. This, too, is a form of disrespect that ought not to be respected.

"Respect for persons" is not, and should not be seen as, unconditional. Respect is an attitude of openness and genuine inquiry that fuels communicative rationality that, in the best of times, leads to the sort of rational choice that Kant envisioned. However, when others refuse to play by these communicative rules, a one-sided attempt to maintain "the game of respect" that is *essentially* intersubjective is not only futile, it undermines one's responsibility to maintain of one's own self respect.

The short answer to the veil question is, thus, that face covering, if apparently a product of personal choice, is disrespectful to others, and hence ought not to elicit respect. If face covering is not a product of personal choice, it is oppressive, and

---

[57] Or, as Sartre says more poetically "I am what I am not, and I am not what I am."

[58] Frankl 1974, p. 98.

hence also ought not to elicit respect. The practice of face covering and respect for that practice are, in other words, incompatible.

Reference list

Ahmed, Leila. *A Quiet Revolution: The Veil's Resurgence from the Middle East to America.* New Haven: Yale University Press, 2011. Print.

Ali, Ayaan Hirsi. *Nomad.* Toronto: Knopf, 2010. Print.

Buber, Martin. *I and Thou.* 2nd ed. New York: Charles Scribner's Sons, 1958. Print.

Buchanan, Allen E. and Dan W. Brock. "Standard of Competence." *Biomedical Ethics: A Canadian Focus.* Ed. Johanna Fisher. Toronto: OUP, 2009. 26-30. Print.

Frankl, Viktor E. *Man's Search for Meaning.* New York: Pocket Book, 1984. Print.

Gardner, Susan. *Thinking Your Way to Freedom: A Guide to Owning Your Own Practical Reasoning.* Philadelphia: Temple University Press, 2009.

Habermas, Jürgen. *The Theory of Communicative Action.* Vol. 1. Trans. Thomas McCarthy. Boston: Beacon Press, 1992. Print.

Kielburger, Craig & Marc. "Designers deserve credit for standing up for tolerance." *Vancouver Sun.* July 19, 2010. Print.

Macklin, Ruth. "Ethical Relativism in a Multicultural Society." *Biomedical Ethics: A Canadian Focus.* Ed. Johanna Fisher. Toronto: OUP, 2009. 47-56. Print.

McInnes, Craig. "Facing up to Multiculturalism's Limits," *The Vancouver Sun.* December 14, 2011. Print.

Papp, Aruna. "Cultural-driven abuse of women must be addressed." *Vancouver Sun.* July 15, 2010. Print.

Sherwin, Susan. "A Relational Approach to Autonomy in Health Care." *Biomedical Ethics: A Canadian Focus.* Ed. Johanna Fisher. Toronto: OUP, 2009. 35-43. Print.

Sajoo, Eva. "Why The West Should Not Abandon Afghanistan." *The Vancouver Sun*, October 21, 2011. Print.

David Kennedy
(USA)

One Argument for Why We Should Listen to Children

In a very persuasive paper from 1999, in which she argues against the claims of several philosophers that children are not capable of philosophizing, Karin Murris wrote, "With the philosophical critique of the Western notion of 'disembodied rationality', awareness is growing that children's thinking is not inferior to that of adults, and that children deserve to be listened to."[1] This would indicate a historical phenomenon, and a process of what Freire called conscientization. We were not aware before, but now awareness is growing. Why then is it happening, and what sort of historical movement does it form a part of? Is it an aspect of "extending rights and respect to all people"—the move to respect difference? Or is it something we've done before—like listening to the "wisdom of the child," or "the voice of innocence"? Although both of those impulses may be involved, I don't think that's exactly what Murris is talking about, or what we're listening for when we facilitate conversations with children. Following her lead, I would argue that we're listening for what follows when the "Western notion of disembodied rationality"—that is, the Cartesian paradigm—breaks up and begins to transform. We're listening for the (r)evolutionary emergence of what the social philosopher Herbert Marcuse, whose thinking I will also be working from here, calls a new form of reason, or even more ambitiously, a "new sensibility." This paper will be dedicated to exploring the part that children may play in that emergence, particularly in the context of the school and of the discourse model we call "community of inquiry."

There is plenty of evidence, at least in the history of Western thought and ethical culture, of epistemological change over historical time, which leads to new ontologies, new anthropologies, and new values and convictions. There are paradigm shifts, and what the history of the last 200 years would suggest is that we are in the middle of one. In our case at least, it is driven by science, by exploration, and, I would argue, by crisis: by *science* in quantum physics' blurring of subject-object boundaries and the consequent crisis of objectivity, by the *exploration* of inner space in psychoanalysis, of cosmic space and nanospace through new technologies, of intersubjective space in cultural anthropology, and the new planetary intervisibility made possible by technology; and finally, by *crisis* in the form of the multiple economic, social and psychological depredations of late technocapitalist economies and their correlates: total war and grave environmental degradation. This change is dialectical in the sense that, first of all, it is urged forward by contradictions within the whole system, and second, in the sense that earlier elements of the system can be

[1] Murris 1999, p. 269.

restated in a "sublated" way in the emerging structure. Compare, for example, classically defined "primitive" animism, children's animism, and the animistic tendencies of process philosophy, or the "quantum animism" of the physicist Nick Herbert, Rupert Sheldrake's morphic fields, and Jame's Lovelock's Gaia theory, all of which are attempts to overcome our deep enculturation into mind-matter dualism, and to rethink some fundamental ontological issues (see Skrbina and Kennedy). We can find statements of each in each of the others, and as such we could say that each is one limited response to a question based on an intuition of the unity of mind and nature that is continually restated in different historical contexts and in different discourses. As such, paradigm change is continuous discursive reconstruction.

Paradigm change is also psychological—it results, not just in a new episteme, but in a new psychoculture. It involves new forms of modal subjectivity. A paradigm has not changed until it changes the thinking—not just the abstract or theoretical thinking but the intuitive insights and the practical, everyday reasoning and decision-making—of a collective. Even more it is, Marcuse[2] insists, "aesthetic" in the original sense of "felt." It is embodied. It is what he calls a "sensibility," a particular form of "human nature" or set of "needs and satisfactions," which is marked most significantly by *the way we experience nature and the lived world.* It operates at the perceptual level, and only from the level of perception—of what we see and touch and how we feel about it, how our body "explains" it—does it lead to the formation of different scientific and moral concepts. In his announcement of a new sensibility, Marcuse foresees a new onto-epistemological model "that replaces the bifurcated practice of separating the social from the natural, the objects from the subjects."[3] This transformed post-Cartesian superstructure is, for Marcuse, what can save us from the culture of domination, violation, exploitation and destruction of our own biosphere, a culture from whose iron grip we are finding it difficult to extricate ourselves. It was a new form of "sensuous reason" that Marcuse, in the late 60's and early 70's, strove to articulate, with the admonition that "liberation presupposes changes in [the] biological dimension, that is to say, different instinctual needs, different reactions of the body as well as the mind," in which "cultural needs 'sink down' into the biology of man." [4] And the goal of this is, he says, a human being whose "second nature" has raised an "instinctual barrier against cruelty, brutality, ugliness,"[5] product of a "revolution in perception which will accompany the material and intellectual reconstruction of society, creating the new aesthetic environment,"[6] where "freedom [has become] a biological necessity," and we are "physically incapable of tolerating any repression other than that required for the protection and amelioration of life."[7]

---

[2] Marcuse 1969.
[3] Quoted in Pierce 2009, p. 148.
[4] Marcuse 1969, pp. 7, 10.
[5] Ibid., p. 21.
[6] Ibid., p. 37.
[7] Ibid., p. 28.

Neoteny and adult-child dialogue

Where might children and children's thinking—and children's thinking in settings of communal inquiry in particular—fit in the dialectical emergence of a new paradigm, and how are children actors, agents of its emergence? In fact Marcuse associates its onset with what he calls the *Great Refusal*, an alienation against alienation, which he finds universally expressed in student and youth movements. These movements could be said to emerge from one high point of the long human childhood—adolescence—as its flower, but its roots must be searched for in earlier childhood. The child is the biological and cultural representative of the new, the emergent, and a concrete, literal embodiment of futurity—a futurity, in fact, *in its own image*. As Ashley Montagu wrote, "The child is the forerunner of humanity—forerunner in the sense that the child is the possessor of all those traits which, when healthily developed, lead to a healthy and fulfilled human being, and thus to a fulfilled and healthy humanity."[8]

But this developmental pathway, this evolutionary possibility, inherent in human embodiment itself, for which childhood is a promissory note, is unimaginable apart from our species' *educability*—our relative freedom from instinctual determinism, and from what both John Dewey and contemporary neuroscientists call the "original plasticity" of the young, which is an aspect of neoteny, or the extraordinarily long period of relative immaturity in humans. Dewey, in fact, sounded the same theme in 1922, when he wrote:

> the intimation never wholly deserts us that there is in the unformed activities of childhood and youth the possibilities of a better life for the community as well as for individuals here and there. This dim sense is the ground of our abiding idealization of childhood . . . [which] remains a standing proof of a life wherein growth is normal not an anomaly, activity a delight not a task, and where habit-forming is an expansion of power and not its shrinkage.[9]

As Montagu argues, the term neoteny describes, not just our prolonged childhood, but the human predilection for ongoing development and learning and consequent reconstruction *throughout* the life-cycle.[10] *Humans are pedomorphs*. Evolution, he argues, "has consisted of a shedding of the adult traits of our ancestral forms, and an increasing retention and development of the juvenile traits of those forms. Together with this has gone a stretching out of developmental periods, so that more time has become increasingly available for growth and development. The same processes clearly have been at work for functional and behavior traits. It would be a great step forward," he writes, "if we ceased to regard childhood as a phase of development which terminates at whatever arbitrary age we decide upon and to per-

---

[8] Montagu 1989, p. 106.
[9] Dewey 1922, p. 99.
[10] Montagu 1989, p. 106.

ceive it for what it is, an extended period of growth which slows down, if at all, only after many years."[11] Where then will a new psychoculture emerge except in and through the young *and* those adults who retain youthful characteristics?

Joseph Chilton Pearce, another prophet of our evolutionary potential, which in his latest book (2002) he frames in terms of brain development during the primary neotenous period of childhood and adolescence, argues that for evolutionary change to occur, a *model* is necessary—that, "from the beginning of our life, the characteristics of each new possibility must be demonstrated for us by someone, some thing, or an event in our immediate environment . . . "[12] In the case of the adult-child relation, both at home and at school, life-course neoteny-theory would suggest that the model is bi-directional. If the result of successful education is that the child retains childlike characteristics into adulthood, and if we associate Marcuse's "new reality principle"—the "new sensibility which expresses the ascent of the life instincts over aggressiveness and guilt," and "the vital need for the abolition of injustice"[13]—with these characteristics,[14] then the adult models for the child and the child models for the adult.

The child models these characteristics as a Novum, a utopian horizon, a "not-yet"—as forms of potential social transformation, not yet formed into fixed patterns, which challenge the more fixed patterns of the adult to transform by reinvoking her own neotenous strivings. The adult models the culture, the given, the inherited, the accumulated patterns of the species, the current forms of adaptation, the structures of understanding, the knowledge base, the ethos, the ethical and moral superstructure. It is in the child's interactive experience with these models that the neuronal structure of each individual brain develops, through synaptic exercise and consequent myelination, which preserves the emergent neuronal architecture against the periodic hormonal purging of unused potential pathways. The "original modifiability" or neuronal "plasticity" of which both Dewey and the neuroscientists speak is literal: the immature brain is in fact physically organized differently by interaction with different experience. I would suggest, then, that the educational model that opens a space for paradigm shift is one of *dialogue* between emergent structures, here standing for "child," and relatively fixed structure, here standing for "adult." The assumption of dialogue is that both terms of the relation are liable to change through their interaction. That assumption of mutual modifiability of adult and child in relation is, I would suggest, the key difference between traditional and neotenic forms of education.

Child-adult dialogue can be described on different levels and with different vocabularies. One useful formulation is Dewey's (1922) notion of a dialogue be-

---

[11] Ibid., pp. 61, 98.

[12] Pearce 2002, pp. 5-6.

[13] Marcuse 1969, pp. 23-4.

[14] Montagu identifies 27 of these characteristics: "love, friendship, sensitivity, to think soundly, to know, to learn, to work, organization, curiosity, wonder, playfulness, imagination, creativity, open-mindedness, flexibility, experimental-mindedness, explorativeness, resiliency, enthusiasm, sense of humor, joyfulness, laughter and tears, optimism, honesty and trust, compassionate intelligence, song, dance" (107).

tween "impulse" and "habit." The two are in continual interaction—whether struggle, uneasy partnership, or some kind of conversation. Both are fundamental to individual, dyadic, and group experience. Habit represents naturalized, or reified, or codified initiative and response patterns to the novelty of every situation—even situations that are themselves highly habituated, for even those situations appear in the vertigo, the open space of the now, the "pure mobility" as Bergson called it, of "duration." We use things that worked before. The problem is that the now has irrepressible emergent characteristics—it keeps changing. If we were completely unhabituated, we would be in a fugue state—mad—to the extent that, as Dewey said, habits ". . . constitute the self. In any intelligible sense of the word will, they *are* will."[15] If we were completely habituated—if every response and initiative were based on a response to a past situation—we would also be mad, because our habits or habitus would no longer be adapted—we would be responding to a projection from the past. Given that "selfhood (except as it has encased itself in a shell of routine) is in process of making, and . . . any self is capable of including within itself a number of inconsistent selves, of unharmonized dispositions,"[16] intelligent behavior requires habits that are flexible—permeable constructs, capable of revision and reconstruction in adaptive response to duration—and that can distinguish projection from what reality there is in the open space of the now.

Impulse is Dewey's word for the spontaneous experience of the now, which we may associate with Peirce's "firstness," with the psychoanalysts' "libido," Bergson's *elan vital* or vital impetus, Buber's "originator instinct" and the astropsychologist's "Mars"—instinctual energy, nisus, Mead's "I" as opposed to the "me" of habit—desire. It can manifest in many forms, destructive as well (although the phrase "impulse-ridden" describes a kind of habit), but in children it is often identified with all the traits that Montagu associates with the permanent childlike characteristics of the human species—"questing, striving, questioning, seeking . . . wide-eyed curiosity and excitement in the enjoyment of new experience."[17] It is the energy that challenges habitual response, that acts to break it up, transform it. In optimal situations, its effect is to loosen it, to open it up, to bring it into the present, to reconstruct it. It signifies, not just the individual's "power to re-make old habits, to re-create,"[18] but "a future new society of changed purposes and desires."[19]

Typical child-adult interaction embodies a conversation between impulse and habit. The adult brings models of habit to the table, including the habits of categorical thinking that divide the scholastic world into fields and disciplines—which Dewey calls the "logical"—and the child brings the "psychological" in the form of impulses that encounter habit as expressions of her "own vital logical movement"[20] in the desire to investigate, to make or construct things, to speak and communicate, and

[15] Dewey 1922, p. 25.
[16] Ibid., p. 137.
[17] Pierce 2002, p. 53.
[18] Dewey 1922, p. 97.
[19] Ibid., p. 96.
[20] Dewey 1986, p. 181.

to express thoughts and feelings,[21] all in the interest of a highly personal inquiry with profound social implications. The adult brings the habitus of the age: implicit epistemological beliefs, doctrines, felt truths, proscriptions, aesthetic rules, attitudes and relational styles, all of which imply ontological convictions, often pre-conscious, whether based on scientific or religious or cultural epistemes. These, as we have seen in Marcuse's formulation, are encoded in perception itself, and have immediate implications for how we *experience* what is alive and what is not, about whether we *feel* that killing animals for food is a fundamental violation or not, about what we can be said to "own," about whether what is right for me can always be the "right thing to do," and so on.

The child brings, we might say, the mother of all standpoint epistemologies, dramatically illustrated by Paul Ritter, who at the University of Nottingham in 1968 created a mock-up of two rooms two-and-a-half times actual adult scale. A paper mache man sitting on the paper-mache couch is completely hidden by the newspaper he is holding. The couch has to be climbed like a cliff. The lamp on the table looms above one like the Eiffel Tower; ". . . it brought gasps of astonishment from the visitors."[22] And how do other animals appear from the view of childhood? Or those psychological characteristics of adults that we adults take to be normal? Or the perceptual world of nature itself? When trees move in the wind, is it a sensuous experience for them? Is there really more than a rather superficial difference between the way humans and animals think?

The child represents what Merleau-Ponty called the "polymorph"[23] —"not an absolute other, nor the same"—which amounts as well to a polyvocalism, which is associated with a heightened (relative to adults) capacity for mimesis—mimicry of multiple viewpoints that arises from being, because one is less "disembodied," in a more direct feeling-relation with the world and with others, and a form of temporality more closely allied with Bergson's "pure duration," or "qualitative multiplicity." Lipman, applied philosopher of childhood that he was, modeled his novels intuitively on the narrative fantasy that the child—in dialogue with others—is in fact capable of reproducing in some form all the major philosophical standpoints in the canon—whether Descartes' cogito ergo sum, Plato's innatism, Locke's sensationalism, Berkeley's idealism, Kant's phenomenalism, James' radical empiricism, and so on.

Four dimensions of neotenic schooling

The neotenic school is an adult-child collective based on dialogue, and as such, its primary pedagogical dimension is the community of inquiry. CI is the public heart of the speech community, and the site where child-child and child-adult dialogue become relatively indistinguishable—where deliberative reason as process and activity trumps personal power or manipulative skill, irrational authority and group-think. As a dis-

---

[21] Dewey 1956, pp. 57-61.
[22] Ward 1978, p. 23.
[23] Merleau-Ponty 1964, p. 110.

course-model, it grounds practice in all the school's curricular spaces, whether science, or mathematics, literature, art, or philosophy *tout court*. Philosophy as identification and critical interrogation of concepts is in fact its primary language: problematizing, hypothesizing instantiating, connecting and distinguishing ideas, reflecting on one's own or the group's thinking. Every school content area has a philosophical zone, a network of concepts held together by epistemological, ontological, and axiological beliefs and assumptions based on those beliefs. CI is the site for the identification and problematization of those beliefs, and in this sense every disciplinary community of inquiry is, by definition, a community of philosophical inquiry. CPI is the zone of confluence, the conceptual Ur-space, where the lineaments of our shared paradigm emerge to view, and where its limits and its frangible margins, its aporias and its contradictions, its anomalies and inassimilable counter-examples show themselves.

In the neotenic school, the adult opens and hosts a conversation in the space of CPI so that children may both express their standpoints and affirm, question and contest the received beliefs—from parents, media, peers, and the "wheels" already inside their own heads—that, they discover, have been "received" differently by different people. One discovers that not everyone thinks alike—not even oneself and oneself—and that our beliefs are based on assumptions which bear examination through the giving and testing of reasons, exploration of implications, and the challenge of thinking normatively. This epistemological skepticism is related to what Marcuse called the "great refusal," the alienation from alienation that he understood as the necessary precursor to new paradigm emergence—necessary in a world in which technocapitalism has colonized our very instinctual structures, our perception, our wants and needs. This is often perceived by adults as a dangerous space, and traditional schooling fears it the way vampires fear sunlight, for it overturns that very construction of the child that legitimates, as Dewey said, "an impatient, premature mechanization of impulsive activity after the fixed patterns of adult habits of thought and affection"[24] that is the signature of "necrophilic"[25] formal education: the child as deficit, danger, impulse-ridden, naïve, raw material for the economy, in need of protection, manipulation, bribery, calculated punishment, "instillation," indoctrination. This open space of dialogue and interrogation of CPI, into which adults enter themselves, not just as models and coaches but as (albeit specialized) interlocutors, requires them to re-arrange their thinking about what they are hearing and who they are hearing it from—not to understand children's formulations as naïve, or random, but as fragments of emergent world-view in the making. Adults as models, coaches and interlocutors preside over a dialogical space that, by its very interactional structure, challenges the natural social-survivalist camouflage-position that children (and adults) most often take of mimicking the cliches they hear from parents and other authorities, peers and media.

CPI is only one dimension of the neotenic school—the school that, through respecting children, encourages the emergence of a new paradigm—although it is

---

[24] Dewey 1922, p. 96.
[25] Freire 1965.

the most pervasive, in that it acts as a discursive model that frames the whole enterprise. A second fundamental dimension is located in the dialogue between *child and curriculum*, and also has concrete implications for the organization of the curriculum, and for children's role in that organization; an emergent paradigm is related to an emergent curriculum. A curriculum that opens itself to the four instincts that Dewey identifies of construction, communication, investigation and expression, and that frames and reframes itself in response to children's neotenic impulses—"curiosity, wonder, playfulness, imagination, creativity, open-mindedness, flexibility, experimental-mindedness, explorativeness" and so on—is one that adapts itself to the purposive interests of the child. This in no way implies that, in entering dialogue with the child, it must necessarily compromise its logical structure, its internal organization, or its status as cultural conservator. Dialogue operates from both sides, and the adult demands of rigor and continuity are as legitimate as the child's for relevance and immediacy. The most natural operative medium for the child-curriculum dialogue is art—the aesthetic—given the expressive and constructive direction of childhood impulse, and the neotenic status of art in human culture—its role in initiating new perceptual experience through exploration and invention. Art and making of all kinds—plastic arts, music, dance, writing, theatre, crafts, cooking, sewing, building, gardening—ground the impulse-habit relation in the body. They express the creative interaction between the conceptual and the material, and so provide wide bridges to the more abstract inquiries of history, psychology, sociology, science and mathematics, which the creative and resourceful teacher brings as responses to the process of artifact-making; for example, coterminous with children's pottery making, she launches a study project on ancient near-eastern archeology, with an emphasis on the use of pottery as texts through which pre-history is read.

The dimension of child-curriculum dialogue is, as we have seen, also directly related to the ongoing dialogue within CPI, in that the latter is the sphere in which the epistemological reconstruction that interaction with curriculum triggers finds a discursive form—where in fact it is *per*-formed. Here, the new scientific concepts or questions that arise from the child's interaction with materials, art, ideas, knowledge-bases, artifacts and practices, are entertained and encouraged, but through interrogating the assumptions that underlie them. These assumptions comprise the epistemological infrastructure of the current paradigm, and the experimental, transitional space of CPI encourages their deconstruction and, if only implicitly, their reconstruction.

The assumptions that are uncovered through the child's interaction with the curriculum tend to revolve around the beliefs associated with the epistemological, ontological, and ethical concepts—"fact/opinion," "belief/knowledge," "living" or "alive," "nature," "human/animal," "individual/group," "fair," "right" (in all its senses)—that inform our paradigm, or "big picture." CPI is the laboratory of their reconstruction—the place where contradictions appear, and the drive for reorganization is triggered. It is in this discursive space that formal schooling redeems its traditional role as a place apart, disassociated from everyday work and knowledge, that has, from its beginnings, distinguished the school from the "village curriculum."[26] The difference here is that it is a space of questioning rather than mindless affirmation, of the evolutionary gambit rather than mechanical socio-economic reproduction of citizens/workers/consumers; it functions in the interest of the new, emergent paradigm that is governed by the neotenic impulse, rather than the old, which is governed by gerontomorphosis.[27]

A third, closely related dimension of neotenic school practice opens directly from the philosophical dialogue of CPI into the practical, ethical, collective action-space of democratic world-making. As an approximation of an ideal speech situation, CPI offers a functional space for shared decision-making and collaborative governance within the adult-child collective. This is a direct realization of Dewey's "embryonic society," one that is already present in the international democratic school movement.[28] It implies a reconstruction of the relations of power, based on the assumption of children's capacity for social self-regulation in the context of an intentional adult-child collective, for the development of habits that allow for mediating and resolving conflicts of interest, and for the reconstruction of authority and personal responsibility and individual-group relations through "direct democracy." The reconstruction of personal and social habits related to governance, group-discipline, individual-group responsibilities, and to ways of dealing with violation of group norms, is a fundamental aspect of a new paradigm, for it addresses the habits—domination exploitation, privilege, inequality, gratuitous hierarchy—that keep the old one in place. As a model of self-governance, the neotenic school works for the emergence of an authentic democratic subject, in whom, in Dewey's words, "habit is plastic to the transforming touch of impulse"[29] in the implicit interest of "a future new society of changed purposes and desires,"[30] and for whom "situations into which change and the unexpected enter are a challenge to intelligence to create new principles."[31]

Finally, a fourth dimension leads from the interaction of the previous three into community expression as group production and activism. Concepts that are encountered in experiencing the curriculum—the concept of "life" in biological inquiry, for example, of "just war" in social studies, or of "form and function" in science in science, art, architecture and town planning—enter a space of interrogation in community of philosophical inquiry. As a result of their interrogation there, they can be translated into an ethical and political space—"what should we then do?" Through a process of democratic group deliberation, they are transformed into specific actions. The activist collective understands itself as implicitly connected with

---

[26] Lancy 2008 and 2010.

[27] Montagu (1989) characterizes gerontomorphosis as "a form of evolution by specialization ['development of special adaptations to a particular habitat or mode of life'] of the adult stages of successive independent developments. Its net effect is to decrease ability for further evolution and to expose species to extinction" (pp. 9, 253).

[28] http://en.wikipedia.org/wiki/Democratic_education.

[29] Dewey 1922, p. 102.

[30] Ibid., p. 96.

[31] Ibid., p. 239.

and responsible to the larger community, where projects that model the emergent paradigm enter the macrosphere of shared (and perhaps conflicting) values and conscientious action. Concrete projects dedicated to saving the biosphere, to speaking out against the depredations of total war and economic disaster, to succoring the vulnerable and the marginalized, to building relationships with other adult-child collectives around the world—these are natural outgrowths of an emergent paradigm that is in the process of reconstructing notions of moral responsibility at the level of the collective. They move child adult-dialogue into an expanded sphere, where the pedomorphic "embryonic society" of school encounters the very often dystopic policies and practices of the larger society, and seeks to engage it concrete solutions to very practical problems.

Conclusion: A new relation to nature

The emergent paradigm, on Marcuse's account, finds its primary narrative in what he calls a "new relation to nature." This relation is the central element of his evolutionary thinking. I quote him at length:

> In the established society, nature itself, ever more effectively controlled, has in turn become another dimension for the control of man: the extended arm of society and its power. Commercialized nature, polluted nature, militarized nature cut down the life environment of man, not only in an ecological but also in a very existential sense. It blocks the erotic cathexis (and transformation) of his environment: it deprives man from finding himself in nature, beyond and this side of alienation; it also prevents him from recognizing nature as *subject* in its own right—a subject with which to live in a common universe. . . Liberation of nature is the recovery of the life-enhancing forces in nature, the sensuous aesthetic qualities which are foreign to a life wasted in unending competitive performances: they suggest the new qualities of *freedom*. No wonder then that the 'spirit of capitalism' rejects or ridicules the idea of liberated nature, that it relegates this idea to the poetic imagination. Nature, if not left alone and protected as 'reservation', is treated in an aggressively scientific way: it is there for the sake of domination; it is value-free matter, material. This notion of nature is a *historical* a priori, pertaining to a specific form of society. A free society may well have a very different a priori and a very different object; the development of the scientific concepts may be grounded in an experience of nature as a totality of life to be protected and 'cultivated', and technology would apply this science to the reconstruction of the environment of life.[32]

I have tried to suggest that the neotenic school is a cultural site—in our time and place anyway—where the historical a priori of a free society has a place within

[32] Marcuse 1972, p. 235.

which to emerge and grow, through a process in which both child and adult are active participants. This is in direct contrast to the historical function of schooling under capitalism and the nation state; in fact it may be found to be in direct contrast to traditional education in all its forms, beginning with the tribal initiation hut, which is dedicated—if not by its own nature, then by those who control it from above—to minimizing difference, creativity and ongoing social reconstruction in the interest of gerontocratic structures of domination. This suggests to me that at this crisis point in our species history, our global situation of crisis has obliged us to undertake a radical re-evaluation of the value and role of childhood in bio-cultural (i.e. brain-based) and cultural and social evolution, a re-evaluation that is summarized in the biological and psychological concept of neoteny, which in fact only emerged in the latter half of the 19th century (Montagu 1989). It is just the qualities of childhood that adults require in order to reverse the trend towards planetary dystopia; and it is just education in the form of the adult-child collective of school—understood as a laboratory for the germination of a form of modal subjectivity that is, in Marcuse's words, "grounded in an experience of nature as a totality of life to be protected and cultivated"—that provides the developmental niche[33] for such an ongoing evolutionary project. Why then do children deserve to be listened to? Because our lives depend on it.

Reference list

Dewey, John. *Human Nature and Conduct: An Introduction to Social Psychology*. New York: Henry Holt & Co., 1922. Print.

Dewey, John. "The Child and the Curriculum." Ed. John Dworkin. *Dewey on Education: Selections*. New York: Teachers College Press, 1956. Print.

Dewey, John. *How We Think*. Revised Edition. Ed. Jo Ann Boydston. *The Later Works, 1925-1953, Volume 8: 1933*. Carbondale, IL: Southern Illinois University Press, 1986. Print.

Freire, Paulo. *Pedagogy of the Oppressed*. New York: Continuum, 1965. Print.

Herbert, Nick. *Elemental Mind: Human Consciousness and the New Physics*. New York: Dutton, 1995. Print.

Kennedy, David. "Young Children, Animism, and the Scientific World Picture." *Philosophy Today* 33, 4 (Winter), 1989. Print.

Lancy, David F. *The Anthropology of Childhood: Cherubs, Chattel, and Changelings*. Cambridge: Cambridge University Press, 2008. Print.

Lancy, David F., Bock, John, and Suzanne Gaskins (Eds.). *The Anthropology of Learning in Childhood*. Lanham, MD: AltaMira Press, 2010. Print.

Lovelock, James. *Gaia: A New Look at Life on Earth*. Oxford: OUP, 1979. Print.

Marcuse, Herbert. "The New Sensibility." In *An Essay on Liberation*, 23-48. Boston: Beacon Press, 1969. Print.

Marcuse, Herbert. "Nature and Revolution." In *Counterrevolution and Revolt*, 59-78. Boston: Beacon Press, 1972. Print.

Merleau-Ponty, Maurice. "Methode en Psychologie de L'Enfant." *Bulletin de Psychologie* XVIII 3-6, 1964. Print.

Montagu, Ashley. *Growing Young*. Second Edition. New York: Bergin & Garvey, 1989. Print.

[33] Super & Harkness 1986.

Murris, Karin. "Can Children Do Philosophy?" *Journal of Philosophy of Education* 34, 2: 261-279, 1999. Print.

Pearce, Joseph Chilton. *The Biology of Transcendence: A Blueprint of the Human Spirit*. Rochester, VT: Park Street Press, 2002. Print.

Peirce, Clayton. "Democratizing Science with Marcuse and Latour." Eds. Douglas Kellner, et al. *Marcuse's Challenge to Education*. Lanham, MD: Rowman & Littlefield, 2009. 131-158. Print.

Sheldrake, Rupert. *A New Science of Life: The Hypothesis of Formative Causation*. Third Edition. Los Angeles, CA: J.P. Tarcher, 2009. Print.

Skrbina, David. *Panpsychism in the West*. Cambridge: MIT Press, 2005. Print.

Super, C.M. & Sara Harkness. "The Developmental Niche: A Conceptualization at the Interface of Child and Culture." *International Journal of Behavioral Development* 9: 545-569, 1986. Print.

Ward, Colin. *The Child in the City*. New York: Pantheon, 1978. Print.

Barbara Weber
(Germany)

'To Tolerate Means to Insult' (J. W. v. Goethe): Towards a Social Practice of Recognition

The German poet and philosopher Johann Wolfgang von Goethe states in his writings 'On Maxims and Reflections': "Tolerance should only be a temporal attitude. But with time it has to lead into recognition: To tolerate means to insult."[1] At the first glance, this statement sounds rather surprising. After all, isn't tolerance one of our most acknowledged and praised Western values—the basis of democracy and plural societies? And although Goethe is probably one of the earliest critics of tolerance, he is by far not the only one. For example, the German philosopher Herbert Marcuse reveals a social practice of 'repressive tolerance,' i.e. in societies where tolerance is one of its core values, even the most rational and well-founded arguments often remain unheard or ignored. As a consequence, this kind of 'repressive tolerance' leads to a widespread indifference which reinforces the continuation of injustice or violence (e.g., against Human Rights).

> Tolerance is an end in itself. The elimination of violence and the reduction of suppression to the extent required for protecting humans and animals from cruelty and aggression are preconditions for the creation of a humane society. ... Tolerance is extended to policies, conditions, and modes of behaviour which should not be tolerated because they are impeding, if not destroying, the chances of creating an existence without fear and misery.[2]

Marcuse suspects (probably rightly) that tolerance gives the aloof and uncaring majority of people a 'legitimate reason' (in form of an accepted value) to stand back, even when they are direct witnesses of social injustice or violence; and the ruling class welcomes this 'cultivated indifference' in the form of tolerance because they can proceed with their practices and sustain the system of power. Consequently, Marcuse proposes a 'practice of intolerance,' especially against old ways of thinking, the oppressing usage of vocabulary, and unjust or violent practices of the ruling powers.

I agree with Marcuse's general attempt, and so I would like to show, in the first part of my paper, why 'tolerance' indeed leads to a destructive form of 'indifference' or even suppression. In the second part of my paper, I will explore the no-

[1] „Toleranz sollte nur eine vorübergehende Gesinnung sein: sie muss zur Anerkennung führen. Dulden heißt beleidigen.“ Goethe, 2006, p. 151, translated by B.W.

[2] Marcuse 1969, p. 95f.

tion of recognition that is suggested in the works of Charles Taylor and Axel Honneth. In so doing, we will come to the conclusion that neither of these approaches offers a specific way forward when confronted with radical alterity. In the third part of my paper, I will argue that an upright and candid cultivation of mutual recognition requires the courage to openly admit and welcome Otherness,[3] as well as the willingness to argue and challenge those with whom we disagree, and that such recognition is a benefit both to the other and to the self.

Tolerance as Virtue and Vice: a Phenomenological Analysis

Enduring Otherness

'To tolerate' comes originally from the Latin word *tolerare*, which means 'to endure' or 'to suffer.' For example, we can be more or less tolerant of pain and this will determine whether or not we choose an anaesthetic injection at the dentist. But what does it mean when we say that we 'tolerate' another form of life, religion, worldview, appearance, or the like?

When Goethe says 'Tolerance should only be a temporal attitude,' then he assumes that, at a first glance, the challenge of our own worldviews or beliefs by an Other is often accompanied by discomfort: In phenomenological terms, 'encountering Otherness' means that we come across something that is absolutely different from us and/or challenges a core aspect of our identity. Most people experience this encounter as a great discomfort, confusion, or profound irritation.

I would like to illustrate this with an example[4]: let us assume that I'm a Christian and I have gone to church every Sunday since I was born. Then, as long as I live in a homogenous society where everyone goes to church, my way of living remains unquestioned. But as soon as there is an atheist who doesn't go to church, but sleeps in or makes money or spends time with his family on Sundays, my way of living becomes arbitrary, and I have to justify in front of myself and others, why I choose to go to the service on Sundays. Thus, the atheist might become a threat to the meaning that 'attending the service on Sunday' has for me.

In situations like this, toleration is a very important virtue, because it allows me to endure the discomfort and irritation that comes from the encounter with 'Otherness,' i.e., it gives me time to ponder whether or not my choice of actions and beliefs might or might not be the right or best one. Tolerance is a true virtue in this case because it enables me to endure the discomfort of encountering this 'alterity': i.e., I allow the other to challenge my system of beliefs and actions and, at the same time, I take the value of other beliefs or practices into consideration.

The opposite of tolerance (as a first reaction) would be: (a) **hatred**, e.g., I regard non-Christians as 'non humans', evil or devils; (b) **ignorance or negation**, e.g., I simply ignore those people who don't go to church; (c) **assimilation**, e.g., I assume

[3] I will use the phenomenological term 'Otherness' or also 'Alterity' whenever I refer to an encounter with, e.g., different views, behaviour, actions or worldviews that profoundly challenge my own identity and/or set of beliefs.

[4] This example is, of course, a simplification.

that they do 'service' in a different way, but in the end it is just 'like us'; (d) **pity**, e.g., I think that 'those non-Christians' don't know better and we have to educate them, or that those poor atheists or non-believers will go to hell.[5]

Thus, it seems that being able to tolerate the irritation that accompanies the realisation of Otherness is positive and helpful, because (a) it reveals another way of being in the world to us which we recognize as an alternative option and (b) we become aware of the Other as a person on my level, whose decisions I have to take into account. The longer we can tolerate the Otherness of the Other, the deeper we can consider its true value.

Cultivating Indifference

As shown above, the literal meaning of 'toleration' always entails a negative connotation of enduring something unpleasant, painful or disturbing. And when we use this kind of vocabulary for describing behaviour or reaction towards pain, then this makes sense and we all are able to empathize with this kind of description. However, a problem occurs when the same vocabulary is permanently used with regard to other people, worldviews or cultural practices. It becomes problematic because an attitude towards something annoying or disturbing is permanently being transferred onto humans or a human behaviour, which now puts them in the category of 'pain,' 'failure,' or 'disruption,' but at the same time, classifies our attitude of 'tolerance' as something honourable, i.e., we suffer, but we are brave and endure the pain.

When tolerance and 'benevolence' towards behaviour or practices that we do not really recognize becomes a habit, it often results in a 'hypocritical friendliness,' which suppresses feelings *per se* because they might be negative. Consequently, we cultivate a 'cosy relativist culture' of 'I'm okay, you're okay, and it's okay,' within which nobody really cares what other people are doing, or whether or not their cultural practices are acceptable. In addition, this 'false welfare' and 'pseudo friendly' behaviour often reduces the Otherness of the Other whereby we take away the personhood of the other: an animal, for example, that doesn't go to church is not a threat to my own choice; and similarly, but unfortunately, we also find children whose beliefs or behaviour differ from our own much less threatening to our own identity. This is why we similarly often regard those people, whose worldviews or practices we find repulsive or threatening, as 'primitives' or 'not yet human.' And

[5] This last kind of 'welfare' and 'wishing well' can be particularly cruel and Goethe describes this very eloquently in his novel 'Die Wahlverwandtschaften' (Elected Affinities) when he says about the female character Charlotte: 'In allen Familien, wo sie hinkam, erkundigte sie sich nach den Kranken und Schwachen, die nicht in Gesellschaft erscheinen konnten. Sie besuchte sie auf ihren Zimmern, machte den Arzt und drang einem jeden aus ihrer Reiseapotheke, die sie beständig im Wagen mit sich führte, energische Mittel auf; da denn eine solche Kur, wie sich vermuten lässt, gelang oder misslang, wie es der Zufall herbeiführte. // In dieser Art von Wohltätigkeit war sie ganz grausam und ließ sich gar nicht einreden, weil sie fest überzeugt war, dass sie vortrefflich handle." Goethe shows how Charlotte's 'pretending to be good to other people can be much more cruel then an upright selfishness or intolerance. She wants to be good to others only for her own sake and uses other people viciously in order to feel good about herself. I owe this quote to Prof. Dr. Steven Taubeneck from a personal communication that we had in March 2012.

by taking away their personhood, we escape the danger of having to engage with them in a dialogue or controversy.

The suppression of personhood is by far easier and 'cosier' than recognizing the other as a person because the latter, most of the time, has to lead to action: i.e., either it leads into a change of my own set of beliefs through accepting or appreciating the Other's worldview (which doesn't necessarily mean that I will do the same as the other, i.e., I can also just accept the other's choice as a legitimate choice while I at the same time remain with my own way of living or doing) or it leads into a candid challenge and criticism of the other. In both cases, I engage in a sincere dialogue with the other and, thus, become vulnerable to his/her criticism. Engaging in a controversy is also unpleasant, because I might come to the conclusion that I do not want to recognize or even accept certain cultural practices.[6]

This is why wishing to cultivate 'tolerance' as a permanent virtuous attitude in a multicultural society seems inevitably to lead ultimately to the cultivation of indifference and prevent the sincere recognition of 'Others' in their personhood. This, in turn, leads to the suggestion that cultivating intercultural recognition is important.

The Importance of Recognition for Intercultural Relationships

To respect and recognize cultural and ethnic differences and, at the same time, guarantee the equality of treatment, are among the most crucial challenges that plural democracies are faced with. It results in multiple problems, such as the struggle for recognition of cultural minorities or the actualization of universal human rights. However, is the 'recognition of Otherness' at all possible, especially if 'recognition' not only means the perception and identification of Otherness, but, as well, entails an affirmation within the dialogical process of self-actualization in a public space? In the following, I will show the importance of recognition within multicultural societies by referring to Charles Taylor and Axel Honneth. It will demonstrate why tolerance can never be sufficient for the dialectic identity building process in heterogenic societies, but rather, is highly destructive.

Between Identity and Difference: Charles Taylor

Among the first philosophers who revealed the underlying emotional motivations of political actions and intercultural deliberations was Charles Taylor.[7] He claims that human identity in its fullness can only be achieved in interaction with the world and with "significant others." This Hegelian reflection on the dialectical character of identity implies that mutual interdependence is not antithetical to one's ability to achieve individuality, but is rather a crucial aspect of it.[8]

---

[6] But there is no use in making up our "Western mind" about these limitations of recognition before engaging in such a dialogue because we might be surprised: In the end we always have to assume that "the Other could be right." Gadamer 1996, p. 320.

[7] Taylor's call for a "politics of difference" is illustrated in his example of minority francophone Quebecois who seek recognition from the rest of English-speaking Canada (see Taylor 1992, pp. 32ff.).

[8] See ibid. p. 36f.

To illustrate the importance but also the difficulties of the process of identity building, both on a cultural and individual level, Taylor goes back to Hegel's metaphor of master and slave. Hegel claims that every individual strives for recognition. But in our struggle for honour, both, the winner and the looser come from this struggle disappointed: the looser, because he won't get the recognition he wanted, and the winner, because the recognition which he now receives from the looser is of no value. The only recognition that is truly valuable is the one we receive in a symmetrical relationship.[9] Consequently, Taylor asks: is recognition between different cultures ever possible? Or more abstractly: How can we achieve equality within difference?[10]

To answer this question, we have to take a closer look at the struggle for recognition in former times. Here Taylor discloses a significant change throughout history: in the past, recognition was received through 'honour,' and its very idea was based on difference. However, the destruction of hierarchies in modern societies led to the substitution of the notion of 'honour' with 'dignity,' which is based on equality and universalism rather than difference.[11] These are the foundational values of modern democracy, i.e., mutual recognition of the human dignity as well as the equality of rights.[12] In addition, around 1900, individual identity became more important than the affiliation with a group or belonging to a class. Every person was different in kind, but the same in value. From now on, self-realization was a task that everyone had to master by him/herself and in relationship with a heterogenic society.[13]

Hence, for Taylor, the process of identity building and finding social recognition is a rather new process that occurs between the dialectical poles of identity (same in value through dignity) and difference (different in kind through our authentic being in the world). However, Taylor's account of recognition is largely descriptive, and he leaves us with the question of what intercultural recognition would actually entail.

The Three Fundamental Spheres of Recognition: Axel Honneth on Love, Right and Solidarity

With a very similar attempt and around the same time as Taylor wrote his book on recognition, the German philosopher Axel Honneth published his work *Struggle for Recognition* and showed how power, recognition, and respect are linked within public space.[14] In his philosophical analysis of political actions, Honneth discloses three fundamental relationships between humans: (a) love, (b) right and (c) solidarity. He states that in each of these spheres, humans are being recognized in a different way. And of course, recognition can also be withheld in each of these three spheres,

[9] See Hegel's master-slave dialectic in Hegel, 1977, esp. Paragraph 179.
[10] Taylor, p. 38f.
[11] Ibid, p. 37f.
[12] See particularly the notion of human dignity in Kant (1996).
[13] Taylor, p. 36f.
[14] For my following account of Honneth's theory I will mostly refer to Honneth 1992.

which can lead to (a) physical abuse, (b) underprivileging and (c) humiliation. In the following, I will characterize the three spheres of recognition.

A baby or child experiences recognition through the love of his/her mother, father or caregiver. This love and attention are so existential that babies who do not receive this kind of attention will die. Being held and caressed by the loving touch of the parent, the baby develops awareness of itself as an embodied being. The love of parents for the child is unique, but not based on any achievements, i.e., they don't love the baby because of its abilities, but rather their love is unconditioned.

The second sphere is called 'right,' which is fundamentally different from love: whereas the first is limited to only one person or a small group of people, the latter, by definition, applies to everybody (of a state or country).[15] And although love and right are quite different in this way, the very notion and understanding of 'right' in itself is based on the experience of love: it is the reciprocal recognition of the other as the 'generalized friend or family member.' This kind of generalized perspective-taking enables us to grant a person fundamental rights, although we have no emotional bond, i.e. we can imagine how we *would* feel if he was our friend or family member.

The third sphere of recognition is called 'solidarity' and it is based on the achievements within a particular social group that share a specific goal. The recognition of the value of the individual contributions is based on the impact those contributions have for the group's attainment of their vision. Every contribution is being evaluated independently of any emotional bonding, i.e., we don't necessarily need to be friends or like a person in order to acknowledge his/her achievements within a field or for a group, e.g., the ability to talk about god to believers, the ability to hunt in a group of hunters or specific intellectual abilities within a society that is based on knowledge and research. Thus, recognition in the sphere of solidarity is very different from the recognition in the sphere of love or right because it is neither bound to the unconditioned love that we receive from our friends or family members (biased, particular), nor is it a purely law based universal recognition of our equality (universal and the same for everyone).

Solidarity is a particularly important kind of recognition because each member is being seen in his/her difference *and* similarity: i.e., different in kind (e.g. in knowledge, abilities, skills etc.), but similar in value (because they all belong to the same group). Thus, the paradox of the master-slave relationship, which we have come across in Taylor's account (and in relation to Hegel), is partly solved by the belonging to different subgroups or cultures, which are structured symmetrical internally, but hierarchically towards other subgroups or cultures.[16] Hence, the members of one group do not only derive self-value through their value and recognition within this group, but also just 'by belonging to this group,' i.e., to be part of a particular vision (e.g., like a Christian might be proud to be a Christian, and so forth). Thus, in order to secure the stability of the group, as well as their personal value within this group, they will fight for their survival. For each group, it is crucial that they are not

[15] This is why 'Justicia', the goddess of justice, is often shown blindfold.

[16] Also ibid, p. 199.

only 'tolerated' within a society, but that their vision is a legitimate choice, if not 'the only choice.'

On the other hand, solidarity creates problems within heterogenic societies, where core beliefs or visions are not being recognized by other members or might even collide. Then a 'struggle for recognition' arises. Or as Honneth states: "When, in former times, the characteristics of the individual were determined by the collective [e.g., the guild of bakers] and thus the amount of social honour was tied to the status of the guild in society, we nowadays lack this possibility because of the disintegration of the traditional value structures."[17]

Often these underlying struggles for recognition are overshadowed by struggles about money. Money increases power and, at the same time, is an objective way to compare whose abilities and skills are most highly valued in a society (e.g., how much somebody earns per hour shows how valued his/her skills/abilities are). As a consequence, and because of the heterogeneity of modern societies, 'social honour' transforms into 'prestige' and becomes visible to the public by the means of desired consumer items like cars, real estate, watches, clothes, jewellery and the like; these products become 'subgroup transcending' symbols for the social recognition of a person.

And because heterogenic societies are faced with a conglomerate of contradicting visions, the chances of exclusion or disregard of goals, visions or practices are very high. Of course, it becomes especially problematic when a whole culture is not recognized within the 'contest of cultures': "The evaluative degrading of specific patterns of self-actualization means that the person cannot relate with his conduct of life to something that is of high value or meaning for the community as a whole; for the individual this not only leads to the experience of a social degrading, but usually also to a loss of self-esteem; i.e., the chance to see him/herself as being recognized and valued in his/her very own characteristics, skills and abilities."[18] Honneth emphasizes that this kind of degrading of the integrity of human beings is as severe as any other physical sickness and becomes apparent in symptoms like shame and anger.

However, Honneth, too, leaves us alone with the question, *how* we ought to deal with radical cultural differences? Are we required to 'recognize' other cultures, even if their values and beliefs are radically against our own beliefs and worldviews? Or can we just 'tolerate' them? What does the recognition of 'Otherness' really

---

[17] Ibid, p. 203, translated by B.W. In original: „Waren derartige Eigenschaftsdifferenzen bislang kollektivistisch bestimmt, um an der Standeszugehörigkeit des einzelnen das Maß seiner sozialen Ehre festzumachen, so entfällt diese Möglichkeit nun mit der allmählichen Auflösung der traditionellen Werthierarchie."

[18] Ibid, p. 217, translated by B.W. In original: „Die evaluative Degradierung von bestimmten Mustern der Selbstverwirklichung hat für deren Träger zur Folge, dass sie sich auf ihren Lebensvollzug nicht als auf etwas beziehen können, dem innerhalb ihres Gemeinwesens eine positive Bedeutung zukommt; für den Einzelnen geht daher mit der Erfahrung einer solchen sozialen Entwertung typischerweise auch ein Verlust an persönlicher Selbstschätzung einher, der Chance also, sich selber als ein in seinem charakteristischen Eigenschaften und Fähigkeiten geschätztes Wesen verstehen zu können."

mean; or even more radical, is the recognition of 'Otherness' possible? These questions are increasingly pressing because they touch the core of our identity (cultural and personal). I will now turn to those questions.

Recognition in Heterogenic Societies

Neither Taylor nor Honneth offers us specifics with regard to what is required of us for recognizing the other in a heterogeneous society. On the one hand, Taylor argues for importance of recognition but without direction, while on the other, Honneth's theory of the three spheres of recognition appears to leave us with a gap. That is, if the other is neither loved nor recognized in solidarity as contributing to the goals of the society, it appears that we are left only with the sphere of rights, and hence seduced back into the position of mere tolerance.

However, as has already been established, mere toleration of Otherness as a persisting attitude towards a person or group of people is degrading because it repeatedly shows the Other that their goals, visions or worldviews are just being 'endured,' but not welcomed or recognized. The continuation of such an attitude leads eventually to indifference because the person who tolerates develops a 'wall' or inner protection against the disturbing behaviour or belief of the other. In the worst case, the 'tolerated' person or group of people lose part of their perceived 'personhood' because they are not seen as even worthy of being challenged or confronted.

Interestingly, if we look to the contrary of tolerance within a valued relationship (and hence one in which hatred, the assumption of ignorance, of pity would be out of place), we begin to find the answer to what is required of us with regard to recognizing the other. In a situation in which we care for the other, we would never 'tolerate' a behaviour that goes against our core values: e.g., if my partner commits a crime, because I care for him, I will criticize him and bring up all the arguments and reasoning I have to show that his actions were ill-willed. My open disrespect and intolerance towards his actions is a sign for our 'symmetric relationship' where I can candidly express my view because I know that the other is able to lay out his/her own convictions.[19] At the end of such an open confrontation, we may have gained some insight into the other's reasons and feelings, and we may even be able to recognize the other's choice as a legitimate choice, i.e., an extension of ways of being and engaging in the world or actualizing one's identity. What recognition (of the value of relationship) requires, in other words, is authentic communication.

[19] However, I also want to warn against the opposite of a positive engagement with and interest in others. This would be an insensitive intervention in other people's businesses to the degree where it becomes impolite or even impudent. Of course, there is a happy medium of positive and interested engagement with Others, with its extremes of indifference on the one side and brazen interference on the other.

Towards a Forth Sphere of 'Recognition': Authentic Communication

There have been many arguments why people ought to engage in a dialogue with people holding opposing opinions or convictions. Some of those arguments refer to the notion of sympathy (Rorty), some to reason (Peirce, Habermas) and some to understanding (Gadamer). At this point I would like to bring up Mill's argument by referring to his powerful chapter in his book "On Liberty," where he talks "Of the Liberty of Thought and Discussions." Mill assumes three possibilities when we actually engage in dialogue with 'the Other': a. the other is wrong, or b. we are wrong, or c. we are both somewhere in between.[20] He writes:

> If all mankind minus one were of one opinion, and only one person were of the contrary opinion, mankind would be no more justified in silencing that one person, than he, if he had the power, would be justified in silencing mankind. . . .But the peculiar evil of silencing the expression of an opinion is that it is robbing the human race; posterity as well as the existing generation; those who dissent from the opinion, still more than those who hold it. If the opinion is right, they are deprived of the opportunity of exchanging error for truth: if wrong, they lose, what is almost as great a benefit, the clearer perception and livelier impression of truth, produced by its collision with error. ... We can never be sure that the opinion we are endeavouring to stifle is a false opinion; and if we were sure, stifling it would be an evil still.[21]

What is particularly interesting about Mill's suggestions is the fact that he claims that stifling a false opinion is a great evil. Why should this be so? The reason is that the moment we rely and rest upon our past justifications, we miss the opportunity to strengthen our own justifications. Every opportunity for such dialogue carries the possibility of bringing up new perspectives and new details to consider, which in turn may lead to the reformulating and refining of our opinions, worldviews and practices, in the light and the perspective of the other. What we gain is such dialogue, in other words, is a kind of 'continuous becoming to an awareness of who we are,' as well as a deepening of self-reflectedness.[22] Thus, though we may want to escape the need to revisit and re-justify our decisions because it takes effort

---

[20] Mill is talking here about an opinion being 'right' or 'wrong' and one might use a different vocabulary nowadays like 'more or less justified/reflected' or 'taking more or less perspectives into account' or the like.

[21] Mill 1985, pp. 84f.

[22] Mill's argument becomes even more taxing when we link it with Habermas' theory of 'communi cative rationality.' Habermas argues that societies become increasingly heterogeneous and complex. This leads to a diversity of 'lifeworlds' (the preconceptions of how we see and understand the world), which then leads to misunderstanding because each of our beliefs 'rest' upon a different lifeworld-perspective. Usually these 'lifeworlds' remain hidden. But heterogeneous societies offer the chance to disclose each other's preconceptions through dialogue and disagreement. (See: Habermas 1992).

or makes us insecure about who we are and what we believe, nonetheless, we need to keep in mind how much we gain in self-expansion and self-security if we do so.

Lastly we must keep in mind the importance of "choice." As embodied entities, we are ontologically constrained in time and space: our lives are 'a being towards death,'[23] and because we are finite and embodied, we can only be in one place at a time. Consequently, people can only actualize a limited number of beliefs and practices on their own. This condition makes choice necessary (e.g., at every minute we choose to do A instead of B and so on) and every choice suppresses all other choices. We speak about "free choice" (on a very basic level) when we recognize the value of different possibilities from which we choose the best one for us at a given time and with respect to our circumstances. When others make choices that are different from ours, they actually expand the horizon of possibility from which to choose. In so doing, this increase of choices makes my own choice even more valuable because it increases my freedom, i.e., the variety of possibilities from which I choose.[24] In the end, if I only have one choice then I'm not free, but rather forced to do what is required. This awareness of choice expansion transforms diversity into something desirable because it makes our decisions much more valuable, i.e., we form our identity by deciding what we wish to do at a given time. The fact that there are more possibilities than we can ever actualize in a lifetime should make us cautious about what we choose, while the fact that other people will actualize other ways of being in the world should (or can) help us to develop a deep appreciation of the opportunities that such diversity indeed offers.

Reference list:

Gadamer, Hans-Georg. *Über die Aktualität der Hermeneutik*, in: Volker Caysa and Klaus-Dieter Eichler, ed., Philosophiegeschichte und Hermeneutik. Leipzig: Leipziger Universitätsverlag, 1996.

Goethe, Johann Wolfgang von. *Maximen und Reflexionen*. München: dtv, 2006.

Habermas, Jürgen. *Faktizität und Geltung*. Frankfurt am Main: Suhrkamp, 1992.

Heidegger, Martin. *Sein und Zeit.* Tübingen: Niemeyer, 1967.

Hegel, Georg Wilhelm Friedrich. *Phenomenology of Spirit*. Trans. A.V. Miller. Oxford: Clarendon Press, 1977.

Honneth, Axel. *Kampf um Anerkennung. Zur moralischen Grammatik sozialer Konflikte*. Frankfurt am Main: Suhrkamp, 1992.

Kant, Immanuel. *The Metaphysics of Morals.* Trans.Mary J. Gregor. Cambridge University Press, 1996.

Marcuse, Herbert. "Repressive Tolerance," in Robert Paul Wolff, Barrington Moore, jr. and Herbert Marcuse, *A Critique of Pure Tolerance*. Boston: Beacon Press, 1969.

---

[23] Heidegger 1967, p. 235.

[24] The Canadian phenomenologist James Mensch argues that other people do not limit our freedom, but rather increase it. He calls it the 'intersubjective genesis of freedom.'In his book *Embodiments,* he argues that our choices are limited as a child, but as we grow up in a social world, various ways of engaging in the world are being disclosed by our caregivers and friends. See: Mensch, 2009, esp. pp. 129-141.

Mensch, James. *Embodiments: From the Body to the Body Politic*. Evanston, Illinois: North Western University Press 2009.

Mill, John Stuart. *On Liberty*. Ed. Gertrude Himmelfarb. UK: Penguin, 1985.

Taylor, Charles. *Multiculturalism and the Politics of Recognition*. Princeton: Princeton University Press, 1992.

Beth A. Dixon and Charles J. List
(USA)

Breaking the Rules of Respect

In this paper we articulate dissatisfaction with rules about respect in two areas: K-12 character education programs and hunter education programs. We recommend a better way to teach respect in each of these ethical domains, relying on an Aristotelian model of practical reason.

The correct analysis of practical reasoning is a matter of some dispute. We shall not enter this debate except to say that the understanding we have of it is in line with at least some standard treatments.[1] As we see it, practical reasoning requires two kinds of skills. First, it involves *thinking* skills achieved by doing conceptual analysis of ethical concepts against the background of a particular context. Second, practical reasoning requires a set of *doing* skills or habits which enable one to act in the right way at the right time. In some areas one or the other of these skills are more prominent, but ultimately both are necessary.

In what follows we will use this division of practical reason into two parts to organize our discussions of respect. One of us will primarily discuss the kinds of knowledge and understanding necessary for a full and nuanced understanding of the concept of respect in character education. And the other will discuss the more practical and habitual side in hunter education. Together, we hope to illustrate how understanding and practicing respect in two particular areas enables practical wisdom in children and young adults.

How *Not* To Teach Respect

One local school district in upstate New York implements a character education program known as "Positive Behavioral Interventions and Supports" (PBIS).[2] This program is a "team based systematic approach to teaching behavioral expectations throughout the school" in a variety of settings. For example, Stafford Middle School Behavioral Expectations Matrix identifies an array of examples of respectful behavior that should be manifested in a variety of school settings (move quietly and stay to the right in hallways, turn off water in bathrooms, respect equipment in computer labs, report to health office when ill or injured, etc.). The four phases of PBIS implementation are: (1) Define the behavioral expectations under broad themes such as

[1] See, for example, Bloomfield (2000), Homiak (2004), Sherman (1989), and Zagzebski (1996).
[2] Plattsburgh City School District: http://www.plattscsd.org/PBIS.htm (accessed May 2012). See also the main website for PBIS: http://www.pbis.org/default.aspx (accessed May 2012).

"Be Safe," "Be Responsible," and "Be Respectful."[3] (2) Teach the behaviors—conveyed and reinforced by teachers, administrators, school aids, and counselors, in a variety of school settings. (3) Reinforce good behavior by public rewards such as Good Citizen Postcards, Praise Hats, Pizza Parties, etc. (4) Collect data and assess by means of disciplinary referrals to help identify which students are having a hard time complying with behavioral expectations and need more support from teachers, counselors, or staff.[4]

This kind of character education program is an example of what Maughn Gregory calls "values transmission" as well as "behavior modification."[5] The program specifies the *right values* in advance, where the central aim of such a program is to attempt to modify students' behavior to conform to these values.

What should we say about such a program? Well, clearly "Be Respectful" is not a bad value, even though it could be argued that students might benefit from asking and trying to answer themselves what values are worth holding.[6] But even if we concede that the values selected by the school (or by the state) are worth instilling in young people, there are a number of problems with the PBIS program as a way to educate for moral character.

Concepts and Rules

One obvious problem with this particular character education program is that it fails to align the concept of respect with the rules of behavior which exemplify that concept. In fact, it would be a serious intellectual challenge to work out what it is that all the rules of behavior listed under "Be Respectful" have in common. For example, it is not clear what characteristic unites all of the following as instances of respect: "treat books and equipment with care," "turn off water" in bathrooms, and "report to health office when ill or injured."

Now why should this matter that the rules of behavior about respect "pull apart" from the concept of respect? After all, if we are in the business of modifying behavior then we might just as well emphasize rules about behavior, and work hard to ensure that young people comply with these rules by using both positive and negative reinforcement—rewards and discipline. One reason for concern here is that using a finite collection of rules about behavior vastly underdetermines the number

---

[3] For example, see Stafford Middle School PBIS behavioral matrix: http://www.plattscsd.org/SMS/SMSPBIS.htm (accessed May 2012).

[4] PBIS website: http://www.pbis.org/default.aspx (accessed May 2012).

[5] Gregory 2009.

[6] Maughn Gregory (2009) articulates this critical point in the following way when he writes, "Nor do these programs provide opportunity for students to express doubt or criticism of the proffered virtues, or to practice open-ended ethical inquiry. The virtues that constitute good character come pretty much pre-defined in the curriculum materials, and the only thinking expected from children is thinking about how best to implement them; the "moral feeling" expected is appreciation of just these virtues, uncomplicated by doubt. This failure to recognize the ambiguity of children's ethical experience is an adultist fallacy" (p. 10).

and variety of new settings in which we might want young people to act respectfully. There cannot possibly be enough rules about how to behave to cover all of these potentially new contexts that require some judgment about what it means to be respectful in these new sets of circumstances.[7] So even though students may learn how to follow the rules of behavior in 13 school settings, when the rules about behavior fail to capture a univocal concept of respect in the first place it is not likely that students will be able to construct what it means to be respectful in new situations and circumstances.

The defender of the rules approach to teaching respect might reply to this criticism by arguing that we may merely need to align the concept of respect with a different set of rules than the ones used in the Stafford Middle School behavioral matrix. We might begin to do so by first formulating a credible concept of respect. For example, one viable concept might be, "respect those with rational natures." Then the rules of respect would be about the kind of treatment owed to human beings specifically, such as, "Always treat human beings with dignity" or "Never exploit or oppress another human being." Rules about respecting property or inanimate objects would not make it onto this revised list of rules because these would not capture the kinds of things owed respect according to the initial formulation of the concept. Of course, one might still wonder whether or not the selected concept of respect is the right one. But at least the original criticism of the rules approach would be answered. Learning the rules about respect would enable a student to learn something about the concept of respect because, by design, there would be conceptual overlap between the concept and the rules.

Perception of the Particulars

However, there is a deeper problem about using rules of respect as a starting point to educate for moral character. When we assign conceptual priority to any rule like "Be respectful," we overestimate the usefulness of this general rule or principle in guiding behavior in real world circumstances. The rule "Be Respectful" cannot be applied unthinkingly or mechanically. Consider, for example, what I would have to know about the contextual details of a situation in order to work out whether, or how, to act respectfully toward a disloyal friend, a bully who continually demeans me, an abusive parent, or a teacher who may have treated me unfairly. We still have to investigate whether or not *this* situation is one that demands respect from me based on the morally relevant circumstances, e.g., who that person is, what they or I

[7] Lipman, Sharp, and Oscanyan (1980) remark, "If morality were simply a matter of knowing rules and obeying them, then moral education would consist in developing in children a conscientiousness that would permit them to carry out these rules in a happy, unquestioning fashion. But morality is not so simple. It is not clear that there are rules for every situation, nor is it clear that it contributes to children's development that they should accept uncritically those rules that might apply. Consequently, the child must be equipped to cope with situations lacking clear guidelines, situations that nevertheless require that one make choices and that one accept responsibility for the choices one makes." (p. 160).

have done, what our history involves, my interest in preserving good relations, and so on. And if the situation calls for me to be respectful, then I need to also determine what kind of saying or doing is appropriate. In other words, the rule follower still has to decide what features of this situation matter ethically in deciding how to think, feel, say, or act. And, most importantly, the rule by itself does not supply this information. What is needed here is a shifting of attention from the rule to the ethically salient particular circumstances. Aristotle called this acquiring "practical wisdom." In Book II of the *Nicomachean Ethics*, Aristotle describes how finding the intermediate "mean" of each virtue between the vices of excess and deficiency does not depend on knowing a rule about how to act. Rather, it depends on "perception of the particulars."[8] He writes,

> In summary, then, if we do these things we shall best be able to reach the intermediate condition. But no doubt this is hard, especially in particular cases, since it is not easy to define the way we should be angry, with whom, about what, for how long; for sometimes, indeed, we ourselves praise deficient people and call them mild, and sometimes praise quarrelsome people and call them manly. . . But how far and how much we must deviate to be blamed is not easy to define in an account; for nothing perceptible is easily defined, and since these circumstances of virtuous and vicious action are particulars, the judgment about them depends on perception.[9]

Aristotle's general guidelines about developing judgment and perception of the particulars invite an illustrative example.

"The Camel Dances"

Arnold Lobel's fable, "The Camel Dances,"[10] is a poignant story of a camel whose devotion to ballet leads her to practice her "five basic positions a hundred times each day" under the hot desert sun. "To make every movement a thing of grace and beauty," she says. "That is my one and only desire." The camel does not stop practicing even when her feet become blistered and her body aches with fatigue. At last she announces, "Now I am a dancer." But when she dances before invited friends and critics they do *not* applaud. In fact, they are dismissive and cruel in their candid assessment of her abilities. "I must tell you frankly," said a member of the audience, "as a critic and a spokesman for this group, that you are lumpy and humpy. You are baggy and bumpy. You are, like the rest of us, simply a camel. You are *not* and nev-

---

[8] See Irwin (2000) for an interpretation of Aristotle on this point. Further discussion of "moral particularism" can be found in Hooker and Little (2000). Giving conceptual priority to the particular is not an original thesis. See also chapter 9 of Pritchard (1996), Nussbaum (1990), and Garfield (2000).

[9] Aristotle *NE* (1109b12 – 1109b25).

[10] Lobel 1980, p. 22.

er will be a ballet dancer!" But she is not convinced. She reasons that since she has worked so hard she must be a splendid dancer. She continued to dance (for herself), and this brought her great pleasure. According to Lobel, the moral of this story is that "Satisfaction will come to those who please themselves."

Both the story and the moral are delightfully ambiguous. Should we aim to *only* please ourselves? Should we always please ourselves? The plausibility of this fable moral depends on a variety of circumstances that are worth exploring, not just about camels who love to dance, but also about circumstances connected to our own passions, ambitions, and our commitment to these projects. When are we the best judges of our own aspirations and activities? Who should we listen to when critical advice is offered? Consider how we might use this story to explore what it would mean to "respect oneself" as a virtue worth cultivating as part of one's moral character. An Aristotelian-like strategy for identifying what is ethically relevant here is to locate the virtue *respecting oneself* between the vice of excess and the vice of deficiency.

Imagine a person who errs in the direction of having an excessive amount of respect for herself. What kinds of character traits and dispositions would she display and how would she act? Well, she might believe that everything she does is honorable. She might admire herself excessively to the point of reverence. Alternatively, she might admire the wrong features of herself; those that are not, in fact, honorable or admirable. Here we should imagine those people that we know whose self-esteem is grandiose. Such people have an inflated sense of themselves. They may be egoistic and self-centered; thinking only of themselves because they cannot imagine being wrong or misguided about what they say or do. In these cases we say that such a person fails to evaluate herself or her aims and projects, honestly and objectively. Her judgments about herself are skewed and out of proportion to a more realistic assessment of her abilities. To be specific, the vice of excess is *arrogance* or *vanity*; a kind of over-valuing of oneself.

Alternatively, imagine a person who does not have enough respect for himself. This kind of person has low self-esteem and is timid about what he thinks and his capabilities. He may "fold" or acquiesce to others' opinions easily and quickly. He will not stick to his principles but may constantly second-guess himself because he does not value or have much confidence in his own abilities, ideas, or projects. This kind of person also fails to correctly judge oneself. But here one underestimates one's own value and shows disregard, not about others' opinions like an arrogant person does, but about oneself. The vice of deficiency then is *meekness* or being *excessively self-effacing*.

So when *respecting oneself* is a virtue it falls somewhere between the vice of excess—arrogance or vanity, and the vice of deficiency—meekness and being excessively self-effacing. A person who has this virtue is habituated to having the right kind of attitude of respect for oneself, and displays the virtue in the right amounts, at the right times, and in the appropriate circumstances. Does the camel have this virtue, or does she err in one direction or the other? One way of thinking about this is to focus on her remark that she is a "splendid dancer." She says this about herself following the critics' discouraging prediction that she will never be a dancer. If we believe these experts then we might also think that the camel has misjudged herself and her abilities. In this case she would be displaying the vice of arrogance or vanity by persisting in her belief that her dancing is good and denying evidence to the contrary.

On the other hand, we might interpret the camel's aims slightly differently to include a certain feeling that she has when she dances. After all, she expresses her desire to make every movement a thing of grace and beauty. And she only announces that she is finally a dancer after her feet are blistered and her body aches with fatigue. So perhaps she has judged her talent correctly if what she sought to accomplish was to train herself with focus and discipline—to work very hard at something. On this reading of the fable, the camel has displayed just the right amount of value for herself. She identifies what she is trying to do as "pleasing herself," and this she persists in doing by continuing her dancing irrespective of what the critics say. The fable invites us to take either point of view, and to consider other particular contexts that require nuanced judgments about how and when we should value ourselves (what we say, do, or think) in order to hit the mean of the virtue *respecting oneself.* [11]

What matters about this methodology that I've appropriated from Aristotle is that the general rule of conduct "respect oneself," is not the starting point for thinking about what kind of person to be. Understanding what it means to respect oneself is conceptually dependent on the ethically relevant particulars of a (situation, story, or fable). These features include: what I am trying to do, who the critics are, their degree of expertise, what they say, whether or not I am engaged in honorable activities, blindness to my own faults resulting in arrogance or vanity, lack of confidence about my own abilities resulting in meekness or an underestimation of my own worth, and so on. A character education program that cultivates "perception of the particulars" in this way might also contribute to the development of practical wisdom in the sense Aristotle describes.

A Code of Respect in Hunter Education

A close reading of the dancing camel fable above illustrates how a teacher might lead students to a more nuanced and analytical understanding of the concept of respect. This skill is necessary for developing practical reason in the area of ethics but is not sufficient. We must also, as was pointed out, require students to practice respect in varying circumstances. Unfortunately, in the area of hunter education, it seems as if respect means merely memorizing a set of rules. This approach, I know

[11] The interesting ambiguity of this virtue is that *respect* may apply to a person in a more holistic or global way. We sometimes use this word to recommend that every person deserves respect regardless of what kinds of things she says, does, or thinks. This is how the philosopher, Immanuel Kant, uses the concept when he asserts that all human beings are owed respect by virtue of having rational natures. Nevertheless, we do also use the concept of respect to single out certain qualities or traits that we want to commend about a person. This use implies that a person does something to *deserve* respect. In this sense we attribute respect to a person relative to something they do.

from the experience of being a hunter educator, is neither sufficient nor even necessary for teaching respect.

What follows is a quote from "Be a Responsible and Ethical Hunter," a section of *Today's Hunter*.[12] This is the manual used for hunter education classes in New York and many other states. The hunter's ethical code includes:

Respect Natural Resources

- Leave the land better than you found it.
- Support wildlife conservation programs.
- Adhere to fair chase rules.
- Know your capabilities and limitations as a marksman, stay within your effective range, and strive to improve your skills and the likelihood of a clean kill.
- Ensure that meat and usable parts are not wasted.
- Treat both game and non-game animals ethically.
- Abide by game laws and regulations.
- Cooperate with conservation officers.
- Report all game violations.

Respect Non-Hunters

- Transport animals discreetly—don't display them.
- Keep firearms out of sight.
- Refrain from taking graphic photographs of the kill and from vividly describing the kill within earshot of non-hunters.
- Maintain a presentable appearance while on the street—no bloody or dirty clothing.

Clearly there is a lot of respecting hunters are asked to do. In line with the criticisms made earlier in this paper, this code is similarly inadequate. It is organized around the various "interest groups," non-hunters, other hunters, and landowners whose tacit or explicit acceptance is desired by hunters and anglers. To those with a critical philosophical eye, this code will appear ethically mysterious and to some extent duplicitous. The rules or clauses of the code, while certainly sensible, are opaque as to their justification. Respect for "Non-Hunters" seems more public relations than ethics. Some elements of this code concern mere legality and, while these are clearly important, a code surely must go beyond them in its requirements.

It is important to keep in mind as a starting point for the following argument that codes are merely lists of rules and rules are always general. Specific guidance must be supplied by what we've previously discussed as practical reason. We need to act in ways that are appropriate to the conditions in which we find ourselves. That is why virtues—permanent dispositions—are crucial. These are practiced responses to similar situations. A code, as a list of rules of thumb, only hints at this complexity. My motivation in emphasizing the role of practical reasoning in this area comes both

[12] Kalkomey Enterprises, Inc. 2009, pp. 68-69.

from my dissatisfaction with the extremely confined role allowed for ethics in hunter education classes in general, but also, the lack of attention to actual skill development and the formation of good habits. That virtue and skill are connected by practical reason is the working hypothesis for this paper. How they might be actually connected in hunter education is what I now intend to explore in one case.[13]

Excellence and Fair Chase

One's character is a living thing; it grows as we do and as it is nourished by experience. We must then imagine the slow growth of the excellences of character from youth to adulthood. A code, on the other hand, is a set of rules and recommendations without awareness of age and development. As such, the code above, like many others, is set at a minimal level: be safe, obey the law, etc. But, when there is an expectation of eventual excellence in character or the refinement of perception in practical reason, one must seek to attain the highest standards. So codes must somehow state minimal conditions for beginners and, at the same time, urge participants to climb the ladder toward excellence.

Aldo Leopold notes that it is the "peculiar virtue" of hunting that "the hunter ordinarily has no gallery to applaud or disapprove of his conduct. Whatever his acts, they are dictated by his own conscience . . ."[14] This relative isolation places the burden for developing these virtues squarely on the hunter. There are many temptations toward vice: to shoot at animals too distant, to use gadgets that replace skill, to shoot a sitting bird, etc. especially with "no gallery" present. Anglers are similarly tempted. Habitually showing such restraint is a mark of excellence. If one has respect for the biotic community then one will show restraint in these ways.

So why should hunters bother to actually follow these rules if no one is watching? Without a good answer to this question, less charitable critics are more than willing to jump in with their own answers for having such rules: self-deception, social camouflage, etc. Rules about respect, so prominent in the code above, need to be grounded in practice, if these objections are to be met. The rules in a code must be used by mentors to guide beginners through the long and difficult process of developing habits that come to form an environmental character.

Consider then the recommendation to "adhere to fair chase rules." The rules of fair chase typically include a limit on technological advantages for the hunter or angler, the self-imposition of other restraints such as to only shoot at birds when they are flying, or those properly worked by the dog. These self imposed rules make the acquisition of an animal more difficult and hence increase the role of skill. The rules of fair chase thus should be understood as invitations to increase one's level of excellence as measured by skill development. So hunter education faces at least two problems. First, the rules of fair chase are not explored and dissected in the way the dancing camel was. They are merely stated and left for the young hunter to puzzle

---

[13] See List, forthcoming 2013.

[14] Leopold 1969, p. 212.

over. Second, and for my purposes more important, the link between fair chase and skill development is not present. Much better than teaching a rule of fair chase or "respect the natural environment" is the actual guidance of young people to skill development.

One might object at this point that surely there are plenty of highly skilled sportsmen who are also ethically challenged. I guess we have all met those who are masters of their crafts but are still jerks. Perhaps Leopold or Theodore Roosevelt each had highly attuned environmental virtues. Yet in other areas of their lives, they were less than conscientious. This is all true, but not germane, because my claim is much more circumscribed. When young people develop excellent characters and when young hunters develop respect, they have slowly become practically wise. Hunter education offers an activity that has everything necessary for this development to occur: hunting is a self-chosen activity, it has ever higher levels of excellence to induce participants to move forward, it has long traditions and literature valuing these excellences, and finally it recognizes the crucial role of mentoring and the guidance of experience. Unfortunately, these inherent advantages are rarely realized in practice. A pursuit of skillfulness in field sports will inculcate that quest for excellence so necessary for virtue development. So to show respect as a sportsman is a matter of habits formed.

The respect shown by following a rule of fair chase is really a demonstration of skills: the ability to find and pursue animals with minimal technical advantage, for example. Fair chase as a method of pursuit that allows animals the chance to escape is increased by lessening dependence on finders and gadgets by increasing one's own skills of observation and movement. Similarly, respect shown by "not wasting meat" is developed and demonstrated by developing one's culinary skills so delicious meals may be prepared with the meat. One shows respect for landowners by developing skills of friendly interaction. A code is necessary to remind beginners and their teachers of these skills of restraint, but these only become real habits of excellence once expertise is established by skillful performance.

So respect as a rule in a code really means that a host of skills must be developed. For the beginner, these rules are a reminder. For the expert they are a tool for teaching. To the non-sporting public, they need to be explained at every available opportunity.

Conclusion

We have argued that when the concept of respect is interpreted as a set of rules about behavior, it is poorly understood and potentially open to abuse in character education and in hunter education programs. Our suggestion to remedy these problems is to emphasize the role practical reason plays in ethics and especially in virtue development. In this we have highlighted the need for two things. First, particular circumstances demand a kind of dancer's flexibility in ethics to do the right thing at the right time. Second, practice in skill development is required to consistently hit the bull's eye in both ethics and hunting.

Reference list:

Aristotle. *Nicomachean Ethics*. Trans. Terence Irwin. Indianapolis: Hackett Publishing, 1985. Print.

Bloomfield, Paul. "Virtue Epistemology and the Epistemology of Virtue." *Philosophy and Phenomenological Research*, Vol. 60, No. 1. January, 2000. Print.

Garfield, Jay. "Particularity and Principle: The Structure of Moral Knowledge." *Moral Particularism*. Ed. Brad Hooker and Margaret Little. Oxford: Clarendon Press, 2000. Print.

Gregory, Maughn. "Ethics Education and the Practice of Wisdom." *Teaching Ethics*, Spring 2009. Print.

Hooker, Brad and Margaret Little (eds.) *Moral Particularism*. Oxford: Clarendon Press, 2000. Print.

Homiak, Marcia. "Virtue and the Skills of Ordinary Life." *Setting the Moral Compass: Essays by Women Philosophers*. Ed. Cheshire Calhoun. New York: Oxford University Press, 2004. Print.

Irwin, T. H. "Ethics as an Inexact Science: Aristotle's Ambitions for Moral Theory." *Moral Particularism*. Ed. Brad Hooker and Margaret Little. Oxford: Clarendon Press, 2000. Print.

Lipman, Matthew, Ann Margaret Sharp, and Frederick S. Oscanyan (eds.) *Philosophy in the Classroom*, 2nd ed. Philadelphia: Temple University Press, 1980. Print.

Leopold, Aldo. *A Sand County Almanac with Essays on Conservation from Round River*. Ballantine Books, 1969. Print.

List, Charles. *Hunting, Fishing, and Environmental Virtue: Reconnecting Sportsmanship and Conservation*. Corvallis: Oregon State University Press, forthcoming 2013. Print.

Lobel, Arnold. *Fables*. New York: HarperCollins Publishers, 1980. Print.

Nussbaum, Martha. *Love's Knowledge*. New York: Oxford University Press, 1990. Print.

Pritchard, Michael S. *Reasonable Children: Moral Education and Moral Learning*. Lawrence: University Press of Kansas, 1996. Print.

Sherman, Nancy. *The Fabric of Character: Aristotle's Theory of Virtue*. Oxford: Clarendon Press, 1989. Print.

Today's Hunter (Northeast): A Guide to Hunting Responsibly and Safely. Dallas: Kalkomey Enterprises, Inc., 2009. Print.

Zagzebski, Linda Trinkaus. *Virtues of the Mind: An Inquiry into the Nature of Virtue and the Ethical Foundations of Knowledge*. Cambridge: Cambridge University Press, 1996. Print.

Wendy C. Turgeon
(USA)

Bachelard and Korczak on Childhood: Constituting Respect for the Child

Introduction

Where does the child fit into society? Does our society accept children as full-fledged members, equal and co-agents with adults or are they treated as less than the adult members of the human community? What does it mean to "respect a child" or to "respect childhood?" How can we relate to our child selves so as to regain a lost realm of experience in ways that allows us to acknowledge the other that is the child before us? This paper will explore the writings of two quite different 20th century writers on childhood, Janusz Korczak and Gaston Bachelard. Korczak worked with children his entire life and died beside them in a Nazi death camp. Bachelard was a scientist who adopted a phenomenological point of view in order to chart the borders of human experience and the ways in which the natural world shapes our psyches. For him, childhood appeared as a key to understanding the adult experience and as such, needed to be approached through philosophical analysis and poetry as twin forms of human insight. Korczak attempts to re-enter the experience of childhood as a form of critique of society's marginalizing children. Bachelard invites the reader to imaginatively recapture childhood through the poet's voice offering us key insights into our adult lives. Both writers argue for nuanced notions of respect for the child as vital in becoming fully human.

As our guides, Korczak and Bachelard invite us to problematize our own experience of children and childhood through examining our attitudes, behaviours, policies and day to day living, thereby reframing the meaning of respect for the child—those around us and the child within

Korczak's advocacy for the small and disenfranchised

Janusz Korczak led a school in Nazi occupied Poland and argued fiercely against what he saw to be a societal dismissal of children as unimportant or insignificant. His sociological observations offer at the macro level a trenchant critique of societal attitudes that purport to love and cherish children but in fact are deeply flawed through a lack of respect for the lifeworld of the child. In his essays "The Child's Right to Respect" and "When I am Little Again" he details the many small actions of adults that demean children. In the former he offers a political platform on which to argue for the rights of the child and the importance of respecting the very characteristic of childhood that lead us to denigrate it. He opens our eyes to the hidden bias that privilege the adult world experience over that of the child. In the latter essay he imaginatively enters back into his child-self as he spins a tale of dreaming[1] that he is a child again. We go through his days inside his child-self as he faces the mysteries and affronts of everyday life.

In both of these accounts, the theoretical argument and the fictional revisiting of his past, he reveals to us the complicity of the adult world against childhood. Children lack size, possessions, knowledge—all of which signal power. In our world, physical size equates with stature, influence, and thereby significance. Short adults are treated as less significant than tall persons. This partially explains why women have always been held in less regard than men: their smaller physical stature is interpreted as weakness and this translates into less competence in the board room as well as on the battle field. While women have been partially successful in combating these assumptions, children by their unavoidable physical limitations have not. Children can be picked up and moved when convenient for adults, whether the child is trembling in rage, crying or simply needs to be moved. This signals a deep inequality of status between adults and children and the favoured side of that equation is on size, the adult. The world is made for adults and children cannot reach the door knobs, the sink, the toilet, without assistance. Physical stature stands in for a range of limitations of the child. Even in our loving and cherishing manner, we signal that the child is incompetent and we must architect an adult from these "raw unformed materials." We must do everything for the child: [2]

> We nurse, shield, feed, and educate. The child gets what he needs without any worrying; what would he be without us to whom he owes everything? Absolutely everything…We know the way to success; we give directions, advice. We develop virtues, stamp out faults. We guide, correct, train. The child—nothing. We—everything.

Korczak goes on to note the implications of the lack of ownership. All that the child has he is given by adults. Children own nothing and what they do is considered worthless, as junk. Even their clothes, the furniture in their rooms, their computers, and toys are not really theirs to do with as they choose. If the child muddies her clothes or loses her bike, she finds an irate parent chiding her for her carelessness. She cannot give away her possessions without their permission. In "When I was Little Again" Korczak as his child-self trades ice skates for a pen box only to receive a serious reprimand from his parents and he is forced to return the box.[3] When children collect bits of nature, or cards or whatever, these are denigrated as garbage and can be easily discarded if they clutter up the house. As adults we are keenly aware of the status that property ownership gives us. The American dream to own a house and

[1] Here we find a point of intersection with Bachelard's notion of reverie to be discussed below.
[2] Korczak, 1992, p. 163-164.
[3] Ibid., p. 72.

land represents this deeply grounded sense that one's place in a community depends upon the status that ownership conveys. When poor people go into debt to buy expensive cars, TVs, etc., we criticize them without seeing the desperate attempt to achieve a sense of belonging and status in the community through property. Since children have neither money nor credit, they can only achieve status as their parents see fit. To achieve a sense of belonging, children often turn to nature as allies in their world: "A dog and bird are close to his heart, a butterfly and flower are his equals; he finds a soul-mate in a stone or a sea-shell."[4]

One of Korczak's main themes in his writings is the importance of seeing childhood as valuable in its own right and in the present tense. "Children are the future" sounds laudatory and valuing but it also connotes that children are not *now* anything of merit. They will *become* in the future when they become *adults*, become educated, become powerful, become citizens. But the underlying assumption is that they are none of these when they are children. He calls for respecting the events and experiences of the child as intrinsically worthy of recognition and acknowledgement: the effort of learning, the setbacks and tears of a child's day, the child's self-realization of their being a burden and an expense on their family, the difficult task of simply growing, and most importantly, a valuing of the present moment. The child is now, and is fully who she is at this moment; she is not simply a promise for a future fulfilment. Children have the right to be who they are and too often adults project their own desires upon the canvas of the child. We ask them to fix and improve what we failed to do and seemly our expectations are great and burdensome on the child who simply wants to be who they are now. We watch the child, noting his faults, not seeing our own. We have great expectations for their future and too often ignore their present selfhood in favour of our own dreams for them. We ask children to live for us, to represent our own successes. This is a terrible load to lay on their tiny shoulders. Children can sense this paradox: adults negate who the child is even as they celebrate their version of the adult-to-become. How can the child fulfil these heavy dreams from those they love? "Let us renounce the deceptive longing for perfect children."[5]

Korczak reserves some of his most rigorous critique for education. He depicts teachers as too often floundering in inexperience, resorting to brute strength and bullying, or else as incompetent and demeaning to children in turn. He slams them as "a storehouse of admonitions, a dispenser of moral platitudes…agents of cheap virtue."[6] But why do even good children rebel against good teachers? he puzzles. Korczak offers a range of explanations: teachers too often try to push every child into the same mould for uniformity and ease of control and this invites rebellion as a form of self-assertion. Or the teacher and the class use different standards for evaluating behaviour and simply do not understand the other's views. Finally he adds that

---

[4] Ibid., p.165. I have written elsewhere about the relationship of children to nature and to animals in several articles. For example see "Max in His Wolf Suit: The Borders of Animality/Humanity and Childhood as Discovered within Children's Literature" in Hopkins, Turgeon & Macleod, (Eds.) 2011.

[5] Ibid., p. 185.

[6] Ibid., 184.

children can simply get excited and "become intoxicated with the oxygen of the air"[7] and perhaps we need simply to avoid criticism and acknowledge that "this obvious childish intoxication, arouses respect and emotion; it does not estrange and set apart, but draws us closer and binds us."[8]

In his essay "When I am Little Again" Korczak personalizes these ideas as he fictionalizes the experiences of himself thrust back into his child-self. He begins as both but as days go by, the adult-self commentary fades and he is absorbed into the child lifeworld where adults too often treat children contemptuously, assuming that they know better, that they know what the child is thinking and feeling, and can criticize the child for the very ideas that they assume he has! He experiences snow as a child would: a mystical interruption in the school day with a delight so intense and burning as to block out all other thoughts and experiences. He expresses his curiosity about the world at home and in school but quickly learns that his questions only generate advice. "I left off asking questions after that. I tried to answer everything myself."[9] He negotiates the construction of friendship, bartering for favours from the more powerful children in the school yard, and going out into the world and being looked at suspiciously and dismissively by adults. He is easy to push around on the trolley, easy to ignore and discount, even when we tries to participate in the life of the community. He rescues a stray dog that he finds on his way to school, only to lose him to another boy who is in a better position to adopt him. He day dreams in class and his teachers chide him for not paying attention. His mother is notified of his scholastic failures: "is there no place at all in the world for a less gifted child?"[10] he anguishes. The account of Korczak's becoming a child again exudes pathos and tragedy as he struggles against a tide of adult misperceptions and a confluence of events that conspire to bring about his ruin. His passion for a little girl he has met twice is mocked and his poverty means that he cannot solve problems for which money can help. In the end, he despairs:[11]

> There seems to be two kinds of life: theirs—serious, worthy of respect, and ours—as if a joke. Because we're smaller and weaker, it's like a game. And this is the source of neglect.
> Children—these are future people. And so it's a matter of their becoming. It's as if they don't exist yet. But indeed, we are; we live, we feel, we suffer.

At the end of a particularly dark day of accusation and blame, Korczak quietly wishes to be an adult again. He finds himself sitting at his desk, marking students' papers. He finds himself reluctant to redline the spelling error. He has reached across the adult-child divide and he understands.

---

[7] Ibid., p.172.
[8] Ibid., p. 173.
[9] Ibid., p. 8.
[10] Ibid, p. 153.
[11] Ibid., p. 155.

Korczak went to his death, leading the children of his school as they were rounded up from the Warsaw ghetto by the Nazis. In neat rows of four, he and his children marched proudly to the cars in the deportation area. His authoritative demeanour took even the Nazis aback. He honoured his children to the end. As he closes his essay "The Child's Right to Respect" he warns the readers:[12]

Beware, contemporary life is shaping a powerful brute, a homo rapax; it is he who dictates the mode of living. His concession to the weak are a lie, his respect for the aged, for women's rights and kindness toward children are falsehoods...Rather it is really children who are the real princes of feelings, the poets and thinkers.

Respect, if not humility, toward the white, bright, and unquenchable holy childhood.

Bachelard's poetico-philosophical reveries

In *The Poetics of Reverie* Gaston Bachelard includes a poetic-philosophic meditation on our recollections of childhood. He invites us to enter into the nature of imagining, dreaming, and the realm of memory as clues for understanding both child and adult selfhood. Bachelard approaches his topic through the micro-lens of self-reflection or even more so—the experience of *reverie* and the intensely personal encounter with poetry. He is not interested in analysing the child or studying childhood. There are no sociological observations on the structure of adult/child cultural interactions. Instead, Bachelard explains in his *Introduction*, that he desires to do a phenomenology of the poetic impulse. He seeks to trace the psychology of wonder as instantiated in poetry, the "joy of speech."[13]

> Poetic reverie gives us the world of worlds. Poetic reverie is a cosmic reverie. It is an opening to a beautiful world, to beautiful worlds. It gives the I a non-I which belongs to the I: my non-I.[14]

Bachelard wants to fuse the philosophical and poetical by seeking the foundational experiences that underscore all of human experience. Towards this end, childhood proves to be a fertile Ur-source of self and world. One needs to seek the child that one was and poets very often serve as our Virgil-like guides into this land that is both utterly familiar and mysteriously absent from our present self. Bachelard professes his desire to be to construct "an ontological philosophy of childhood which underlines the durable character of childhood."[15] Childhood does not leave us when we grow up; it simply goes "underground."

One finds a meandering path of suggestions, hints, musings, indeed—reveries, on childhood in his chapter entitled "Reveries toward Childhood." It is difficult, if not outright falsifying, to outline and force into a piece of systematic argumentation

[12] Ibid., p. 185-186.
[13] Bachelard 1969, p. 5.
[14] Ibid., p.13.
[15] Ibid., p. 20.

the ideas that Bachelard explores in this chapter. His phenomenological method pushes us to weave in and out of ideas, inviting us to revisit our childhood. "By dreaming our childhood we return to the lair of reveries, to the reveries which have opened up the world to us."[16] Bachelard claims. He wants us to recognize how foundational our child-gaze upon the world is for our adult selves. Here imagination and memory both share a common source in the primitive imaging of the child but also vie with one another in giving us back those very images. Poetry serves as a kind of companion guide, opening up the world where we once roamed familiarly and had not yet layered over with facts, values, estimations, the "animus" of objectivity.[17] While psychologists may offer us understanding of childhood from the outside, the poet takes us back into the self-world experience of the child and we can grasp reality through the act of poetic reverie. Perhaps we might see this as a form of peripheral vision of the world: noted on the side, pressing into us, and yet not quite centered. And yet, this side glance gives us the essential context for all upon which we do focus. This allows us entrance into a phenomenological rich meditation on being human:[18]

> We believe that one can know states that are ontologically below being and above nothingness. In these states the contradiction between being and non-being fades away. A sub-being (moins-etrê) is trying itself out as being. This antecedent of being does not yet have the responsibility of being…In such a state of mind, one feels clearly that logical opposition, with its too bright light, erases all possibility of penumbral ontology. Very much softened keys are necessary to follow, in a dialectic of light and shadow, all the emergence of the human trying itself out at being.

Bachelard's reflections on the elemental forces of nature (shadows, water, air, fire) come into play here as he spools out his account of the poet's task to make present the child-past. Childhood is the "well of being."[19] In another apt phrase, he directs us to the child as "the astonishing being… the astonishment of being."[20] The encounter with childhood brings us back to the beginnings or threshold, the newness, the vibrancy of the world and the co-creative act of becoming a self as discovered within that world. Being manifests itself through the child on the verge of discovering her own ontic presence.

Including fragments from poets, many of them French, Bachelard claims that the most intensely philosophical musings emerge from this return to the child lifeworld. Poets offer us the verbal and imagistic door to the secret, almost forgotten, world. He mentions religious and mythic iconography of the divine child but pays it relatively scant attention in favor of the ways in which the senses, particularly smell, captures perhaps most keenly of all those first experiences of the world.

---

[16] Ibid., p. 102.
[17] Ibid., p. 105.
[18] Ibid., p. 111.
[19] Ibid., p. 114.
[20] Ibid., p. 116.

But where is the theme of respect in all of this? Bachelard never uses the word "respect" nor does he directly attempt to define or delineate this notion and yet, respect for the child hovers above every claim about the ways in which poets offer us access to the child view. To lose one's childhood is to die, he claims.[21] The child and her view of the world offer us a serious and important window into the human event. This becomes the point of connection to respect. Unless I can regain, through poetic reverie, that world of my/the child-self, I cannot begin to fathom what it means to be a person in the world. Far from dismissing the child as pre-rational and therefore not yet fully human, Bachelard returns us to the font of experience that he claims as a richer and more vital source than any objectifying act of analysis and distancing of self from world. Reverie towards childhood captures the essence of a respect which acknowledges the seemingly alien but intimately primordial nature of the child as the parent of the (wo)man.

To apply his ideas to the topic of respect for the child, we can see how no one really knows himself unless he can find the child gaze within and to do this requires an attitude of respect for childhood, an abandonment of a common point of view which priveleges adult experience and dismisses that of the child as insignificant. Bachelard recalls us to our own child-nature by pointing to this foundational encounter with being and we can only marvel at a relationship instantiating respect for the other/self within.

Conclusions: merging visions

What have we discovered about the nature of respect? Respect is a ubiquitous concept in everyday life. As children we are taught to respect our elders; we respect authority, knowledge, talent, skill in people. We are asked to respect Nature and to respect ourselves. We ought to respect the law and respect privacy. In all these uses it connotes an attitude of honouring the superior as well as recognizing a being with equally valid interests and concerns. In its general outline, it suggests a refraining from action: to respect something is to leave it alone, to let it be, to allow it to make its own choices and determine its own course. I "respect your wishes" by non-interference. I step aside and refrain from imposition.

It might be this connotation that so often prevents respect for the child: the child is not perceived to be independent, responsible, capable of making wise—or any—choices. As Korczak outlines the dilemma: it is precisely the lack of stature, power, and the wisdom to make choices that puts the child under our authority. They ought to respect *us*; we have no call to respect them. Anyone or thing which shares these "characteristics of lack" is defined as outside the circle of deserving respect. So nature (from rocks to plants to many animals) need not be honoured because as inert matter, as simply "natural", it has no moral standing. Since nature cannot function as a moral agent, the call to acknowledge its status as a moral patient is still suspect. Children and animals do offer us pause for thought: children as future-persons

[21] Ibid., p. 135.

and animals as metaphorical humans with faces. Too often it is simply a pause and we return to our common ways of treating them.

But we should open up the concept of respect to include that of *action/attitude towards*. Respect entails a reaching out and acknowledging the other as significant, as validating forms of presence in the world. With this conceptual strategy we can activate a richer and more positive form of respect that has as its foundation a kinship of co-action. To respect the other is to reach out and grasp a "hand" and to look within a "face" so as to discover the mystery of being. Perhaps this notion of respect veers into the theological realm but if so, it need not entail the baggage of deity and religion.[22] One is reminded of Temple Grandin's empathetic response to cattle and other animals. She respects their way of being and her relationship with animals allows them to function in their own way in the world while she responds empathetically. True, this relationship might be deemed one-way but a person who can appreciate the animal's presence in the world on its own terms very often receives a kind of acknowledgement and acceptance in return from that animal being[23].

Both Korczak and Bachelard call us to attention by reminding us of the world as literally seen through the child's eyes and as experienced through the child's emotional sense of self and others. The child's exquisite openness to the world allows the full richness and pain of being to be perceived. We were once there ourselves but after years, layers upon layers of culture have obscured our child self and perhaps our own buried memories of the judgement of inadequacy renders us unwilling or unable to own our childhood. Who would want to return to that time of dismissive looks, invisibility, presumption of ignorance and guilt? That time where we had no freedom and our thoughts, wishes, desires were deemed trivial because they were ours, those of a child? In dismissing the child before us, we dismiss the child behind us as well.

However, Korczak breaks this cycle by examining what it means to respect the child, and thereby intimating what it means to respect anyone. First and foremost, it entails not assuming a position of privilege because of one's superior size, number of possessions, mastery of information. These qualities may indicate superiority in some social and political contexts but not within the human one. We must be mindful of the ways in which these extraneous qualities enter into value judgments. Korczak does not claim that children experience the world identically to us; he allows for profound differences. But he refuses to see those differences from adults as axiologically important in determining relationships based on respect. The child who is ignorant of the ways of the world reflects equally a human experience of that world and in many ways, noted beautifully by Korczak in his essays, the experiences of children can recall us to ourselves, to that which is deeply human within adult and child alike. But even beyond the human, we can consider extending his lesson to our relationships with animals and the entire natural world. Respecting the center of experiences, of being, wherever they occur opens up a new modality of relating to both

---

[22] I would suggest that my hinted direction here is towards a Taoist view of the world.

[23] A good example is *The Other End of the Leash*, Patricia B. McConnell, New York: Ballantine Books, 2002.

self and world that invites a reverential attitude towards all being, an attitude exemplifying respect.

Bachelard's homage to poetry as the Ur-spring of philosophical access to being takes a very different route but ends up advocating for the same stance towards the child, in Bachelard's case—the child within. Respect entails a mutual openness and acceptance that allows humanity to span not only gender and culture, but also time. To the extent that we marginalized children, we can also find ourselves treating the elderly as children, as discountable for many of the same reasons. We cannot *be* without having been a child and this is not an insignificant point for Bachelard. We discover our being in the world through the child gaze and unless we can keep that gaze below the surface as still vital, we lose our centre. This demands that we respect the child-within, even as Korczak passionately argues for the children without. Respecting my child-self will open up my vision of the children around me in ways that I can acknowledge and hold in dialogue with my adult self and respecting children around us reminds us of our own child-self. Both movements, within and without, require a relational openness to the other as familiar and sharing in the "astonishment of being."[24] And that movement can open up a window to the larger challenge to respect Being in all its manifestations.

Reference List

Bachelard, Gaston. *The Poetics of Reverie*, translated by Daniel Russell. Boston: Beacon Hill Press, 1969. Print.

Hopkins, Lucy / Turgeon, Wendy C. /Macleod, Mark (Eds.). *Negotiating Childhoods*, Oxford: ID-Net Press, 2011. Ebook.

Korczak, Janusz. *When I am Little Again and The Child's Right to Respect,* translated by E. P. Kulawiec. New York: University Press of America, 1992. Print.

[24] Ibid., p. 116.

Susan T. Gardner
(Canada)

Love Them or Leave Them? Respect Requires Neither[1]

Introduction: What kind of respect do we owe others?

We are often admonished that we ought to respect one another. This notion that we ought to—implying therefore that we *can*—respect one another, is the springboard from which multiculturalists speak, and, indeed, appears to be the prerequisite for the very viability of our global village which seems too often under threat.

Given the fact that our welfare—indeed our very lives—may depend upon it, it is imperative that we understand what kind of respect we owe one another, i.e., what kind of respect has the tenacity to underpin the web of human life. It is to that question that what is to follow is addressed.

Let us begin by first noting that this notion of "respect for persons" is one that is often closely tied to the commonly cited religious adage that "we ought to love one another." It thus appears to give rise to a command that we are all obliged to nurture some kind of positive regard toward others—or at least that we ought to attempt to limit our negative judgment—an assumption that vigorously fuels the fire of postmodern relativism.

Speaking to the "politics" of positive regard (or its lack), Charles Taylor, in his inaugural address entitled *Multiculturalism: The Politics of Recognition* presented at the University Center for Human Values at Princeton University in 1990, argues that a person suffering from the lack of "adequate" (presumably positive) recognition is an evil that can be ranked in the same echelons of harm as inequality, exploitation, and injustice.[2] It is for that reason, Taylor argues, that due recognition "is not just a courtesy we owe people. It is a vital human need." [3]

Kant would worry about any suggestion that "sensuous" positive regard can be commanded. Nonetheless, with regard to negativity, it follows from his theoretical framework that condemnation is an illegitimate response to choices made by rational agents. This is so because, according to Kant, the freedom that is purchased through self-conscious rationality is an individual accomplishment. Thus, since self-conscious rational freedom is the foundational value of self-conscious rationally free agents, such agents ought to act in ways that give freedom maximum room to flourish. And this is true—as R. M Hare noted in his seminal book, *Freedom and Reason*

[1] This paper is also published in the *International Journal of Applied Philosophy.* Spring 2013.
[2] Taylor 1994, p. 64.
[3] Taylor 1994, p. 26.

—even with regard to universalizing "evildoers." Thus, when faced with a fanatical Nazi who claims that he would wish to be exterminated if he were a Jew, reason has no right even to condemn.[4] And then, of course, there is Kant's infamous attempt to lay homage to "isolated" reason by claiming that we cannot condemn a person for telling a vicious murderer the location of his victim because the alternative, i.e., lying, cannot pass the universalizability test. Specifically Kant suggests that it would be immoral to lie even to a murderer because if you lie about the fact that the victim is in the closet, saying instead that she ran out the back door, unbeknownst to you, the victim may very well have run out the back door, and thus your lying has sent the victim right into the arms of the murderer.[5] Condemning such a truth-telling victim-betrayer is, therefore, out of the question.

Both of these views will be challenged in what is to follow. It will be argued that not only do we *not* owe all persons respect in the sense of positive regard, but that attempting to adopt such an "I'm OK, you're OK, everyone is OK"[6] attitude is ethically contemptible. And it will be argued, as well, that giving wide birth to "rational" choices can be similarly ethically indefensible. It will be argued, by contrast, that, although we do owe "respect to persons," we owe respect in the specific sense of being prepared to hold persons "**communicatively-accountable**." Specifically, it will be argued, referring to the works of George Herbert Mead, Peter Strawson, Stephan Darwall, and Jürgen Habermas (amongst others), that self-consciousness, rationality (in the practical reasoning sense), and freedom, are **inter**-, rather than **intra**-, subjective phenomena and that, since they emerge only as a result of persons holding one another "communicatively-accountable," **that** is what we owe one another. And because holding one another "communicatively-accountable" requires hard-nosed intersubjective communicative-interaction (Habermas) about the sort of values and ideals that ought to guide all reasonable people, and since such communicative interaction necessitates the interchange of both positive AND negative attitudes and judgements, it turns out that "respect for persons" requires neither that we love them, nor leave them alone. Respect requires, rather, that we engage.

Let us turn first to the development of self-consciousness.

The emergence of self-consciousness

In his book *Mind, Self, and Society,* Mead presents a compelling case that self-consciousness, rather than being some sort of exudate of the brain, can be described as an imaginative awareness of self that emerges as a result of social interaction—a view that has strong empirical support.[7] George Horton Cooley refers to this as "the looking-glass self." However, this imagined awareness of self, this self-consciousness, emerges **not** as a result of just any kind of interaction, but rather, an interaction of a particular sort, namely one in which the recipient, let's call him

[4] Hare 1965, pp. 157-185.
[5] Kant 1964, pp. 95-96.
[6] Weber 2012.
[7] Gallup 1977.

Johnny, is able to detect a clear correlation between his actions, say throwing cereal on the floor, and a ***change*** in the evaluatively-charged attitude or behavior of another, e.g., the disapproval of his mother. This evaluatively-charged attitude on the part of mother is one that we will refer to, following Peter Strawson's lead in his article "Freedom and Resentment," as **a participant reactive attitude**. Strawson describes participant reactive attitudes as "**non**-detached," i.e., non-objective. They involve "attitudes and reactions of offended parties and beneficiaries; of things such as gratitude, resentment, forgiveness, love, and hurt feelings." [8]

Strawson contrasts participant reactive attitudes with what he refers to as an "objective attitude."[9] According to Strawson, "to adopt the objective attitude to another human being is to see him, perhaps, as an object of social policy; as a subject for what, in a wide range of sense, might be called treatment; as something . . . to be managed or handled or cured or trained."[10]

Strawson's notion that we "mark" the freedom of others to do other than they do by evaluatively-tinged responses echoes the case made by Antonio Damasio in his book *Self Comes to Mind*, following up on his earlier book, *Descartes' Error*. Specifically, Damasio argues that Descartes got it wrong when he failed to recognize that reason and emotion are inextricably linked. Damasio articulates what he refers to as "the somatic marker hypothesis," i.e., that what we see is always a function of the degree of emotion that serves as a "marker" for the relative importance of the image, i.e., what the mind sees is always value laden.[11] If we apply this notion to Strawson and Mead, it follows that for me to see my freedom (to do other than I am doing) in your eyes, I must see value (i.e., the possibility of a fluid change between positive and negative judgements) reflected in your responses.

Participant reactive attitudes thus signal to others both our belief in their freedom, or agency, and our evaluation of their actions (these two being intrinsically tied). What is particularly intriguing about this summation is that, if we infuse it into Mead's depiction of the emergence of self-consciousness, we come to the thesis that the emergence of self-consciousness is not a value-free awareness as the name implies. It is, rather, an awareness of the **value** of one's action as reflected through the participant reactive attitudes, i.e., judgments, of others, along with an awareness that the other believes that one is **free** to do other than one did. In other words, aside from gifting Johnny an *awareness* of his cereal-throwing behavior, and aside from gifting Johnny an awareness that this behavior is *negatively valued* from her point of view, Mother is also gifting Johnny the ***belief*** *in his own agency to do other than he is doing,* and in so doing—or so it is being argued here—gifts him that freedom. That is, mother's participant reactive attitudes send the clear message that she believes that Johnny has the power to do otherwise, and since she believes it, he too comes to believe it, and it is this belief that he is free to do otherwise that actually gives him the power, i.e., freedom, to do otherwise—presumably by introjecting im-

[8] Strawson 2005, p. 3.
[9] Ibid., p. 6.
[10] Ibid., p. 7.
[11] Damasio 2010, p. 76.

ages of others' responses to his actions as imagined positive and negative stimuli.[12] We will refer to this interchange as the **responsibilizing** of one another, i.e., that it is by holding others responsible that freedom is created (rather than freedom being a prerequisite of responsibility, as is so often assumed).

Responsibilizing others through participant reactive ATTITUDES.

This emergence of agency through "responsibilizing" one another becomes readily apparent if we examine the training of a pet. When Fido pees on the floor, I admonish Fido even though I know he can do no other than he did. However, because Fido is able to detect a consistent correlation between my ***changing*** participant reactive attitude and his behavior, Fido comes to believe that he can do other than he did, and in so doing, Fido indeed acquires the capacity to do other than he did, i.e., Fido becomes house-trained. And since Fido can thus view the value of his behavior from my point of view, and can respond appropriately, he, like any other trained animal, can be considered self-conscious—though minimally so.

To make the claim that trained animals are self-conscious, though only minimally so, mirrors Mead's thesis that self-consciousness is not an all-or-nothing phenomenon, but rather a matter of degree. Mead describes the initial emergence of self-consciousness as one in which the child (and, as is being argued here, also trained animals[13]) learns the value of his/her behavior from the point of view of **particular** others. Mead refers to this initial stage as the **play stage**.

The next stage in the development of self-consciousness requires that one learn to perceive one's behavior from the point of view of the more abstract perspective of rules, as in rules of a game. Appropriately, Mead refers to this as the **game stage.**

What is fundamentally different about the game stage is that signalling by participant reactive attitudes alone is not sufficient to prod awareness to this level of abstraction. In order to explain the rules of the game and what counts as an excuse or mistake, **symbolic language** is required.

Thus, the responsibilizing relationship that emerges between **symbolically interacting** humans is qualitatively different from the kind of relationship that we humans have with our pets. This is so because, aside from the interchange of **participant reactive *attitudes***, we **symbolically interacting** humans address one other with **participant reactive *reasons***, i.e., evaluatively infused practical reasoning.

---

[12] Gardner 2009, pp. 11-18.

[13] Mead described the interchange between animals as "a conversation of gestures." He did not specifically utilize the notion of the "play stage" when describing animals.

Responsibilizing others through participant reactive REASONS.

"Johnny, you shouldn't throw your cereal on the floor because we all need to do our part to keep our home a clean and tidy place that we can all enjoy." Note the difference between this kind of reason and saying to Johnny, "you shouldn't throw your cereal on the floor because, if you do, you will get spanked." Though cloaked in words, the latter is a raw *participant reactive* ***attitude***. Mother is evaluating Johnny's behavior solely from the point of view of her own wishes. The former, however, is a *participant reactive* ***reason***: though it carries an evaluation, it does so *not* by reference to the authority or the evaluative point of view of a *particular* speaker, but by reference to a person-neutral evaluative authority that the speaker is assuming all reasonable people ought to recognize.

In his book *The Second-Person Standpoint: Morality, Respect, And Accountability,* Stephan Darwall, Professor of Philosophy at Yale University, refers to what is here being called "participant reactive reasons" as "**second-personal reasons**." Darwall says that "Addressing second-personal reasons of any kind always carry certain presuppositions concerning second-personal authority, competence, and responsibility of the addresser and the addressee alike."[14]

Thus, reasoning with one another is *not* a "struggle to the death" as to whether my idiosyncratic evaluation of you prevails or your idiosyncratic evaluation of me prevails. Second personal interchange may be a struggle, yes, but this is a struggle to get the other to see what each view as **the correct person-neutral or *objective* evaluative depiction of the situation at hand**. Thus, to the degree that "hell really is other people" as Sartre suggests in his play *No Exit*, this is so in a second-personal interchange not because of the *personal* negative evaluation of the other (something that understandably worries post-modern relativists), but rather because one has been found wanting with reference to what the other sees as a person-neutral set of rules, i.e., a set of rules that the other presumes that every other rational person would accept.

In reasoning with one another, in other words, we see ourselves as tied together by normative rather than merely power relations. If I give you a reason to stop what you are doing, what is important to me is not simply that you desist, but that you come to believe that you *ought* to desist (i.e., you have recognized the rules), and in so doing, you do your part in the maintenance of this normative freedom-creating relationship (i.e., freedom in the sense that we can reason our way beyond the control of behavioristic stimuli).

This is a freedom that is only possible between reasoning beings. In support of this point, Darwall quotes Fichte who says that pure second-person address always presumes to direct an agent's will through the agent's own self-determining choice.[15] Only in this way, Fichte argues, can reasons simultaneously address and direct another as a free agent. Thus, what is important to reasoning beings is not so much how we want the world to be but how we are to relate to one another—a relationship

---

[14] Darwall 2006, p. 20.

[15] Ibid.

that presumes and thus creates mutual freedom grounded in reasoning with each other.[16]

The requirements for engaging in a personhood-maintaining practical-reasoning process.

In saying that interpersonal judgements are not only permissible but, *ceteris paribus*, because of their freedom supporting-properties, ethically required, it is critical to keep in mind that this is so exclusively with regard to participant reactive **reasoning**, and *not* with regard to raw participant reactive attitudes (the latter being—perhaps—exclusively appropriate in fiduciary non-linguistic relationships). One's job, in other words, is not merely—and perhaps not ever—to be judgmental *per se*; one's job, rather, is to be "participantly" reasonable, i.e., to be prepared to continuously reason with others to try and parse out what sort of rules ought to govern the behaviors and judgements of all reasonable people.

Given that only genuine second-personal reasoning can contribute to the maintenance of our mutual freedom (as opposed to raw judgemental attitudes or the mental manipulation of "faux reasoning" that can be destructive of our freedom), it is imperative that we make explicit the implicit assumptions that reasoners must make in order for this sort of reasoning to be efficacious. These assumptions are as follows. We must assume (1) that we agree on a common *non-subjective position-guiding* reasoning process, (2) that the goal is a common perspective *anchored by reason*, (3) that our initial positions are different and that we are comfortable with that, (4) that there is some common value-overlap, and (5) that we see one another as equal in this freedom-producing accountability relationship.

Let us deal briefly with each of these in turn.

1) A Common Non-Subjective Position-Guiding Reasoning Process

If we are to genuinely reason together, we must assume that we are both committed to a common non-subjective position-guiding reasoning process, i.e., that we both recognize that **how** we reason and **what** we conclude is not up to us. Darwall quotes Pettit and Smith as pointing out that, in taking up a conversational stance, both participants must assume that there are norms that govern what each should believe, that each can recognize these norms, and that each is capable of guiding their beliefs by them. In a similar vein, Jürgen Habermas, in his book, *The Future of Human Nature,* argues that "how speakers and hearers make use of their communicative freedom to take yes- or no-positions is not a matter of their subjective discretion. For they are free only in virtue of the binding force of justifiable claims they raise toward one another. The *logos* of language embodies the power of the intersubjective, which precedes and grounds the subjectivity of speakers."[17] Kant likewise notes the necessity of assuming a common process in depicting the "kingdom of ends" which

[16] Ibid., p. 38.

[17] Habermas 2008, p. 10.

he describes as a "systematic union of different rational beings under common laws" and that our duty "is in no way based on feelings, impulses, and inclinations . . .".[18] What follows from all of the above, then, is that to engage in the sort of second-personal reasoning that underpins freedom, reasoners must be committed to a common non-subjective reasoning process and, in so doing, must recognize that it is the **process**, not persons, that ultimately determines which of competing alternatives has the strongest justification. A genuine commitment to this process would thus appear to require that all participants be prepared to change their minds in light of stronger competing arguments. If one is not prepared to change one's mind, one must accept the verdict that one is more interested in power than in freedom.

2) The Goal of a Common Perspective Anchored by Reason

The second presupposition that we must make if we are second-personal reasoning with one another is that achieving a common perspective is possible, otherwise reasoning together would have no point. It is important to emphasize again, though, that the goal does not trump the way. In second-personal (freedom supporting) reasoning, I am **not** simply trying to manipulate or convert your perspective (nor do I concede just to achieve agreement). In utilizing participant reactive reasons, we address one another as beings capable of following person-neutral (though somatically marked) reasons wherever they lead—as beings capable of *freeing* ourselves from otherwise determining, i.e., biased, influences. It is in addressing one another as accountable, i.e., as responsible, that we gift one another freedom in this sense. Thus, I want you to adopt what I believe to be the correct perspective only if and because you see that this is the most reasonable thing to do. My aim, in other words, is not just that we have a common perspective, but rather that we have a common perspective *because* we both see it as the one that has the strongest justification of all competing alternatives, i.e., we both see it as "objectively valid." In so doing, we both testify to our mutually interdependent freedom.

3) Different Initial Positions

The third presupposition that we must make if we are second-personal reasoning with one another is that we begin with differing perspectives. That is, if I am giving you a reason for doing something other than what you are doing, then I must be presuming that you **do not** see the situation as I do.[19] What is intriguing about this initial position is that it is this difference in perspectives that serves as the catalyst for reasoning—the very reasoning that underpins our mutual belief in, and hence the emergence of, our mutual freedom. Thus, if reasoning with one another is the agar out of which our mutual sense of responsibility and hence freedom emerge, and if reasoning with one another requires the assumption that we do not see the situation in the same way, it follows, interestingly, that our *differing* perspectives turn out to be a necessary condition of human freedom. To the degree that we understand this, and to the degree that these differences are not extreme (see below), and to the de-

[18] Kant 1964, p. 100.
[19] Darwall 2006, p. 45.

gree that those with differing perspectives are eager to genuinely engage in reasoning together about which of competing alternatives has the strongest justification, we ought to learn to celebrate and indeed seek out, rather than become annoyed with, difference.

4) Some Common Value-Overlap

Though *differing* perspectives are a necessary condition of human freedom, these differences cannot be extreme. This is so because individuals who reason with one another must presume that there is sufficient value-overlap that the reasons that either offer to the other are of the sort that it is reasonable to presume that the other might accept. Reasoning, in other words, is like a fishing expedition: each is fishing around for a common value in order to reel the other in. Thus, a Nazi telling a Jew that he is vermin and that that is the reason why it is ethically permissible to exterminate him is not actually second-personal reasoning with the Jew, i.e., is not making an attempt to speak to **the will** of the other. What looks like a reason here is a raw participant reactive attitude dressed up as participant reactive reason. A "will-directed" reason requires that I believe that you *should* and *would* accept my reasoning if only you could step out from behind your own personal bias and adopt an *impartial* perspective.

5) Equal Players in an Accountability Relationship

The last presupposition that we both must make when we reason together is that we see one another as equal players in this game. It is only by seeing one another as equal players that we can *participantly* react to perceived responsibility, accountability, and freedom. Thus, Poole, in his book *Morality and Modernity*, quotes Hegel as noting that the life of the master, in Hegel's classic master/slave dialectic, is defective because his identity is not conferred by an independent other.[20] Because a master is not addressed in an accountability relationship, he is not addressed as a free being in the sense of being responsible for the narrative of his life. And from the slave's point of view, since he too is not addressed with reasons, he cannot blame himself for what he does—though he can fear sanctions.[21] Thus, while self-consciousness *per se* and a sense of agency can emerge in unequal power relations (e.g., parent/child, owner/pet), freedom in the sense of rational self-legislation cannot. Both the master and the slave are confronted solely with participant reactive *attitudes*; thus the mirror into which each peers is impenetrable, i.e., they cannot see *themselves* in the attitudes that they take toward one another. If the master and slave confronted one another as equals with participant reactive *reasons*, each would presume that both their own and the other's perspective, along with its evaluative tone, could change with reasoning, i.e., they would see both themselves and the other as free.

---

[20] Poole 1991, p. 143.

[21] Darwall 2006, p. 79.

Adding more texture to the above Hegelian gloss, American philosopher Robert Brandom likewise suggests that "Hegel's discussion of the dialectic of the master and slave is an attempt to show that asymmetric recognitive relations are metaphysically defective, that the norms they institute aren't the right kind . . . to make it possible for us to think and act. Asymmetric recognition in this way is authority without responsibility, on the side of the master, and responsibility without authority, on the side of the slave. . . Hegel's argument is that unless authority and responsibility are commensurate and reciprocal, no actual normative statuses are instituted."

What is our responsibility if the other cannot or will not genuinely engage?

In his famous and lovely book *I and Thou*, Buber describes what he refers to as "meeting in the in-between" against the background of the world divided in two, in accordance with humanity's twofold attitude. These attitudes are characterized, according to Buber, by the primary words of *I-Thou* and *I-It* (where *He* or *She* can replace It). The primary word *I-Thou* can only be spoken with the whole being,[22] and relationship within *I-Thou* must always be direct; it cannot be mediated by a system of ideas, or foreknowledge, or fancy, or aim, or lust.[23] I cannot approach the other as a problem to be solved or as a person to be fixed. However, I can meet the other in the middle only if the other comes out to meet me, i.e., *this is a relationship that cannot be managed from one side or by one person.*

This distinction between an *I-Thou* and an *I-It* relationship finds a reflection in Jurgen Habermas' description of "communicative" as opposed to "strategic" action. According to Habermas, the former strives toward reaching understanding, while the latter strives toward exerting influence.[24] And like Buber, Habermas emphasizes that success in communicative action is always a function of both the speaker *and the hearer*.[25] Thus, according to Habermas, participants in communicative action must recognize that whenever they speak, they raise what he refers to as a "criticizable validity claim for the proposition *p*, a claim that the hearer can accept or reject *with good reason*." [26] As a result, participants must understand from the get-go that what will ultimately be accepted as true will be a function of what *both* participants bring to the table. Participants cannot, in other words, assert that their claims are true merely by referring to some *a priori* metaphysic such as a universalizing technique (hence the penetrating title of one of Habermas' book, *Postmetaphysical Thinking*); participants must, rather, remain constantly open to the challenge that their claims may turn out to be inadequate from the other's viewpoint. Specifically he says:

> Anyone participating in argumentation shows his rationality *or lack of* it by the manner in which he handles and responds to the offering of reasons for

[22] Buber 1958, p. p. 3.
[23] Ibid., p. 11.
[24] Habermas (PMT) 1992, p. 79.
[25] Ibid., p. 80.
[26] Habermas (TCA) 1992, p. 11.

> or against claims. If he is "open to argument," he will either acknowledge the force of those reasons or seek to reply to them, either way he will deal with them in a "rational" manner. If he is "deaf to argument," by contrast, he may either ignore contrary reasons or reply to them with dogmatic assertions, and either way he fails to deal with the issues rationally.[27]

Habermas goes to quote Robin Horton who, in studying Evans-Pritchard's observations of the justificatory practices of the Azande, says:

> Here then we have two basic predicaments: the "closed"—characterized by lack of awareness of alternatives, sacredness of beliefs, and anxiety about threats to them; and the "open"—characterized by awareness of alternatives, diminished sacredness of beliefs and diminished anxiety about threats to them.[28]

Habermas, thus, like Buber, is urging us to whole-heartedly embrace what, in our terms, would be referred to as "second-personal interaction" or "engaging in a personhood-maintaining practical-reasoning process." However, neither Habermas nor Buber provide guidelines for how to proceed when confronted with those buried by "a closed system" or who would be horrified about the very thought of "meeting in the in-between." They thus leave us without a compass when confronted with people like Hare's Nazi fanatic (and the myriad of less extreme others) who approach dialogue with no intention of changing their mind (breaking rule #1 above), who dialogue merely to persuade (breaking rule #2), whose positions makes it impossible to celebrate our differences (breaking rule #3) because there is no possibility of value overlap (breaking rule #4), and, hence, since they have no intention of playing the freedom-producing practical reasoning game, there is no possibility of seeing one another as equal players (breaking rule #5).

It is beyond the scope of the present enterprise to attempt a detailed account of how to optimize one's approach in situations in which others are unwilling (as in the case of fanatics) or unable (as may be the case with some children) to play by the same rules. Nonetheless, there are several sign posts that we can glean from the model heretofore presented. First and foremost, we need always to remember that autonomy, in the sense of freeing oneself from one's sensuous nature and/or from the determining influence of others, cannot be purchased alone. The capacity to rise above such freedom-destroying pressures lies in one's commitment to "objective" practical ideals that can emerge only through the sort of on-going communicative **inter**action of which Habermas and Darwall speak. Though "meeting in the in-between" (in the sense of engaging in the process) is clearly ideal for all persons, in real-life situations, one can never know in advance if the other can or will engage in this freedom-supporting enterprise. Given that this is the case, the model admonishes us that "respect for persons" requires that *persons respect the process out of which*

[27] Ibid., p. 18, emphasis added.
[28] Ibid., p. 61.

persons emerge and are maintained, i.e., that "respect for persons" requires that persons recognize this process as a foundational value. As a result, the model requires of persons that they always be prepared to "walk out to the middle," in the hope that they might find someone there.

Thus, in contrast to the Bubarian/Habermasian framework outlined above, the model suggests that there are more the two basic attitudes of I-Thou and I-It, that there are more than merely communicative or strategic approaches, that there is more to either having it all or having nothing, that there is more than either both of us being fully present or both of us attempting to out-bully the other. The model suggests, rather, that there is a third option, namely that I ought to do my part in honouring the process by *working the process* as best I can, in the hope that others may join the team.

Obviously there is much more to be said with regard to how to maintain an open communicative stance in the presence of varying kinds of non-cooperation. However, with regard to what is *not required* in such situations, the model is quite specific. We can know for sure, for instance, that "respect for persons" not only does not, but cannot, require that we refrain from being evaluatively engaged. This is so because such an emotional or participatory blank-slate would mask the sort of mirroring message that is critical for the emergence and/or maintenance of the other's self-consciousness and freedom. And we can be certain, too, that rather than backing off in the face of positions that we find untenable, this conception of self-conscious, rationality, and freedom is such that "respect for persons" not only permits, but indeed requires, that we challenge the other to engage in "personhood-maintaining practical reasoning," e.g., you need to give me reasons, other than your ability to universalize your bias, as to why eliminating Jews, or voluntarily surrendering a victim to a murderer, is permissible. I, in turn, will offer reasons for an opposing position, on the assumption that both of us will embrace the least-weak of the two positions[29] (condition #1 of "personhood-maintaining practical reasoning," i.e., that we are both committed to a common non-subjective position-guiding reasoning process).

Of course, the other may not rise to the challenge, i.e., may not agree to engage in such a reasoning process, or may play around in the arena of 'faux' reasoning. However, if such is the case, this conception of "respect for persons" is such that one can nonetheless "reasonably" condemn the other without fear of transgressing the "respect for persons" edict. And one can know too, that, by confrontation, one is potentially enhancing the other's freedom, rather than blocking it.

Is the freedom that emerges through intersubjective interchange "real" freedom?

The command that we ought all to maximize our commitment to participant reactive reasoning is grounded in the claim that it is only by so responsibilizing one another

[29] Gardner 2009, p. 33.

that the belief in, and hence the actualization of, mutual freedom becomes possible. This claim that freedom is a product of a *belief* that emerges as a result of intersubjective second-personal *interactive* reasoning rather than being an end-point of a causal chain emanating from localizable neurons may, to some, send a worrisome message with regard to its reality. Is this freedom really real?

If we root around in *Kant's Critique of Pure Reason,* we find the touchstone of an answer. Even modern neuroscience does not argue against Kant's claim that the *belief* in the reality of physical objects is inevitably a function of the *interaction* between the see-touch perception of perceiving entities and whatever is in fact there. However, the fact that I know this to be the case, i.e., I know that what I now inexorably believe to be real would be utterly different if I were a colour-blind electron-sized entity, does not in the least undermine my commitment to what I perceive as reality, nor does it mitigate the power of what I perceive to move my behavior; dark chocolate is still an appetitive stimulus even though I know that it makes no sense to say that in and of itself, i.e., in a noumenal sense, it is sweet and chocolate brown. Likewise, my sense of self is no less real because I know that it emerged as a function of being exposed to participant reactive attitudes and reasons in intersubjective space. And likewise, the fact that we both know that we are both free only in the sense of being accountable for following reasons wherever they lead, in no way mitigates our power to follow those reasons, and hence indeed to feel responsible in the makes-life-worth-living sense for who it is that we are becoming. As Strawson points out,[30] we either view one another as participants in this game and hence react accordingly, e.g., with contempt or admiration, guilt and pride, (i.e., attitudes that continue to energize our mutual sense of responsibility), or we view one another as not capable of playing this game, i.e., as out of the reach of reason and hence as something to be managed and manipulated, but not something "worthy" of participant reactive attitudes. Like Dumbo's feather, it is our combined belief in, and response to, one another's freedom that produces its efficacy. We none of us can do this alone.

Freedom's fragility

Though freedom's reality ought not to be doubted simply because it is a product of a *belief* in freedom, freedom's fragility because it is a product of a *belief* in freedom ought to be taken seriously. That is, since the *fact* of freedom is a function of the *belief* in freedom, it can be presumed, can it not, that to the degree that the belief in freedom is weakened, so the capacity for freedom (or self-control) will correspondingly weaken? The answer appears to be "yes." In a recent experiment, social scientists[31] showed that when subjects are exposed to the deterministic message "that free will contradicts the known fact that the universe is governed by the lawful principles of science," those subjects were far more likely to cheat both in a quiz situation and

[30] Strawson 2005, p. 6-7.
[31] Vohs and Schooler 2008.

one in which money was involved than those who are not so exposed. That is, exposed to the subliminal message that they could not be responsible, these subjects acted in ways that could be characterised as non-responsible behavior.

In his book, *The Future of Human Nature,* Habermas echoes a similar theoretical concern with regard to the fragility of freedom when he worries that the future (potential) genetic engineering of humans will undermine our belief in human freedom and, in so doing, undermine freedom *per se.* Specifically, he says that "the biotechnical dedifferentiation of the habitual distinction between the 'grown' and the 'made,' the subjective and the objective, may change our ethical self-understanding as members of the species and affect our self-understanding . . ."[32] Thus, the "possibility of a self-critical appropriation of one's own developmental history is not available in regard to genetically manipulated dispositions. . . For this poor soul there are only two alternatives, fatalism and resentment." [33]

Both these positions, then, suggest that our confidence in "the lawful principles of science" and/or the future bioengineering of humans have the potential, though perhaps surreptitiously, to undermine our belief in human freedom and, in so doing, threaten freedom itself. However this need not necessarily be so. After all, beliefs are only fragile to the degree that they lack the underpinning of evidence and/or a strong theoretical base. Certainly if we presume that freedom is some inexplicable non-natural mystical force that emanates we-know-not-how from neural meat (perhaps from the chaotic movement of sub-atomic particles), then our belief in the reality of that freedom will be sabotaged by the more compelling physicalistic narrative. However, if, instead, we move our understanding of freedom into the arena of a reasoned theoretical framework of the sort provided here, the belief in human freedom can be correspondingly strengthened (much to our combined benefit). We must be clear, then, that though not physical in the sense of being emitted by a brain in a vat, self-consciousness and freedom are *not non-natural.* The theoretical framework presented here has shown explicitly from where self-consciousness and freedom come, namely from the responsiblizing interaction between reasoning persons who approach one another with the presupposition of a common non-subjective reasoning process, with the goal of a common perspective anchored by reason, with the assumption of (and comfort in) different initial positions but that have a common value-overlap, and with a commitment to equal standing in the accountability game (a picture similar to what Kant referred to as the "Kingdom of Ends"). Once we have faith in our combined ability and commitment to play the responsibilizing reasoning game, we can have faith in ourselves.

---

[32] Habermas 2008, p. 23.

[33] Ibid., p. 14.

Conclusion: What kind of respect do we owe others?

Self-conscious rational beings owe one another what Darwall calls "recognition respect"[34] in the sense of always being prepared to participate in the game of interpersonal practical reasoning. We owe this to one another because such interpersonal interchange is mutually supportive of our capacity for self-consciousness, rationality, and freedom, none of which are possible on one's own.

It is imperative to keep in mind, however, that participant reactive reasoning is inherently judgmental. I can send the message that I believe that you are *free* not to do what you are doing only through the message that you *ought* not to be doing what you are doing (or sending its mirror image of praise). Though attitudes of disapprobation and indignation may short-circuit what Darwall calls "appraisal respect"—at least in the sense of positive regard,[35] they are not in the least disrespectful in the sense of suggesting that I view you as other than a member of the moral community. As Strawson points out "The partial withdrawal of goodwill . . . is, rather, the consequence of continuing to view (the other) as a member of the moral community; only as one who has offended against it."[36]

Such, then, is the paradox of this game of "self-consciousness maintenance" that since playing by "objective" rules is a testament to our mutual freedom, our interaction under the authority of these objective rules requires non-objective interpersonal responses. That is, it is precisely because the rules of reasons are presumed to be "objective" that we do not view each other as such because it is the "objectivity" of the rules that frees us from determining bias, and it is this freedom that warrants non-objective or participant reactive responses. If you are committed to everyone playing by the rules, in other words, you must be prepared to call a "foul."

Self-consciousness is thus a relationship that is *essentially* a normative. Given that that is the case, it follows that it is not only misguided but potentially unethical to refuse the responsibility of making reasoned interpersonal judgments (assuming, of course, that etiquette, and prudential and efficacy considerations, are taken into account). To refuse (where appropriate) to make such reasoned interpersonal judgments is to treat another with a neutral (objective) attitude; it is to treat that other as a mere object to be manipulated; it is to view the other as not really free and not really capable of "choosing" to act as she does. In so doing, one undercuts one's own and the other's freedom.

With regard to the original question of what kind of respect we owe one another, the answer seems to be that respect requires that, individually, we have the responsibility to engage in the game of inherently normative practical reasoning whenever willing, or potentially willing, players are available. It also suggests that, collectively, we have the responsibility to foster in others (particularly our youngsters) both the capacity and the motivation to engage in this mutually-reinforcing freedom-producing practical reasoning process. In this light, we need to keep in

---

[34] Darwall 2006, p. 122.
[35] Ibid.
[36] Strawson 2005, p. 16.

mind, that since good/bad judgments that are rationally supported (though perpetually open to revision) are inherent to the process, blanket edicts that we all ought to love, tolerate, and accept one another "no matter what," or that we ought to revere choices that are a product of isolated "reasoning," whether universalizable or not, will shut this process down. "Respect for persons" requires neither that we love others nor leave them alone. Respect requires, rather, that we engage.

Reference list

Robert Brandom. Interview, summer 2008. Video: http://video.google.com/videoplay?docid=-1034802594689246468. 15m: 25s. Web.

Buber, M. I and Thou. 2nd Ed. New York: Charles Scribner's Sons, 1958. Print.

Cooley, Cooley, C. H. *Human Nature and the Social Order*. New York: Schocken Books, 1964. Print.

Darwall, Stephan. *The Second-Person Standpoint: Morality, Respect, and Accountability.* Cambridge, Mass.: Harvard University Press, 2006. Print.

Damasio, Antonio R. *Descartes' Error: Emotion, Reason, and the Human Brain*. New York: G.P. Putnam's Sons, 1994. Print.

_____. *Self Comes To Mind: Constructing The Conscious Brain.* New York: Pantheon Books, 2010. Print.

Gallup, Gordon G. "Self-Recognition in Primates: A Comparative Approach to the Bidirectional Properties of Consciousness." *American Psychologist.* May 1977, vol. 32, pp. 329-338. Print.

Gardner, Susan T. *Thinking Your Way to Freedom.* Philadelphia: Temple University Press. 2009. Print.

Habermas, Jürgen. *The Theory of Communicative Action. (TCA) Vol. 1: Reason and the Rationalization of Society.* Trans. Thomas McCarthy. Boston: Beacon Press, 1992. (German text 1981.) Print.

_____. *Postmetaphysical Thinking: Philosophical Essays. (PMT)* Trans. William Mark Hohengarten. Cambridge, Mass: MIT Press, 1992. Print.

_____. *The Future of Human Nature*. Cambridge: Polity Press, 2008. (German text 2001). Print.

Hare, R. M. *Freedom and Reason.* New York: Oxford University Press, 1965. Print.

Kant, Immanuel. *Groundwork of the Metaphysic of Morals*. Trans. H.J. Paton. New York: Harper and Row, 1964. Print.

Mead, George Herbert. *On Social Psychology*. Ed. A. Strauss. Chicago: University of Chicago Press, 1934. Print.

Pettit, Philip, and Michael Smith. "Freedom in Belief and Desire." *Journal of Philosophy 93.* 1996. 429-449. Quoted in Darwall. Print.

Poole Ross. *Morality And Modernity.* London: Routledge, 1991. Print.

Sartre. Jean Paul. *No Exit.* New York: Vintage Books, 1955. Print.

Strawson, Peter F., "Freedom and Resentment," *The Determinism and Freedom Philosophy Website,* (Spring 2005), Ed. Ted Honderich, *URL*=<http://www.ucl.ac.uk/~uctytho/dfwstrawson1.htm>. Web.

Taylor, Charles. *Multiculturalism.* Ed. Amy Gutman. Princeton, New Jersey: Princeton University Press, 1994. Print.

Vohs, Kathleen D. and Jonathan W. Schooler. "The Value of Believing in Free will: Encouraging a Belief in Determinism Increases Cheating." *Psychological Science*, Vol. 19, number 1, January 2008. 49-54. Print.

Weber, Barbara. *"'To Tolerate Means to Insult' (J. W. V. Goethe): Towards a Social Practice of Respect and Recognition."* Paper given at the 2012 NAACI conference.

Richard "Mort" Morehouse
(USA)

Response to Susan Gardner's "Love Them or Leave Them? Respect Requires Neither"

The purpose of my response to Gardner's paper is to support her position on the development of the self and its relationship to the development of respect. To do this, I will expand on her position by extending the idea of Mead's conception of the construction of the self, using some ideas of Jerome Bruner and to a lesser extent the work of Carol Gilligan.

Mead understood self-consciousness as a product of social interaction. Mead argues that self-consciousness emerges from interplay between communication partners, both singular and multiple, and eventually with the larger culture. It is this interplay of communication partners that connects Bruner and Gardner with regard to respect. Gardner states that there is a deeper message within Meads theory of self-consciousness. Self-consciousness, she argues, demands that we communicate across our differences because self-consciousness also requires that we respect ourselves. Implicit within that demand is what Gardner calls an engine of self-development. To better understand the relationship between self-development and the demands of self-consciousness that lead us to respect, I now turn to a tool used in human resource training.

Luft and Ingham[1] characterize the relationship between two individuals as a self-regulated process of self-disclosure. The self-disclose process they articulate provides a framework for understanding how respect develops from the understanding of Self and Others. What follows is a short explanation of what Luft and Ingham have self-labeled as the Johari Window. The Johari Window has four openings: the arena or open area, the façade or hidden area, the blind spot, and the unknown area. The open area of the Self is readily knowable by members of one's family and by close friends and even many acquaintances. The blind spot is knowable to others but initially remains unknown to the Self. The façade is known to the Self but more or less consciously hidden from others. Neither Self nor the Other know what is in the unknown area, the inner Self. By giving feedback (and specifically in the case argued by Gardner correcting the inappropriate behavior of the child), one not only influences that Other, but also changes one's understanding of the Self as the unknown area becomes known to both Self and Other. If I make an ethical remark regarding your behavior, I am also revealing a good deal about my ethics. Implicitly my ethical comments to the child, to the Other, involved in the communication

[1] Luft & Ingham, 1950.

transactions are about you, me and the world. It is through this process that the child learns first to know herself and to gain respect for Self and the Other, and eventually she begins to develop some understanding of the world, the larger society.

Respect for self, then, begins with some sense of understanding our Self and the selves of others. And as our understanding of ourselves grows, so does the understanding of the Other and the respect for the Self and the Other. Jerome Bruner provides some insights into what it means to know a Self (one's own self and other selves) in *Acts of Meaning*[2] and in particular in "A narrative model of self-construction.[3]" Bruner writes about autobiography and self in order to extend Mead's ideas about self-consciousness. Susan Gardner adds to Bruner's point by specifically connecting autobiography with self-development. Self-development begins, Bruner argues, with self-understanding as well as an understanding of other selves. Bruner constructs a picture of Self by articulating a process of looking inside as well as looking out to the world. Self is both private and public; that is, Self is both inside the person, and in the world, a view in sync with the explanation provided by Luft and Ingham. "So the experienced world may produce Self, but Self also produces the experienced world."[4] Bruner goes on to write that we shape and develop our Selves by offering "justifications, excuses, and reasons."[5] Implied in this statement is Bruner's observation, as well as the observations of Luft and Ingham, that when we receive advise, criticism and support, we also are required to provide the context on which we make these justifications and excuses, as well the context for giving and accepting complements.

Bruner goes on to present some additional conjectures regarding the nature of the Self. He speculates that the Self may not be as private or as indescribable as it is purported to be. For the Self appears to be, in part, a cultural product, a product of discourse. Our self-story is a retrospective prose that narrates a real person's concern with her or his existence. This narrative, this story has both a cultural and an individual function, and here is the connection to Gardner's paper, this individual and cultural function aids in the regulation of interpersonal transactions.

This interpersonal transaction is based on what Bruner calls the enhancement of species mutuality. Species mutuality is premised on the idea that "other minds operate as ours do, that we can share attention with others, and that as the system grows, we share common beliefs, expectations, and other intentional states." In a slightly different context, Bruner argues that to "tell a story is inescapably to take a moral stance."[6] This supports Gardner's claim regarding moral demands as the "communication engine that fuels self-development.[7]" This human capacity for interpersonal transaction "seems to require not only mutuality, but also the establishment of a shared conception of legitimacy: what particular beliefs may be expected of others and what may be expected of us, what endeavors can be legitimately pur-

[2] Bruner, 1990.
[3] Bruner, 2006.
[4] Bruner, 2006, p. 147.
[5] Ibid, p. 147.
[6] Ibid, p. 151.
[7] Gardner, Love Them Or Leave Them? This volume.

sued, how values should be applied, etc."[8] Under these circumstances, our way of conceiving our own and others' selfhood is established. In her article, Susan Gardner writes:

> In reasoning with one another, in other words, we see ourselves as tied together by normative rather than merely power relations. If I give you a reason to stop what you are doing, what is important to me is not simply that you desist, but that you come to believe that you *ought* to desist (i.e., you have recognized the rules), and in so doing, you do your part in the maintenance of this normative freedom-creating relationship (i.e., freedom in the sense that we can reason our way beyond the control of behavioristic stimuli)[9].

The idea of the Other recognizing the rules for their own behavior and the behavior of others is consistent with Bruner's idea of the self as distributed and build on Mead's idea about the emergence of self-consciousness through interpersonal exchanges. Bruner points out, that the Self is perhaps better understood as distributed, rather than as an "enduring, subjective nucleus,"[10] again these ideas connect with Mead's "social games" and the development of the Self.

In my view, the idea of a distributive self is similar to Gardner's view that acceptance of a rule is based on the possibility of two beings reasoning together. To reason together is to direct another being as one self-directing agent to another self-directing agent. According to Gardner, a second-person address always presumes to direct an agent's will through the agent's own self-determining choice.

Only in this way, Fichte argues, can reasons simultaneously address and direct another as a free agent. Thus, what is important to reasoning beings is not so much how we want the world to be but how we are to relate to one another—a relationship that presumes and thus creates mutual freedom grounded in reasoning with each other (Darwall 38)[11].

Susan Gardner's point is tied together, in my view, with the perspectives of Mead, Luft and Ingham, and Bruner by exemplifying the strength and value of communication across differences. It is these types of efforts at discourse, among and between culturally different groups, that lead to respect.

One last comment regarding Susan Gardner's thoughtful and instructive paper. Carol Gilligan writes about some of the ways to understand gender as a cultural issue in need of conversational engagement. Carol Gilligan cites several lines from Emily Dickinson "Ourself behind ourself concealed / Should startle most." Gilligan understands this quote as "a startling discovery of a hidden self."[12] In *Joining the Resistance*, she outlines a method for listening that is important for understanding respect. The four steps for listening in a research interview are: (1) listen for the

---

[8] Ibid, p. 115.
[9] Gardner, Love Them Or Leave Them? This volume p. 81.
[10] Bruner, 1990, p. 107.
[11] Gardner, Love Them Or Leave Them? This volume.
[12] Gilligan, 2011, p. 10.

plot, (2) listen for the "I", (3) listen for different voices, (4) and assembling the evidence. Each step is complex and interconnected. For example, the plot includes listening for disruption, gaps, and emotional "hot spots." Listening for the 'I' includes following the associative stream and constructing an 'I' poem – a series of I statements that use stanza breaks to mark a psychic cadence. The final task for the interviewer/listener is to assemble the evidence, that is, to put it all together in a narrative that supports and affirms what was said and what was heard.

The position taken here with support from Ingham and Luft, as well as Bruner and Gilligan, may seem at odds with Gardner's position regarding second person reasoning. But my point is that second person reasoning ought to begin with understanding first person narrative, as the first person narrative is essential to the first stages of understanding of the emergent consciousness. This emergent consciousness is built on the understanding of Self and Other. And as presented earlier, Selves are distributive, connected. The following quote characterizes the spirit of my critique of Susan Gardner's paper.

> For self-doubt to lead to self-reflection, the environment must be relatively safe and supportive. The cost of making mistakes must not be too great. This requires that other people be patient, sensitive, and responsive. Even when a person is acting or conversing inappropriately, her purpose must be recognized and satisfied. In this manner, the consequences of her failure will be diminished. This may then provide the security the individual needs to creatively play with her own understanding of social interaction.[13]

Rosenberg's statement is in harmony with Gardner's paper, and Philosophy for Children classroom orientation, the spirit of Community of Inquiry and hopefully my comments to Gardner's paper.

Reference List

Bruner, Jerome. "A Narrative Model of Self-Construction." *Annals of the New York Academy of Sciences*, pp 145 -161. 17 Dec 2006. Print.

Bruner, Jerome. *Acts of Meaning*. Harvard University Press: Cambridge, MA,1990. Print.

Gardner, Susan. Love Them or Leave Them? This volume.

Gilligan, Carol. *Joining the Resistance*. Polity Press: Cambridge, UK. 2011. Print.

Luft, Joseph. & Ingham, Harry. "The Johari Window; A Graphic Model of Interpersonal Awareness." *Proceedings of The Western Training Laboratory In Group Development*. Los Angeles: UCLA, 1950. Print.

Mead, George. Herbert. *Mind, Self, and Society: From the Perspective of a Social Behaviorist*. Edited, with an Introduction, by Charles W. Morris. Chicago: University of Chicago Press, 1934. Print.

Rosenberg, Shawn. W. *The Not So Common Sense*. New Haven, CT: Yale University Press, 2002. Print.

[13] Rosenberg, 2002, p. 58.

Wayne I. Henry
(Canada)

Respect and Non-Human Animals[1]

The topic I am concerned with in this address is respect for animals. Specifically, I want to explore particular answers to the following questions. Which non-human animals are deserving of respect? And what would this respect require of us? The particular approach I will be exploring is that of Tom Regan and it has been around for a while. My concern here is to defend it against a couple of objections in a way that, I think, strengthens the theory. I will conclude, though, by raising an objection for which I do not have a completely satisfying answer. In fact, as I will argue, this latter objection raises difficulties for rights theories generally.

The view

Most contemporary discussions of respect begin with Kant's Practical Imperative and for good reason. Kant insists that respect for another demands of us, at the very least, that we never use another as mere means. This amounts to insisting that when we use another, it must be on the basis of informed consent, absent of all coercion or manipulation, and that it must be mutually beneficial. A reasonable reconstruction of Kant's argument is this.

P1: All and only rational beings have inherent worth.
P2: All beings that have inherent worth have it equally.
P3: The inherent worth of another demands respectful treatment (i.e., their inherent worth must never be compromised for some other goal we might set for ourselves, no matter how worthy).
C: Therefore, all and only rational are equally deserving of respectful treatment.

It is well known that the term 'rational being' as used by Kant is a metaphysically rich notion. It means much more than the notion used by economic theory, for example, which implies merely that one is capable of means-to-ends reasoning, the ability to calculate the most efficient means of satisfying our wants. For Kant the notion implies that one is rational in the economic sense to be sure, but more importantly, it implies that one is self-aware and autonomous. Being

[1] Thanks to John Russell (*Douglas College*, Vancouver) and Jim Robinson (*University of British Columbia Okanagan*, Kelowna) for helpful comments. Thanks also to Susan Gardner (*Capilano University*, North Vancouver) for much assistance throughout the project.

autonomous one is capable, in principle, of acting on the basis of laws (maxims) as opposed to mere instinct. Indeed, it implies that one is capable of understanding that the laws that properly determine our behavior transcend our subjective wants and impose objective obligations on us to treat our fellows respectfully. As Kant would put it, we are capable of acting out of respect for the law itself.

For Kant, this is quite an exclusive club. I have always thought that when Kant says, "Now I say that man, and in general every rational being, exists as an end in himself, not merely as a means for arbitrary use by this or that will,"[2] he meant to leave open the possibility that there might be rational beings other than human beings, say aliens on other planets perhaps. But it is equally clear that on planet Earth, Kant was convinced it included only human beings. Famously he said of non-human animals that they are mere things. They have certain analogies to us which makes it wrong to treat them cruelly deliberately, not because of the harm it might do to the animal but, rather, because of the harm that might indirectly result to other human beings. Thus, Kant claims that, so far as non-human animals are concerned, we have only indirect duties that arise out of our direct duties to our fellows.

It might come as a surprise, then, to discover that Regan bases his defense of the respect of non-human animals on a Kantian framework. But the reason is the recognition that only a Kantian framework can provide an adequate defense of respect for others however 'others' may be defined. I will return to this point below. Here is Regan's argument as I reconstruct it.

P1: All subjects-of-a-life have inherent worth.
P2: All beings that have inherent worth have it equally.
P3: The inherent worth of another demands respectful treatment (i.e., their inherent worth must never be compromised for some other goal we might set for ourselves, no matter how worthy).
P4/C: Thus, all subjects-of-a-life are equally deserving of respectful treatment.
P5: Many non-human animals are like us in being subjects-of-a-life.
C: Therefore, many non-human animals are deserving of respectful treatment.

A further feature of this argument that deserves comment is that, unlike Kant, Regan is not concerned to be exclusionary, and I mean this in a sense that goes beyond the inclusion of some non-human animals. Note that in the first premise, it is claimed that all subjects-of-a-life (hereafter: S-O-L) have inherent worth, not "all and only." I think his point here is that we may, as a result of future deliberations, discover compelling reasons for extending the boundary of inherent worth (the charmed circle if you will) even further. In any event, no theory should rule out the possibility. His central point is that we have good and sufficient reasons now for recognizing the inherent worth of many non-human animals by recognizing their obvious and morally significant affinities with us. And what this requires of us is that we never treat them as mere means to our ends. However, as I will argue later,

[2] Kant 1964, p. 95.

this inclusive feature of Regan's theory raises difficulties that are not easily resolved.

Which non-human animals are included in the category S-O-L? Regan explains the notion of S-O-L as follows:

> To be the subject-of-a-life, in the sense in which this expression will be used, involves more than merely being alive and more than merely being conscious. To be the subject-of-a-life is to be an individual whose life is characterized by [such features as having] beliefs and desires; perception, memory, and a sense of the future, including their own future; an emotional life with feelings of pleasure and pain; preference- and welfare-interests; the ability to initiate action in pursuit of their desires and goals; a psychophysical identity over time; and an individual welfare in the sense that their experiential life fares well or ill for them, logically independently of their utility for others and logically independently of their being the object of anyone else's interests.[3]

As such, the notion of being an S-O-L is one that applies to individuals, not species or groups of beings. Indeed, any particular human being may not be an S-O-L, or may not be an S-O-L through the entire span of its life (e.g., those in a permanent vegetative state). And similarly for any non-human animals that may be S-O-Ls. We aren't carving out a charmed circle that includes, say, bears, monkeys, elephants, whales, etc., as such, but it is certainly likely (I think) to include many individual bears, monkeys, whales, elephants, and so forth.[4]

Objections

Let me now turn my attention to the objections I wish to consider. The first two are due to Mary Anne Warren from a frequently reprinted paper titled "Difficulties with the Strong Animal Rights Position." Here, in her words, is the first difficulty.

> Inherent value is a key concept in Regan's theory. It is the bridge between the plausible claim that all normal, mature mammals – human or otherwise – are subjects-of-a-life and the more debatable claim that they all have basic moral rights of the same strength. But it is a highly obscure concept, and its obscurity makes it ill suited to play this crucial role.[5]

---

[3] Regan 1983, p. 243.

[4] Clearly this raises an issue regarding what duties, if any, we might have to, say, a loved who, as a result of trauma or disease, falls below the threshold for being an S-O-L. The problem can be dealt with in Regan's theory but, in so far as it is beside the main point of the discussion, I will leave it for another occasion.

[5] Warren 1987, p. 165.

She goes on to point out that it is "defined almost entirely in negative terms" and that it "appears as a mysterious non-natural property which we must take on faith."[6] I concede from the outset that the concept of inherent worth really is the crucial notion in Regan's theory that Warren claims; it is the bridge between the (plausible) claim that many non-human animals are S-O-Ls and the conclusion that they are equally deserving of respectful treatment. But if this is a problem for Regan's theory, it is worth pointing out that it would be a problem equally for all deontological and consequentialist theories, at least as I understand them. When she claims that it is defined negatively, she alludes to the fact that inherent worth is usually defined as being *not* in any way relational. Specifically, it is the value a thing has in itself and *not* in relation to any other thing. Thus, we understand inherent worth as a member of the contrasting pair, intrinsic worth versus extrinsic worth.[7] Extrinsic worth is entirely relational; it is a conditional worth that a thing has in relation to something else that has intrinsic worth. For example, for the Utilitarian, money has value only in relation to its capacity for bringing about pleasure by, perhaps, satisfying the desire of a particular sentient being to eat. Or, in more modern guise, money is the means to satisfy the preferences of some sentient beings. The money, and for that matter the sentient beings and their preferences, have no worth in themselves. It is the satisfaction of the preferences of sentient beings that has value intrinsically.

In deontological theory, it is individuals that have intrinsic worth and everything else has a mere extrinsic (i.e., conditional) worth in relation to the goals and values of these individuals. Thus Kant, who locates intrinsic worth in human beings, is driven by his theory to claim, as we have seen, that animals are mere things. Kant means this quite literally as the only value they have is in relation to their capacity assist us in the realization of our goals and plans. In this sense, they are like any other resource (e.g., the oil in the ground), i.e., the means to our ends. But, as Kant says, our fellow humans are of unconditional (i.e., inestimable) worth and this is why it is never permissible to use a fellow human being as mere means, not even for some goal that might seem quite worthy. To return to the point promised earlier, this also explains why it is only some form of deontological theory that can ground a notion of respect for others. By locating intrinsic worth in individuals, it is the individuals themselves that matter, not their pleasures or other states of mind. Consulting Regan's definition of S-O-L above, confirms that, while it is significant that S-O-Ls are sentient (i.e., feel pains and pleasures) and have preferences, it is not the pains, pleasures, and preferences themselves that matter. What is significant is that these beings, S-O-Ls, are capable of being in such states and, thus, subjectively their lives can go better or worse for them.

So, the claim is that all consequentialist and deontological theories rely on some assumption of intrinsic worth. And now we see why. As normative ethical theories, these theories are in the business of justifying value judgments, but such

---

[6] Ibid.

[7] I use the terms *inherent worth*, *intrinsic worth*, and the Kantian term *inestimable value* as synonyms.

judgments presume a standard. *That which has inherent worth is the standard against which all else is measured.* As Kant says, "unless this is so (i.e., if it's not the case that some things – in Kant's case "persons" - have objective, intrinsic worth) nothing at all of *absolute* value would be found anywhere. But if all value were conditioned – that is, contingent – then no supreme principle could be found for reason at all."[8] Moreover, it is this assumption that determines the entire character of normative ethical theories. Arguably, this is the crucial difference between consequentialist and deontological theories. It is, I believe, the presupposition we must make to engage in normative moral discourse.[9] Thus the significance of the claim from Kant above that "no supreme principle could be found for reason at all." By this he means, I think, that if there is no such thing as intrinsic worth then no objective normative principle to guide us in ethics is possible.

One might accept all this but wonder why it must be that all who have inherent worth have it equally. Why can't inherent worth come in degrees? The usual reason given is that consistency would demand that we accept the same point within the class of humans. Some human beings will have less inherent worth than others. Mentally challenged people, for example, will have less than us and we will have less than, say, Albert Einstein and Immanuel Kant. Now if someone is willing to accept this consequence, I have no problem with that. We agree to disagree and there is probably little left to say to each on this topic. But the discussion above reveals another and more important reason, in my view, for resisting the claim that inherent worth comes in degrees. If we accept this claim, then it really does begin to appear that inherent worth is nothing more than a subjective projection of value; it is no longer a claim about objective and unconditional value. It becomes difficult, if not impossible, to see how it could function in the role of foundational principle for an *objective* ethics.[10]

I have just recently been made aware that G.E. Moore argued for something very much like this view of inherent worth about a century ago. He is alleged to have claimed that the notion of inherent worth is the foundational premise of all normative ethical theories and that, as such, it determines the character of the theory that flows from it. He is also alleged to have claimed that inherent worth is some sort of indefinable, non-natural property[11] but this is what I reject. My argument is explicitly Kantian at this point in so far as I am claiming that the notion of inherent worth is a presupposition, a foundational principle if you will, that makes normative ethical discourse possible.

Turning now to Warren's second objection:

[8] Kant 1964, p. 96 (emphasis in original; material in brackets mine).

[9] This is so, it seems to me, unless you go with some form of constructivist theory (e.g., subjectivism). John Mackie's view argued in *Ethics: Inventing Right and Wrong* comes to mind.

[10] I am reminded of the difficulties that plagued Mill's attempt to draw a principled distinction between qualities of pleasures.

[11] This is perhaps the origin of Warren's concern, noted in the quote above, that inherent worth must be some sort of strange non-natural property.

> Perhaps the most serious problems are those that arise when we try to apply the strong animal rights position to animals other than normal, mature mammals. Regan's theory requires us to divide all living things into two categories: those which have the same inherent value and the same basic moral rights that we do, and those that have no inherent value and presumably no moral rights. But wherever we try to draw the line, such a sharp division is implausible.[12]

She goes on to muse about whether insects and spiders are members of the exclusive club.[13] Part of the problem here is that the objection rests on a misunderstanding of Regan's position. Although it is true that in his book, *The Case for Animal Rights*, Regan focuses his attention on normal, mature mammals he is not identifying the notion of S-O-L with normal, mature mammals. Rather they are used as examples for expository purposes because of their familiarity for most readers (e.g., family pets, etc.).[14] In any event, you will recall that, as I have reconstructed Regan's argument, the first premise claims that all S-O-Ls have inherent worth, not all and only; it is admitted that there may be other reasons forthcoming for extending the boundaries of inherent worth beyond even S-O-Ls. But we can be sure of this much at least: all S-O-Ls have inherent worth, thus it would be wrong to treat them as mere means to our ends. He admonishes us to avoid misusing those individuals of whom we can be certain they are deserving of respectful treatment. Thus, although it is true that Regan's theory divides all beings up into two exclusive categories, the real division is between those that are S-O-Ls and those that aren't. So the point I've just made might be summarized in the following way. The notions of being a S-O-L and having inherent worth are not coextensive for Regan and this is one sense in which, I claim, Regan's theory is not exclusive in the way that Kant's is.[15]

Still, perhaps Warren's concern carries force. We might put it this way: Regan's theory requires us to draw a sharp division between those individuals that are and those that aren't S-O-Ls. But no matter where we try to draw such a line, no sharp division seems plausible. If this is the claim, then I think the premise can be rejected: there is no reason why the theory should be committed to the claim that we must be able to draw such a sharp line.[16] Metaphysically, an individual either is or is not an S-O-L, but epistemologically we may not always be able to tell. There is no reason in principle why Regan's view cannot be consistent with the claim that there may be borderline cases. As long as there are clear, paradigmatic cases of individuals that are S-O-Ls and clear paradigmatic cases of individuals that are not S-O-Ls, the notion is serviceable for the purposes of this theory. There may be a

[12] Warren 1987, p.165.

[13] Warren 1987, p.166.

[14] I think there is something more to it than this would suggest, namely their psychological proximity to us relative to non-mammals, a point to which I shall return shortly.

[15] My response to Warren's objection, then, amounts to the claim that she is guilty of conflating the notion of "inherent worth" and the notion of "S-O-L" and, thus, the objection rests on an instance of equivocation.

[16] I am indebted to John Russell for making this clear to me.

penumbra surrounding the clear paradigmatic cases that remains epistemologically undetermined for us. Perhaps there will always be such borderline cases.

This might leave some uneasy, concerned that the borderline cases may turn out to be rather large. But here is an obvious fact about the sort of properties that are constitutive of S-O-Ls: they are not found in such things as rocks or bricks, or (I will argue) in such things as insects and spiders. And when you compare paradigm examples of S-O-Ls with paradigm examples of entities that are not S-O-Ls it is clear that the former share another feature lacking in the latter: internal complexity. To put it bluntly, the sorts of properties that are constitutive of being a S-O-L don't just float about like Humean impressions. They supervene on complexly organized structures (i.e., functioning brains or something relevantly like brains). In fact, it's not merely the presence of a functioning brain that is required for sustaining these properties. In mammals, these properties are causally grounded in the part of the brain known as the cerebral cortex, the most complexly organized part of the mammalian brain; that multiplied folded mass of tissue that sits on top of older, more primitive structures (i.e., the mid-brain – the limbic system - and the reptilian complex – the basal ganglia). This kind of complexly organized structure is simply not found in such things as bricks or rocks, or insects or spiders for that matter.

At one point, Warren muses about whether birds are to be considered S-O-Ls, "Some birds (e.g., crows, magpies, parrots, mynahs) appear to be just as mentally sophisticated as most mammals and thus are equally strong candidates for inclusion under the subject-of-a-life criterion."[17] Well, here is an interesting fact about birds: they don't have a cerebral cortex. There used to be a pejorative expression, "bird brain," that implied one was not very bright, to put it politely. We now know that, as an attribution to many birds, this is quite false. Many of them are surprisingly intelligent.

In a book published with the disarming title "Bird Brains: The Intelligence of Crows, Ravens, Magpies, and Jays," Candace Savage reveals that although birds don't have a cerebral cortex, they have another structure equally complex (perhaps more so). Instead of resembling a pile of worms, these structures resemble deeply folded corduroy (the neostriatum/hyperstriatum ventrale). But, and here is the point, it is a case of what biologists call parallel evolution. Specifically, the evolutionary problem of fitting a complexly organized organ into a relatively small skull was accomplished by separate evolutionary processes (because mammals and birds had already split into separate evolutionary lines long before the evolution of the sort of intelligence found in S-O-Ls). You get a similar result manifested by different means but, and this is crucial, the properties that are constitutive of being a S-O-L found in both birds and mammals are grounded in structures of similar complexity. I venture to assert (what Regan does not, at least not to the best of my knowledge) that the notion of being a S-O-L is coextensive with some suitably defined notion of "complexly organized structure." I don't pretend to have such a definition, but I don't need it to answer Warren's objection; since an intuitive grasp is sufficient to enable us to pick out paradigm examples of both S-O-Ls and non-S-O-Ls, it is

---

[17] Warren 1987, p.165.

sufficient to make the notion serviceable for purposes of this normative theory (and without implying that we can resolve all borderline cases).

While I think the above is sufficient to answer Warren's objection, I'd like to sketch the outlines of a more speculative approach to this particular problem. At the same time, this may shed light, I think, on a further reason Regan relies so heavily on examples of normal, mature mammals in explicating his theory. When originally thinking about this problem, I kept asking myself, "Well, how do I know when an individual is an S-O-L? How do I recognize another to be an S-O-L?" And the answer I kept coming to is, "They're the sorts of beings with whom I can have a meaningful relationship." After all, the notion of "appropriate internal complexity" can't be functioning as a criterion for recognizing S-O-Ls in so far as none of us has access to the interior of others.[18] Yet we all of us make such judgments routinely, so the question arises "What do we rely upon as a criterion for recognizing another as an S-O-L?"

The obvious problem is to come up with some sort of philosophically adequate analysis of what constitutes a meaningful relationship. As a first approximation to such an analysis, consider Sartre's notion of "the gaze." Recall that, for Sartre, we recognize each other as persons (i.e., as individuals that impose obligations on each other) in that instant where our eyes meet and we hold each other in a gaze. And what is it that we recognize in the gaze? The answer is, we recognize each other's subjectivity. That is, we recognize the other to be, like ourselves, an S-O-L. It is in that space of inter-subjectivity that opens up in the gaze that we see the other returning our gaze. Please note that we must not place too much emphasis on eye contact as the means whereby we come to recognize the subjectivity of another. Although it is certainly prominent in our normal daily interactions with one another, it clearly isn't necessary as the case of Helen Keller demonstrates. The real point to be emphasized is that we can, by various means, come to recognize the subjectivity of one another and it is in the space that is opened by this inter-subjectivity that meaningful relationships are possible.

I am aware, of course, that this raises a host of difficult questions that I can't adequately address here. I would, though, like to briefly consider two of them. First, one might say, "Well, but what about the person who says, quite sincerely, that when they look into the eyes of a dog (monkey, whale, take your pick), they don't see any subjectivity reflected there as they do when looking into the eyes of a fellow human being." Sartre is aware, of course, that we don't always recognize others as like ourselves in being persons; we can always deny the personhood of another and refuse to meet the other's gaze.[19]

And this, for Sartre, plunges us into false consciousness. Hegel, too, speaks of this in his discussion of the relationship between master and slave. The master, in refusing to recognize the personhood of the other (i.e., seeing the other as slave, something less than a person), involves himself in a contradiction, or what we might

---

[18] This applies, of course, to our encounters with other human beings as well.

[19] I am reminded of a particularly powerful scene in the film "Schindler's List" involving the woman POW walking across the court yard as Amon Goeth (Ralph Fiennes) cleans his rifle.

today call cognitive dissonance. To have one's status as master recognized by the other requires the other to be a person; only another person can recognize the master for what he is. But this cognitive dissonance can only be resolved by recognizing the personhood of the other and, thus, it is simultaneously recognized that, as a person, it is no longer possible to treat the other as slave. Similarly, animals are our slaves and it is in our self-interest to refuse to recognize their subjectivity.[20] To recognize their status as S-O-Ls would require significant sacrifice for us and, thus, it is easier to refuse to meet their gaze, to treat them instead as mere resources. And for some of us at least, the experience of cognitive dissonance is what ultimately leads to adopting vegetarianism as a moral attitude.

But second, and coming from the opposite direction as it were, one might say, "Just because you say that when you observe the goldfish, you don't see anything like subjectivity reflected there, how do you know that this implies there is none?" This is a much tougher problem, though not for the reason one might first think. Let me start with the relatively easier cases and approach the borderline cases by and by.

I'm aware that some people believe, apparently quite sincerely, that their houseplants thrive when classical music is played. And Warren herself alludes to the belief that spiders and insects might be S-O-Ls. After all, they exhibit what appears to be intelligent (i.e., goal-directed) behavior don't they? I can't make the argument here for reasons of space, but I assert that the apparently intelligent behavior of houseplants, insects and spiders, indeed of goldfish and guppies, is merely instinctive behavior.[21]

Moreover, not only is there an alternative explanation for the apparently goal-directed behavior, but there is nothing with the requisite internal complexity to support subjectivity.

It is for these reasons, sufficient in themselves, that we can say these are paradigm cases of individuals that are not S-O-Ls. I don't for a moment deny that there may be troubling borderline cases, but I don't need to deny that for the point to stand: in regards to paradigm cases of animals that are S-O-Ls, we are able to meet them inter-subjectively if we choose and, coincidentally, they have the requisite internal complexity.

Let us now consider the tougher cases, for example the octopus, that demonstrate intelligent behavior but in other ways are so alien to us that we have no idea what it would be like to meet them inter-subjectively. I think it is cases like this that sheds light on the real nature of the borderline cases. There are no real reasons to believe that spiders might be S-O-Ls in the relevant sense, but an octopus presents a much more troubling case.

Its behavior seems to be genuinely intelligent, not merely tropic, yet is so psychologically alien to us that we don't or can't recognize its subjectivity. Inevitably we contemplate the possibility that there might be some other explanation for the behavior.

---

20 Consider, for example, the case of Descartes and his response to critics regarding his experiments involving vivisection on live animals.

21 I have in mind here, the well-known example of the experiment involving digger wasps widely discussed in the literature.

Thus, normal mature mammals will always function as paradigm cases of S-O-Ls for us because of their psychological nearness to us and borderline cases persist, at least in part, because of their psychological distance from us. Perhaps future research in neurophysiology and ethology will clarify these isues.[22] Perhaps we will, one day, have an adequate understanding of internal complexity to decide the troubling borderline cases but I'm not holding my breath.[23]

I turn now to the last objection I wish to consider. This one is not raised against Regan directly but arises out of reflecting on a view defended by Paul W. Taylor in an article titled, "The Ethics of Respect for Nature." In this essay, Taylor is arguing for the reasonableness of a view known as "respect for nature," or alternatively, "the biocentric view," according to which we ought to extend moral considerability to all living things on the grounds that all living things have intrinsic worth. In speaking of the usual justifications of anthropocentric views for ascribing intrinsic worth to all and only humans, Taylor says the following.

> The human characteristics mentioned are all valuable to humans. … Clearly it is from the human standpoint that they are being judged to be desirable and good. It is not difficult here to recognize a begging of the question. Humans are claiming human superiority from a strictly human point of view, that is, from a point of view in which the good of humans is taken as the standard of judgment.[24]

Clearly the point can be generalized. Regan's theory, although it extends intrinsic worth to include many non-human animals, is anthropocentric in the sense that it is in relation to ourselves that we define the notion of S-O-L and magnanimously include these non-human animals in the charmed circle. If one gives up the notion of human superiority, on the grounds that all attempts to establish such are question-begging, then the conclusion follows that humans are simply members of the community of living things on the same level as all others; naturally evolved beings with no special status. Thus, all living things have intrinsic worth and are equally deserving of moral considerability on the grounds of being "teleological centers of life." This feature of being a teleological center of life is sufficient to distinguish those beings deserving of moral consideration from those that aren't (because teleological centers of life have interests – things can go better or worse for them). But any attempt to further restrict the boundaries of moral considerability is merely parochial and, thus, begs the question at issue.

I'm honestly not sure how to meet this objection. Of course Taylor's theory is not a theory of rights. It is a theory of moral considerability and nothing more. So, perhaps this is exactly the sort of argument that Regan anticipated might compel us

---

[22] In regards to ethology and the meeting of minds as it were, have a listen to a podcast by Irene Pepperberg titled "Alex and Me" about her years spent studying the behaviour of Alex, an African Grey parrot.

[23] On the general point of psychological nearness to us and its relevance to this, I am again indebted to John Russell for help in clarifying my thoughts on this.

[24] Taylor 1981, p. 212.

to extend the boundaries of intrinsic worth even further. Moreover, it reinforces what was said above in my response to Warren's second objection, namely that the notion of S-O-L is not coextensive with the notion of intrinsic worth. Then perhaps we could go on to say that S-O-Ls impose stronger obligations on us, obligations to never use them as the means to our ends, while those living things that are not S-O-Ls are deserving of our moral consideration (i.e., we must take their interests into account in our moral deliberations) but they are not deserving of respectful treatment as we have defined the term.[25]

Unfortunately there is something deeply unsatisfying about this response. Regan's argument depends crucially on the claim that all S-O-Ls have intrinsic worth and that all beings that have intrinsic worth have it equally. It is on this basis that we are obliged to treat them respectfully. But now, if we grant that some beings that are not S-O-Ls are possessed of intrinsic worth, then why aren't they similarly deserving of respectful treatment? Are we forced to recognize that intrinsic worth comes in degrees after all? Or alternatively, if the notion of bearer-of-intrinsic-worth has come apart from the notion of bearer-of-rights, then what, if anything, is to ground the notion of bearer-of-rights? No matter which way we turn, there is no easy answer to this dilemma.

Conclusions

A few concluding remarks are in order. First, I think this theory is still a live option for answering the questions we began with, notwithstanding the issue raised concerning rights theories. There are non-human animals numbering in the billions exploited by us each year for food, entertainment, experimentation and sport. These animals are like us in being S-O-Ls and, thus, are deserving of respectful treatment. At the very least this means that we must cease to treat them as resources, mere means to our ends. But secondly, in regards to the notion of intrinsic worth, I have argued that it is not some sort of indefinable, non-natural property but, rather, a presupposition of normative ethical theories. Yet important questions remain unanswered. Does intrinsic worth then depend, in some sense, on some natural property or properties? In which case, what is the nature of this dependence? Is it causal? Supervenience perhaps? And if it is not in any way dependent upon natural properties of any kind, what good reasons have we got for believing in it?[26] In a sequel to this essay presently in progress, I intend to address these issues. Thirdly, although not essential to the defense of Regan's position, the notion of S-O-Ls as the sorts of beings with whom one can, in principle, have a meaningful relationship, and what it means to meet one another *as* subjects, offers intriguing possibilities for exploring the related notion of psychological proximity and its role in recognizing

[25] At least two people who have commented on this paper have told me that they don't see problem with drawing a distinction between respect and moral considerability along the lines I have sketched here. Regrettably I have not yet been able to see my way past the difficulties with perfect clarity.

[26] Thanks to Jim Robinson for getting me to (reluctantly) accept the force of this point.

the subjectivity of others. Or more accurately, we would like to know what role psychological distance (i.e., *alien*-ness) plays in obscuring the subjectivity of others. Be all that as it may, however, in broad strokes the case made herein is that, details aside, human animals, who are "subjects of a life," are ethically obligated (on pain of hypocrisy and contradiction) to treat other "subjects of a life" (many of whom are non-human) with the sort of respect that being a "subject of a life" so clearly demands.

Reference list

Kant, Immanuel. *Groundwork of the Metaphysic of Morals*. Trans. H. J. Paton. New York: Harper Torchbooks, 1964. Print.

Regan, Tom. *The Case for Animal Rights*. Berkeley: University of California Press, 1983. Print.

Savage, Candace. *Bird Brains: The Intelligence of Crows, Ravens, Magpies, and Jays*. New York: Random House, 1997. Print.

Taylor, Paul W. "The Ethics of Respect for Nature." *Environmental Ethics*, vol.3, no.3 (Fall 1981): 197-218. Print.

Warren, Mary Anne. "Difficulties with the Strong Animal Rights Position." *Between the Species,* 2, No. 4, (Fall 1987): 433-441. Print.

Lena Green
(South Africa)

Teaching Respect in South African Classrooms: Challenges and Possibilities

The context

Respect is a particularly sensitive and important topic in South Africa, given this country's history of lack of respect for the majority of its citizens during the apartheid era. The Preamble to the new Constitution published in 1998 emphasizes the need to establish 'a society based on democratic values, social justice and fundamental human rights'. Moreover, the notion of respect is deeply embedded in African culture. Professor Nhlanhla Mathonsi, head of the school of Zulu Studies at the University of KwaZulu-Natal, was recently reported as saying that "In Zulu culture you respect adults. It is not earned – it is predetermined".[1]

In the immediate post apartheid period, there were high hopes that a reformed system of national education, explicitly aligned to the political values of the new government, would be a powerful tool to facilitate the transformation of South African society. A policy document emanating from the Department of Education in 1997 states that the curriculum aims to "...foster learning which encompasses a culture of human rights, multilingualism and multiculturalism and sensitivity to the values of reconciliation and nation building."[2] The report of the working group on values in education[3] subsequently identified respect as one of the values to be taught within the new National Curriculum.

The new curriculum was widely researched internationally, resulting in a final design that emphasized the integration of knowledge across disciplines and teaching that was outcomes based and learner centred. 'Learning areas' rather than subjects were identified and outcomes specified for each. Drawing on the frameworks of Ryle[4] and Mason,[5] each area was to be taught in such a way that students would acquire not only knowledge, but relevant skills and values associated with that knowledge. Solomons offers the following example:

> In a lesson on natural resources in environmental education one could address:

[1] Mail & Guardian, May 25-31, 2012.
[2] Cited in Solomons 2010, p. 41.
[3] Department of Education 2000.
[4] Ryle 1971.
[5] Mason 1997.

a) The state of water resources [propositional knowledge];
b) How to save water [skills, or procedural knowledge];
c) The will to act in accordance with[6] [values, or dispositional knowledge].

The notion of respect is embedded in the South African curriculum in various ways. The learning area named Life Orientation includes the following outcomes.

"The learner will be able to demonstrate an understanding of and commitment to constitutional rights and responsibilities, and to show an understanding of diverse cultures and religions" and

"The learner will be able to use acquired life skills to achieve and extend personal potential to respond effectively to challenges in his or her world." [7]

In addition, the curriculum document specifies a number of 'Critical Outcomes' that span all learning areas. These include being able to work effectively with others, being culturally and aesthetically sensitive across a range of social contexts, and participating as responsible citizens in the life of local, national and global communities. As Solomons points out, if the above principle of identifying knowledge skills and values is applied to values education, then the teaching of respect would have to involve equipping students with *understanding* of the concept, providing them with *practice in acting* respectfully in different contexts (because skills are not acquired without practice), and encouraging in them the *disposition* to be appropriately respectful.

Two important assumptions made by the original framers of the curriculum were, firstly, that it would be possible and unproblematic to teach respect in South African schools and, secondly, that local teachers would be able to devise their own contextually appropriate means of arriving at the specified outcomes. Both these assumptions are problematic.

Conceptual challenges associated with the teaching of respect in schools

The teaching of values in schools is widely regarded as problematic for a number of reasons. It is, for example, claimed that education should not prescribe the nature of 'the good life.' Solomons[8] points out that many authors contend that education should be about equipping students to make informed choices about their own values rather than 'indoctrinating' them with pre-selected values or nurturing pre-selected virtues. She adds that notions of 'the common good' may be a means of promoting social cohesion but can be difficult to defend, citing Gutmann[9] who maintains that societies united by a common good are frequently repressive. The tension between social values and personal autonomy is apparent in the wording of the South African curriculum documents but unacknowledged as an issue that might trouble teachers in classrooms. Even if it is accepted that certain common values are desirable, the fact

[6] Solomons 2010, p. 59.
[7] Department of Education 2002.
[8] Solomons 2010.
[9] Gutmann 1990.

remains that individuals' values are social constructs embedded in historical and socio-political contexts. They cannot be replaced by simple prescription.

Secondly, it is sometimes claimed that it is neither possible nor desirable to teach values in schools because, in a multi-cultural society in which different religions and norms co-exist, groups do not necessarily share the same values. If cultural identities are to be respected, schools must either teach a multiplicity of values, some of which may conflict, or refrain from explicitly promoting any particular value system. From this perspective, it is parents and communities who have the right and the responsibility to inculcate the values they consider important and determine the persons or principles they consider worthy of respect. A recent address by Professor Jonathan Jansen, Vice Chancellor of a South African university, appears to support this view. According to a local newspaper report[10] he recently argued that education should start at home by inculcating the core values of a strong moral code, respect for one's elders and a deep respect for learning. The tension between respect for diversity and the notion of common values is also present in the South African curriculum documents. Teachers are aware of the need to respect diversity, but it is far from clear at what point diversity becomes unacceptable and is no longer a right. As Gardner[11] has argued, there are circumstances in which approval and respect may not be appropriate.

The third issue that I wish to highlight is the question of schools, and the education system itself, as models of democratic practice. Education in South Africa under apartheid was notably authoritarian and discipline frequently involved corporal punishment. Students did what teachers told them and teachers did what 'The Department' told them. The new curriculum was intended to transform schools, but was presented to teachers in a top-down manner that did not model the practices it wished to introduce. Most schools have retained traditional authority structures although these are frequently, and sometimes justifiably, challenged by both parents and students on the basis of their rights. This has undermined the authority of teachers who, notwithstanding the structures in place in the school, no longer receive automatic respect (or at least respectful treatment) on the basis of their status or their licence to punish. There is apparently no intention on the part of education policy makers to introduce the kind of school reform that would make schools democratic institutions. The assumptions of school authorities, teachers, parents and students regarding authority and respect are, therefore, often different. The way in which respect is conceptualized cannot be separated from the way in which it is seen to operate in the wider social world which school-children, their parents, and their teachers inhabit. The ten year old who said, "Now that we have democracy and everyone can do what they like…", was not alone in this view. In general, in South Africa, a widely shared understanding of the meaning and importance of democratic practice is yet to be established.

---

[10] People's Post, May 22 2012.

[11] Gardner 2009.

Practical challenges to the teaching of respect in South African schools

Further challenges to the teaching of values that are particularly evident in South African schools include levels of poverty in many communities (that make survival the primary value), widespread frustration that expectations raised by the change to democratic government in 1994 have not been met, and, on occasion, a somewhat alarming sense of entitlement.

Moreover, it fairly soon became apparent that, for a number of reasons, the assumption that the majority of teachers in South Africa would have the confidence and the skills to create their own curricula and learning materials was flawed in terms of almost all learning areas. Already in the 1990's concerns were being expressed about the capacity of the curriculum to achieve the many admirable goals expected of it[12]. The main criticism was that the curriculum did not take into account the historical and social contexts of schooling in South Africa and their implications. Curriculum planners urged the teaching profession to make a paradigm shift, but, in keeping with outcomes based principles, offered no specific guidelines to teachers accustomed to a prescriptive curriculum regarding what to put in place of their old teaching methods. South Africa spends a great deal on education (21% of the national budget in 2011), but despite the new curriculum, school results remain poor. For example, the Western Cape Education Department's Diagnostic Assessment[13] results indicate that the Grade 6 literacy rate was 44.8 % in 2007 and 48.6% in 2009. This province is considered to have one of the better functioning education departments and yet less than half its children are literate after six years of schooling. As a consequence, criticism of the curriculum and of teachers is rife and teacher morale is low. The profession itself no longer enjoys the status it once did and it is not a popular career choice among young people. The national curriculum has, therefore, been the subject of several revisions. While retaining its overall goals, it has become increasingly prescriptive in terms of how they are to be achieved, particularly in the basic areas of literacy and numeracy. It still retains, however, an overall commitment to the nurturing of democratic values and nation building, including the teaching of respect.

How do teachers in South Africa understand the teaching of respect?

An empirical study involving 350 teachers from 36 schools in one province[14] suggests that, despite the above challenges, teachers still see the teaching of values as part of their professional responsibility. But although claiming to believe in the crucial importance of fostering goal-setting and planning, reliability and trustworthiness, punctuality, and persistence, only 30% or less of the teachers in the study admitted to working actively to promote these dispositions. Although Ohlsson[15] and

[12] Jansen & Christie 1999, 2001.
[13] Western Cape Education Department 2010.
[14] Green 2004a.
[15] Ohlsson 2009.

others have made a strong case for their importance, teachers in this study did not prioritize the cognitive, or intellectual, virtues that would enable meaningful value judgements, or perceive effective thinking to have any bearing on the teaching of respect.

A second study[16] investigated teachers' practices. It confirmed teachers' sense that they had a professional responsibility to teach values and their awareness of their importance as role models. However, they made use of only a limited range of possible strategies and tended to conceptualize their task as managing undesirable behaviour rather than as a positive endeavour. The most commonly used strategies were: to insist that rules are obeyed (83% of teachers claimed to do this); to warn learners about negative consequences (79% of teachers claimed to do this); and to model the qualities they wished to encourage (67% of teachers claimed to do this). Although 43% of teachers claimed to give regular practice in reasoned discussion, the nature of these discussions was not clarified.

Possible approaches to the teaching of respect

What are the options for teaching the package of knowledge, skills and values said to constitute 'respect'? What theories of learning might inform what teachers do? With regard to knowledge, traditional teacher centred instruction based on behaviourist theories of learning might equip students with an understanding of one specific meaning of the word/concept 'respect' and information regarding what they were to consider worthy of respect. The meanings would be fixed and to a large extent dependent on either individual teachers' own beliefs about respect or the direct instructions of the curriculum. Similarly, certain behaviours believed to demonstrate respect could be modelled and reinforced by rewards. If a disposition to respect socially desirable objects were to develop, it could be interpreted as a habit based on the rewards one personally received or observed others to receive.

As illustrated above, the teaching of respect in local classrooms tends to focus on the behaviour that is considered an indication of respect in particular contexts. In other words there is little attention to respect as a concept and the questions that it might raise, for example, about who or what deserves respect and why. One might conclude that genuine deferential regard (a disposition) is either assumed to exist on the basis of the outward signs of respect under controlled circumstances or considered to be beyond the scope of a teacher's role.

Piagetian and Kohlbergian developmental theories emphasize the importance of the personal construction of meaning in discussion with peers. In a Piagetian and learner-centred classroom, students might generate a number of meanings around the concept 'respect' and a number of ways in which respect might be displayed, and would not necessarily internalize identical understandings. If a disposition to respect socially desirable objects were to develop, it would be seen as the result of a personal choice on the part of individual students. The theory assumes that innately reason-

[16] Green 2004b.

able young people will inevitably discover and choose for themselves values that are at least close to those that policy makers wish to establish in society, and adopt them as their own.

Given the state of South African society, its emerging role models and its crime statistics, many teachers would not consider this a valid assumption. Students might know how to show respect and be disposed to do when it was in their interests, but few teachers would claim to be confident that their students would independently choose appropriate objects to hold in deferential esteem. Although some teachers in the study referred to above claimed to encourage discussion, it was not clear what role they took in guiding or challenging its conclusions.

Recent thinking about learning and teaching emphasizes the ideas of Vygotsky[17] and Feuerstein[18], both of whom stress the importance of mediation for the construction of meaning and for the shaping of intelligent thought and action. Children and young people do not discover meaning in a vacuum. A more knowledgeable other, and/or the social and cultural artefacts that currently shape their contexts, mediate and influence their interpretation of existing knowledge and their acquisition of the mental tools that have been constructed in human society to enable careful, consistent, reasonable, yet flexible thinking. It is from this foundation that new knowledge and new ways of understanding human thinking processes are creatively generated.

In a classroom where learning is based on Vygotskian theory, the generation of meanings around respect and the ways in which it might be displayed would not be wide open, but required to meet certain criteria for effective thinking and at least take into account certain socially and culturally constructed criteria of human worth. The disposition to be appropriately respectful, if it did develop, would be a shared accomplishment of teacher, student and peers. This approach requires the teacher to teach not only knowledge, but ways of thinking about and interacting with knowledge, a process sometimes referred to as cognitive education. The teacher would, as in community of inquiry practice, mediate thinking processes as well as knowledge about the world.

Philosophy for Children as a promising strategy for the 'teaching' of respect

If teachers in South Africa are required to 'teach' respect, Lipman's[19] approach is well worth considering. Not only is *Philosophy for Children* highly consistent with the most recent theories of development and learning, it also offers an opportunity to enhance cognitive and moral development concurrently and to do so within a structured but democratic process. If practiced regularly with a skilled teacher, it can equip students of all ages with a repertoire of thinking and reasoning moves that will serve them well in all areas of learning and as future citizens of a democracy. Lip-

---

[17] Vygotsky 1962, 1978.
[18] Feuerstein Klein & Tannebaum, 1991.
[19] Lipman, 1991.

man's ideas are aligned with cognitive psychology in that he believes it is important to become aware of thinking processes and to practice the use of specific thinking moves (which in other contexts, might be called skills). The moves that he advocates are those culturally constructed ways of enquiring together that have evolved in certain human societies and are considered most likely to generate movement towards truth. He is Vygotskian in his emphasis on meanings co-constructed in language in a social context that includes a knowledgeable mediator. The teacher's role in a philosophical inquiry is not just to facilitate discussion but to ensure that the discussion makes some progress towards truth, or at least a position that can be defended by reason. She is required to model, nurture, and insist on the use of specified thinking moves.

Philosophical inquiry can be stimulated in many ways – for example by a picture, an incident, or a news report. The advantage of Lipman's narrative texts is that, while incorporating potentially philosophical questions, they also provide a cumulative model of the process of inquiry for both students and their teachers. In addition they engage students because they can recognize their own environments and identify with the characters portrayed.

For a number of reasons,[20] Lipman's original materials are unlikely to be used optimally in the majority of South African classrooms, even supposing them to be affordable, which they are not. But his ideas suggest a promising direction for the teaching of concepts such as respect and his generosity in sharing them permitted the development, in collaboration with local teachers learning about community of inquiry practice, of simple, locally relevant stories designed to reflect the realities of one of South Africa's many contexts. Each story booklet is accompanied by a brief manual containing guidelines and suggestions for teachers. The manuals suggest questions that might arise for discussion and include simple classroom exercises, although they do not approach the richness and complexity of Lipman's manuals.

The story booklets and manuals were subsequently distributed to other groups of local teachers who received brief training in community of inquiry methods on various occasions between 2002 and 2009. The classroom report below comes from one such teacher working with a class of 10-11 year olds in 2012. The story she used is included as an appendix to this paper. After sharing the story and engaging in community of inquiry discussion, the children were asked by their teacher to write their personal answers to a number of questions, giving reasons for their opinions.

The questions were selected by the teacher from those listed in the Manual as options from which children may select a topic for exploration if they do not generate questions of their own. It has been found that local children have some difficulty in formulating questions, and teachers have had to rely more than is desirable on the suggestions in the Manual. In this case the teacher also chose to use the questions for a written exercise.

---

[20] Green 2008.

The first question to which the children responded was:
Is it possible to care about someone but not respect them?
Two thirds of the class said it was not, providing the following type of justifications:
What's the use of caring about someone if you don't respect them?
Everyone deserves respect.
Everyone should be respected.
It is impossible because caring comes with respect.
That person might be older than you.
But others saw it differently.
Yes it is possible because you can give your granny food and still be rude.
Yes - Some people need to earn respect but you can still care about them.
It's OK if you at least pretend to respect.
It is possible to care and not respect because if you think your little sister is stupid and annoying if she dies you'd be sad because she's a part of you.
When the question was turned around the class was more or less equally divided about whether or not it was possible to respect someone but not care about them.
No, everyone deserves respect
No, everyone is supposed to care about everyone the way we want to be cared for the same way.
No, if you can't care about someone you can't respect them.
No, I think it's the same thing.
Yes because it depends on what happened.
Yes you can be nice to them but not care about them because caring is deep like a family member when you care about someone you love and admire them, but respect someone...you can respect anybody, a homeless person or by carrying bags for a lady...
Yes, it is possible to respect a person as very important.
Yes it is possible to respect someone but not care for them because you maybe don't like them but you must respect them if they earned it.
The final question related to respect was:
If someone is 'family' should we always help them and look out for them?
Most children answered yes, emphasizing the importance of a family bond and reciprocal caring, as the following examples show.
It's your family. You will be nothing without them.
You should always look out for them because you only get one family.
He or she would do the same for you.
Family sticks together.
When something is wrong he will help you, even if he does not want to.
If you need help no-one will help you [without family].
One realist acknowledged that children's power is limited.
We should most of the time help and look out for them – if it is an adult and they have a problem at work sometimes we can't help them but we can try.
There were, however, some reservations.

> *Well you do respect them and help them but I would never back up badness ever.*
> *Yes and no because even if the person IS family it only depends on what you're helping them with.*
> *If someone is family you shouldn't always help them because what if they rob a bank.*

Discussion

It is clear that the curriculum formula of knowledge, skills and values does not fully accommodate the teaching of respect. Respect as a value is not the same as, for example, honesty, or justice. The disposition to be respectful involves not only the skill or habit of behaving with apparent respect, but the ability to make judgements about what or who is worthy of respect. The examples provided illustrate that these young students were beginning to develop an awareness of what might be problematic about respect and to see the need to provide reasons for their opinions. But the evidence also suggests some recognition of the complexities involved in understanding the need to respect human dignity, the need to respect one's elders and family, and the notion that respect must be earned. In several cases it seemed that their opinions represented what ought to be rather than what is. Slightly older students at a different school displayed a similar tendency when they insisted that a community was always a group of people who *help* each other. This emphasis on the importance of helping and respecting others may reflect the values of the Constitution but, equally, it may signal the anxiety of a generation of adults who are far from confident about what the children of the new South Africa may grow up to respect.

The community of inquiry offers a space to explore, although not necessarily resolve, confusion about concepts. But, in South African classrooms, it is difficult to find space in the curriculum for such time-consuming activities. The skilled teacher in the example above chose to use time allocated for 'shared reading' for the reading of a locally produced text, followed by a group discussion with certain 'rules' and finally a written exercise. For this activity, she chose the traditional format of question and answer, using the questions for inquiry proposed in the manual. It is not clear to what extent this format might influence students' sense that a 'right answer' could be found or to what extent the preceding discussion was shaped by the teacher. It is nevertheless encouraging that students seemed to be beginning to think for themselves. It would be interesting to see how they would respond to the exercises suggested in the manual, which would be a means of building on their ideas. At this time, such follow up depends entirely on the teacher's ability to integrate work of this nature with the requirements of the national curriculum. Lipman's approach does not guarantee results but it is, in the long run, more likely to encourage genuine and appropriate respect than a method that informs students who and what they ought to respect and how they ought to display such respect.

Reference list

Department of Education. *Report of the Working Group on Values in Education.* Pretoria: Government Printer, 2000.

Department of Education. *Revised National Curriculum Statement Grades R-9.* Pretoria: Government Printer, 2002.

Feuerstein, R., Klein., P, and Tannenbaum, A. (eds.). *Mediated learning experience: Theoretical, psycho-social and learning implications*. London: Freund. 1991.

Gardner, S. 'Love thy neighbour? Maybe not, in E. Marsal, T. Dobashi & B. Weber (eds.). *Children Philosophize Worldwide*. Frankfurt: Peter Lang. 2009.

Green, L. Nurturing democratic virtues: educators' perspectives. *South African Journal of Education, 24(2).* 2004, pp.108-113. 2004a.

Green, L. Nurturing democratic virtues: educators' practices. *South African Journal of Education, 24(4).* 2004, pp.254-259. 2004b.

Green, L. Cognitive modifiability in South African classrooms: the Stories for Thinking Project, in Oon Seng Tan & Alice Seok-Hoon Seng (eds.). *Cognitive modifiability in learning and assessment*. Singapore: Cengage Learning. 2008.

Gutmann, A. *Democracy and democratic education*. Princeton, NJ.: Princeton University Press. 1990.

Jansen, J. & Christie, P. (eds.). *Changing curriculum: Studies on outcomes based education in South Africa*. Kenwyn: Juta. 1999.

Lipman, M. 1991. *Thinking in education.* New York: Cambridge University Press.

Mail & Guardian, May 25-31, 2012.

Mason, M. *Good thoughtful teachers make the difference*. Cape Times, 1997.

Ohlsson, R. Some connections between moral and intellectual virtues, in E. Marsal, T Dobashi & B Weber (eds.). *Children Philosophize Worldwide*. Germany: Peter Lang. 2009.

People's Post Claremont-Rondebosch 22 May 2012.

Ryle, G. Teaching and training, in *Collected Papers,* vol. 2, pp.451-465. 1971.

Solomons, I.D. A conceptual exploration of the teaching and assessment of values within the South African outcomes-based curriculum. Unpublished doctoral thesis, University of the Western Cape. 2010.

Vygotsky, L. S. *Thought and language*. Cambridge, Ma.: MIT Press. 1962.

Vygotsky, L. S. *Mind in society*. Cambridge, Ma.: Harvard University Press. 1978.

Western Cape Education Department. Ministers press release 18 February 2010. Available at www.wced.wcape.gov.za, accessed 23 February 2010.

Appendix

Story 4: Respect

The children were happily walking to their favourite corner shop. Suddenly, just in front of them, an old man stumbled and fell at the edge of the road. Everyone got a big fright. Shariefa felt sorry for the man and wanted to rush over to help him.

"Shame," she said, "let's help him. He must be sick. Maybe he has TB."

Short strong Ricardo grabbed her by the arm and scolded, "Why do you say shame? He is just an old drunk." He turned around to look at Michaela and said, with a grin on his face, "Ask Michaela, it is family of hers."

Michaela did not feel bad because all she knew about the man was that her father gave him a place to stay in their backyard.

"You think you know everything. You don't even know the man," she shouted at Ricardo.

Candice was afraid to walk nearer as she thought drunk people were really bad and smelly. Also you never knew what they would do next.

Riyaad wondered if the man was really so bad, just because he was drunk. He was still lying at the edge of the road and seemed quite happy to stay there. There was not much traffic so Riyaad did not think he was in danger. Maybe he was a nice person even if he was drunk. No-one ever touched alcohol in his home. It was against their religion. But he had heard people speaking about what it could do to you. It could make you get sick, or even die.

Nomsa, who was at the back of the group, watching from a distance, tried to imagine what kind of a job the man must have had – or maybe he did not ever have a job? Maybe that was why he drank? Or maybe he was dismissed for drinking?

Sipho stepped closer, lifted his glasses and tried to get a better look. 'I wonder if he drinks all the time, and why he does it,' he thought.

"Come on," said Shariefa. "We can help him to get up Children are supposed to help older people."

"He does not seem to want to get up," answered Riyaad.

Just then two men came out of the shop and pulled the man to his feet. He walked away towards the back of the shop.

"Drinking is disgusting," said Ricardo.

"Well, my dad drinks, but he never becomes drunk like that," said Candice. "He is not disgusting," she went on, "He will never make me sad. I love him."

"How can you love someone who drinks?" said Ricardo scornfully. He hated it when his uncle visited and shouted at everyone.

Nomsa wondered how it was that some people seemed to know when to stop drinking and others ended up falling in the streets.

But Shafiek was puzzling about something else. At school Mrs Van Schalkwyk often talked about respect, and how it was important to respect everybody. But did that mean that you should respect people even when they were drunk?

Ricardo gave him a push. "Come on now, what's the hold up?" he said. "Stop thinking about that old drunk. This is nothing to do with us. Last one at the shop is a rotten egg!" he called out, and began running towards the shop.

Classroom activities suggested in the Manual:

1. ***In each of the following situations say what you might do to show respect. Then say what you might do to show that you care about the person. Then decide if you think there is a difference between respect and caring.***

	respect	*care*
An older person is trying to cross the street		
A pregnant woman is standing in a bus		
A teacher does not notice that she has dropped her keys		
You are competing with your class mates in a race		
Guests from out of town are visiting your house		
One of your parents is sick		

2. If it is true that every human being is entitled to respect, how would you show respect to the following persons:
(1). A teacher who is giving an interesting lesson?
(2). A class mate who received a prize for high achievement?
(3). A famous singer?
(4). One of your class mates who was punished for breaking a school rule?
(5). A friend's parent who lost her or his job?
(6). A famous singer who committed a crime?
(7). A teacher who is giving a boring lesson?
(8). An old man who is drunk on the street?

3. Decide whether the behaviours below are a sign of respect, a sign of disrespect or could be either. Remember to give reasons for what you think.

Listening carefully	*Opening the door for someone*
Being punctual	*Taking someone's advice*
Knocking on a door	*Calling a person Sir*
Being friendly	*Looking down*
Speaking politely	*Shaking hands with someone*
Ignoring someone	*Smiling*

Jessica Davis
(USA)

Respecting Our Being: Philosophical Dialogue as Non-Instrumental Pedagogy[1]

In this essay I aim to do two things: I argue that students and teachers ought to respect one another as human beings who are mutually dependent, and I also argue that philosophical dialogue thus ought to be included in all classrooms regardless of the subject matter – indeed, I insist that without the space for dialogue in classrooms, mutual respect is absent.[2] I examine some reasons why philosophical dialogue, or in particular, the Socratic Method (SM), is alleged to be educationally meaningful, and show that a number of impressions regarding the value of SM are mistaken, insofar as they approximate the very form of education which Socrates and, indeed modern educational reformers, contest. As such, my overall thesis in this essay is that philosophical dialogue is educationally meaningful because it entails as intrinsic respect for persons regardless of merit or instrumentality. So long as one is participating in dialogue to the extent one is capable, an affectionate educational 'aim'– and one which I insist is necessary for all other meaningful education and flourishing in general – is satisfied.

Part 2 | Introduction

The dialogue format in Plato's works is often described as a method conducive to eliciting interlocutors' inherent knowledge, or as a tool by which elenchus, valued for its own sake, can be achieved. However, to understand Plato in either of these ways is to miss the significance of the dialogue format, i.e., the metaphysical underpinnings of the dialectic relation, predominant in his corpus. In this essay I interpret the limitations of knowledge in Plato's corpus as a correlate of one's claims to independent possession of knowledge. As this essay proclaims, a teacher must demonstrate how to corroborate her beliefs with those of others, and acknowledge her interdependence with her students and her community by way of respectful dialogue –

[1] A version of this paper has previously published under the title of "Being Participation: The Ontology of the Socratic Method." *Analytic Teaching and Philosophical Praxis* 2012, vol. 33, no. 1, pp. 19-29. Website. It is reprinted here with permission from the publisher.
[2] I have in mind here secondary school education, but the same argument can be applied to primary school. I believe it is important to make these arguments regarding mandatory education as opposed to university-age instruction wherein students presumably make a choice to go to school.

else any proposed benefit of education *for each student* will inevitably be thwarted in the name of dogma or mob rule.

In the present section, Part 1, I begin by offering a contrast between what I call the 'instructional approach' to education, which is common in our nation's educational institutions, and the SM, which we find in the Platonic corpus.[3] In Part 2, I describe how some interpretations of SM can be seen as faulty because they view the SM merely as instrumentally valuable to our *becoming* something else. In Part 3, I offer my interpretation of the SM, which is based on an ontological reading of SM as intrinsically valuable insofar as it entails respect for persons engaging in dialogue.[4] Let us begin with some context: the problematic, instructional approach to knowledge, or what Socrates referred to as sophistry.[5]

The Problematic Instructional Approach

It is typical in popular education approaches for students to be seen as passive recipients of knowledge, and for teachers to be seen as bearers of knowledge which they can impart on the students.[6] There is a sharp distinction between teacher and student, and students are taught certain pre-determined curricula which essentially contains other people's beliefs. However, the students are not instructed on how to develop and evaluate their own beliefs.[7] Students memorize isolated and fragmented bits of information without ever learning the connections between facts, and without being able to give an account of how things are related.[8]

"Teaching to the test," which is now widely admonished by educational reformers, is an exaggerated manifestation of this problem.[9] Our schools teach content that is required of them in order to get funding, rather than having concern for the form that education takes, or with the overarching principles that guide our schools. Funding for secondary schools is largely contingent on test results and on end results in general. It may be results that we want from schools – certainly we want all students to graduate, for example – but this approach leaves no mechanism for checking whether or not our collective goals are *good* goals. When teaching to the test we

[3] Pang 2005, pp. 28-31, Leonardo 2004, pp. 12-15.

[4] Interestingly, Paul Woodruff argues that in the early Platonic dialogues, in which there is some scholarly agreement that the historical Socrates is more accurately portrayed than in later dialogues, Socrates himself is not committed to an ontological framework. Specifically, because "early dialogue Socrates" does not adhere to the Platonic Forms, Woodruff claims that Socrates was ontologically neutral. This view gives credence to the aspect of my argument which holds that the Socratic Method does not limit us to a dualism. However, because Woodruff bases his conclusion on the content of the Platonic corpus, rather than on the SM itself, Woodruff remains in the ontologically-neutral position regarding Socrates. See Woodruff 1978, p. 113-114.

[5] See Plato's *Republic* Book 6, 493a-d, and *Republic* Book 9, 576b-c, *The Complete Works of Plato* for some discussion of this sophistry.

[6] Plato, *Republic* Book 7, 518b-c, *The Complete Works of Plato,* and Freire 2000, p. 72.

[7] Pang, 2005, p. 14.

[8] Ibid., p. 21 and p. 29.

[9] Ibid., pp. 422-423.

are vulnerable to the possibility that the mob, as Socrates might say, is wrong; we evaluate students and faculty based on an allegedly universal criterion, without preserving an internal structure capable of evaluating individuals on a personal level that respects their haeccity, nor capable of questioning our notion(s) of the good.[10]

It is most likely because of these problems – of structuring schools around the demands of our funders, of being subject to assessments which discount qualities like integrity or morality in our students, and of being dependent on quantifiable results in general – that educational reformers today advocate for use of the SM.[11] In the following section I will explicate just how the SM in general serves as an alternative to the instructional approach, before delving into my interpretation of the ways in which the SM is viewed as instrumentally valuable by its proponents today.

The Socratic Method

The SM is generally viewed as an alternative to the instructional approach toward education because it prioritizes the investigation of the beliefs that students have, and their processing of those beliefs, rather than on beliefs or information which teachers have and *give* to students.[12] The qualities derivable from a survey of the myriad of examples of the SM in Plato's corpus have been nicely summarized as consisting of epistemic humility, a collective pursuit of truth, curiosity, honesty, humor, and hope, among other things.[13] The SM has also been described as consisting of at least two key steps: the 'gadfly' step, wherein students are brought to doubt their claims to knowledge, and the 'midwifery' step, in which students are led to critically evaluate their beliefs and elicit 'improved' or 'correct' beliefs.[14]

Generally, the instructional approach as described in the above section is concerned with 'the destination,' or particular conclusions and results of education, while the SM in general is concerned with 'the journey,' or the form which education takes. The instructional approach assumes that education itself is of *instrumental* value because the process of instilling information in a student is analogous to using information as a *tool* by which to 'do something to' a student. The end result, in this framework, is a knowledgeable student who has been 'filled.' In the following section I aver that, despite its alleged dissimilarity with the instructional method, the SM has *also* been interpreted (and/or implemented) primarily as instrumentally valuable.

---

[10] See *Republic* Book 6, 493a-d *and* Book 9, 576b-c, in *The Complete Works of Plato.*

[11] It should be noted, too, that in this framework, students are assumed to be individuals who, although needing to be 'filled with knowledge,' are culpable if unsuccessful. This blame is based on the assumption that students ought to meet universal standards. And to the extent that teachers are then to blame in terms of these high-stakes tests, the assumption is still that teachers ought to be able to mold students into these universal standards.

[12] Wolz 1981, pp. 14-15, Portelli, 1990, pp. 143-144.

[13] Corlett 2005, pp. 48-49.

[14] Matthews 2009, p. 441, and Wolz 1981, pp. 14-15.

Part 2 | *Becoming*: Instrumental Interpretations of the Socratic Method

Many of Plato's dialogues have been classified as either embodying a "radical openness," or as typifying the instructional or consensus-aimed methods of education.[15] Kevin Decker avers that because elenchtic dialogues can only refute invalid beliefs, and cannot themselves give birth to viable new philosophical theses, we ought to either abandon elenchtic dialogues all together, or decide that the dialogical format is itself the wisdom for which we should strive.[16] The SM must either be instrumentally valuable or intrinsically valuable. Let us examine two interpretive schemas which take the SM to be instrumentally valuable, before taking a closer look at a schema which is *closer* to viewing the SM as intrinsically valuable.

The Instrumental Recollection and Instrumental Emergence Approaches

Regarding the relevance of the dialogue format within education studies, the emphasis seems to be either on the benefits of using the method due to the uncovering of knowledge otherwise buried within the student, *or* due to the possibilities which are made available when education is led by inquiry rather than predetermined curricula.[17] Within the former framework – which has been derived from various Platonic dialogues – it is assumed that students have knowledge within themselves and that the SM brings out and gives birth to this knowledge.[18] The object of value in this case is the knowledge that each student possesses. The latter view holds that the SM *creates* value by maintaining a kind of ground for possibility. The object of value in this case is 'the possibility itself,' or the properties which consequently emerge, such as the equality which obtains when neither teacher nor student is said to possess knowledge, or the self-improvement which results from the student's process of disregarding false beliefs.[19] Critical theory of education, though its affinity with the SM may be limited to its questioning of beliefs, may also be seen to fit into this category, insofar as it utilizes analytical methods in order to reach certain valued ends in education.[20]

With respect to the view that beneficial possibilities emerge from the use of the SM, one problem is that, if we have a fixed notion of potential in mind, we may actually thwart potential because of our own ignorance of capacities and possibilities.[21] Similarly, if we take this fixed notion of potential for our students – be it a

---

[15] Decker 2000, p. 6 and 22, Matthews 2009, p. 441.

[16] See Decker 2000, p. 22, and Matthews 2009, p. 2.

[17] Margonis 2011, pp. 433-439.

[18] See *Meno* for discussion of recollection. In *Euthydemus* 719c-d, and 303b -306a, Socrates agrees that wisdom can be taught, but that this type of wisdom is likely sophistic. See *The Complete Works of Plato*.

[19] See Freire 2000, p. 89 and Lipman, Oscanyan, and Sharp 1980, pp. xv, 157 and 207, Overholser 2011, p. 5 and Vansieleghem and Kennedy 2011, p. 173.

[20] Leonardo 2004, pp. 12-15.

[21] See Margonis 2011, p. 436 and Colebrook 2008, p. 40.

quality conducive to egalitarianism, or a quality of achievement – to be our *end*, we may come to find that there are other ways of achieving this end that do not wholeheartedly respect the students. And yet, this concern is precisely what is wrong with assuming *a priori* knowledge: it reduces knowledge to the status of an object which can be possessed. This objectified notion of knowledge takes wisdom as constitutive of the fragmented, isolated bits of information upon which the instructional method of education thrives. Furthermore, in each of the instrumental and emergent value approaches, the role of the interlocutor, and thus, the SM itself, can become problematic and even superfluous if *a priori* knowledge or emergent qualities can arise otherwise. In both interpretations, as explicable as they may be within the context of Plato's works, the operative notions of wisdom are problematically consequentialist. Let us move on now to a third interpretation of the SM.

Instrumental Aporia Approach

Having gone through the conceptions which take the SM as instrumentally valuable – because it elicits *a priori* knowledge or because it opens us up to some other extrinsically valuable quality such as possibility – we can now assess the accounts which take the *aporia* resulting from the SM as 'intrinsically valuable.'[22] My argument here is that this approach also interprets Plato incorrectly, attributing too much to the ideas expressed by Plato's interlocutors by concluding that our ontology entails a gap between our existence and Truth. The instrumental *aporia* approach, I argue, takes the SM as *a means* to realizing our epistemic ineptitude and to realizing, essentially, the chasm between ourselves and certainty. This view thus remains an instrumental account of the value of the SM.

It may be the case that dialogue is doubly instrumentally valuable, insofar as it both brings forth *a priori* knowledge and opens us up to possibility. There is certainly evidence of this within the text. We also see, however, many occurrences in which *something else* is alleged to occur as a result of the SM. In *Sophist*:

> **Visitor:** And you'll assign this dialectical activity only to someone who has a pure and just love of wisdom.
> **Theaetetus:** You certainly wouldn't assign it to anyone else.
> **Visitor:** We'll find that the philosopher will always be in a location like this if we look for him. He's hard to see clearly too, but not in the same way as the sophist.
> **Theaetetus:** Why not?
> **Visitor:** The sophist runs off into the darkness of *that which is not*, which he's had practice dealing with, and he's hard to see because the place is so dark. Isn't that right?
> **Theaetetus:** It seems to be.

[22] See Matthews 2011, p. 441. An intermediary view is expressed in passing in Lipman, Oscanyan and Sharp 1980, p. 207.

> **Visitor:** But the philosopher always uses reasoning to stay **near** the form, *being*. He isn't at all easy to see because that area is so bright and the eyes of most people's souls can't bear to look at what's divine.[23]

Even the philosopher, who is engaging in the SM and is closest to truth, is only near it. The instrumental *aporia* approach recognizes this philosophically alluring element in Platonic dialogue and deems it a valuable end.

Plato's corpus includes many passages which indicate that Socrates (or Plato) believed elenchus *itself* to be truth because our bodies act as a barrier to knowledge; we can only know our limitations.[24] And there is much scholarly discussion regarding the disparity of metaphysical beliefs which obtain in the elenchtic dialogues and the more robust and theoretical later dialogues.[25] Some interpreters hold that while the earlier dialogues are aporetic, the later ones, insofar as they articulate more elaborate metaphysical and civic accounts, such as those found in *Laws* or *Timaeus*, represent Plato's abandonment of the 'the value of aporia' in favor of certainty.[26] I believe that these concerns only arise when one seeks justification for use of the SM – and of philosophy itself – by appealing to its instrumental capacities, rather than on its possible intrinsic value.

It need not be a surprise that interpreters attempt to justify use of the SM in terms of the results it affords; we live in an age, as Padraig Hogan and Richard Smith write, in which "nothing seems to have value unless it has demonstrable, quantifiable outcomes." However, as they go on to say, "To the mentality that fetishizes the performance-indicator, the Socratic dialogue is likely to remain a lasting puzzle."[27] Whether you take Plato's older dialogues to be indicative of fixed metaphysical positions or not, what can be said is that the dialogue *format* obtains throughout the corpus.

When advocates of SM argue that dialogue is an alternative to (or a supplement for) the instructional approach to education, they seem to focus on the benefits that dialogue has for students and teachers.[28] These same advocates seem to conceive of Plato and the SM, understandably, as entailing a certain metaphysical position.[29] In particular, this position holds that one's knowledge is limited insofar as one is part of a changing, material world, and that one's knowledge is *confirmed* to the extent that one connects with the unchanging Forms inhering in the soul; we are limited to the status of *becoming*.[30]

---

[23] Bold emphasis by author. Plato, *Sophist* 253e-254b in *The Complete Works of Plato.*

[24] McCall 2011.

[25] Benson 2000, pp. 57-95.

[26] Hogan and Smith 2003, pp. 167-168.

[27] Ibid. p. 175.

[28] Estarellas 2007, pp. 12-15, Shah, 2008, p. 268.

[29] There are even advocates of the Socratic Method's potential to "turn the soul" of students, who attribute this metaphysical framework to Plato but decide to simply circumvent his metaphysics altogether while still using the SM. See Haroutunian-Gordon 1991, pp. 5-6.

[30] Plato, *Phaedo,* 66c-d, *Parmenides,* 133b, and *Timaeus* 50d-e in *The Complete Works of Plato.*

I agree that the SM is beneficial, and I agree that the metaphysics mentioned above are easily derivable from the Platonic corpus. However, I argue that it is just as plausible, and more *powerful*, to view Plato, and the method he portrays, as pointing to a fact of our *being,* rather than as a fact of our *becoming*. In my view, it is the dialogue form itself which we ought to view as the most conclusive metaphysical and normative assertion within the corpus: engaging as such is what it means to *be*. Let us examine just how this plays out, and why it is important for an educative space.

PART 3 | Respect for *Being:* The Intrinsic Value Approach Based on Ontological Interpretation

In the remainder of this paper I argue that in order to truly preserve SM as distinct from the instructional approach to education we must appreciate the necessary educational goodness that it entails, i.e., an intrinsic respect for students and teachers regardless of their performance or outcomes. In this section, I first summarize the problem with instrumentality when it comes to educational goods within discussions of educational justice in order to explain the detriment caused to humans when their available pedagogies are merely instrumental. Next, I clarify the function and significance of interlocutor and self within SM, in order to reiterate the necessity of respect in educational spaces, before I conclude.

Underlying the discussion of educational goods is too often a treatment of both students and educational goods as concrete and finite objects, rather than as comprising an interconnected and complex whole. It is precisely this reification of knowledge as a transferrable good that characterizes the problematic instructional approach to education described previously. Along similar lines, assessment based on performance outcomes could be seen as predicated on the idea that private property (as consumable, finite and quantifiable goods) is the utmost value which our democratic citizenship is meant to protect. In contrast with the factory model of schools wherein knowledge and good students are the products or *parts*, a concern for the qualitative nature of the form of our schools as *wholes* has a different nature.[31]

While efforts to create equality among students are certainly well-intentioned, there is a sense in which the basis for their comparisons relies much more on the products of life and an attempt to equalize the products, rather than a comparison of the plurality of individual interests, perspectives, and voices in our society and an attempt to accommodate the myriad interests, perspectives and voices equally. Hence, the need for a respectful pedagogical practice emerges: dialogue permits us to allocate respect to all individuals without having to compare arbitrary qualities. But what is it more precisely that is required of us in order to respect a person? While it is typically agreed that Plato's later dialogues contain a theory of literal oth-

---

[31] Indeed, obsession with inputs and outputs has its roots in our industrial development as a country, and in the administrators that tried to model schools after business. See David B. Tyack, 1974, p. 136.

er-worldliness regarding truth, my interpretation takes the SM throughout the entire corpus as representative of the nature of being: we do not exist in isolation, and neither does our knowledge. To respect a person thusly will involve acknowledging this condition of our being. Whether we look at 'ourselves' as individual human beings or as the human race, we cannot rightly lay claim to *certain* knowledge because we can only occupy *our* place in relation to *otherness*.[32] As such, it is disrespectful to allow someone to carry on with a belief that does not truly correspond to reality, without offering our relation as *other* through dialogue. With that, let us turn our attention to the individual functions of the interlocutor, and then the self, in order to get us further in our analysis of the respect entailed by SM.

The Role of the Interlocutor

The *Republic* and other works emphasize a distinction between wisdom of the self, and the knowledge claims of sophists, the mob, and interlocutors – even when the interlocutor is Socrates himself. Socrates often presents the ideal of knowledge as that which one uncovers within one's soul, regardless of the material world and other people, and yet we are faced with the brute fact that it is dialogue, not diatribes, which are predominant in the corpus. While many of Plato's passages indicate that it is up to the individual to order themselves properly, and to not succumb to group dynamics or pressure from majority rule, other dialogues clearly dismantle the kind of knowledge a Pythagorean might express, wherein "every man (is) self-sufficient in wisdom."[33] But if the role of the interlocutor or teacher is nothing more than the leading out of *a priori* knowledge within the student, then the interlocutor may not be necessary if the student has some other way of accessing their knowledge. What exactly is Plato's stance on the role of other people as interlocutors, as teachers?

One way to begin answering this is to consider Socrates' commitment to the ideal state of justice in *Republic*:

> But perhaps [...] there is a model of it in heaven, for anyone who wants to look at it and to make himself its citizen on the strength of what he sees. It makes no difference whether it is or ever will be somewhere...[34]

Just because our ideal does not presently exist, it does not mean that we should not *act* as though it does; our ideals ought to effect what we do.[35] But why

---

[32] A further, very interesting claim is that Socrates took the elenchus as a tool by which incongruity could be identified not with respect merely to varying beliefs that a person has, but with respect to their beliefs and the way they live their lives. This too, is an interpretation of the Socratic Method which views its value in terms of its good-making consequences. See Kahn 1996, p. 302.

[33] Plato, *Theatetus* 169d in *The Complete Works of Plato*.

[34] Plato, *Republic* Book 9, 592b *The Complete Works of Plato*.

[35] William James echoes this when he asserts that "It is quite obvious that something more than the mere possession of ideals is required to make a life significant in any sense that claims the spectator's admiration. Inner joy, to be sure, it may *have,* with its ideals; but that is its own private senti-

does Plato bother having his characters bring this up throughout the corpus, if at the same time, his dialogues exemplify the value of bouncing your ideas off of others? Plato confirms, time and again, that reason can help us edit our ideals, but that ultimately, the ideals come from outside of ourselves. We get ideals from others, even if from the World of the Forms, and can use our own reason to sort out illusions from Forms. But what else can we learn about the self through the Platonic dialogues?

The Role of the Self

Plato's dialogue format, wherein people can check their conceptions of the world with each other, and confirm their most reasonable mode of behavior, should be seen as an exemplification of practical identity.[36] As Christine M. Korsgaard writes, in the Kantian spirit, in order for us to be efficacious agents, we must act on beliefs, or reasons, which consistently cohere with our reality. In order to do this, she continues, we must presuppose the existence of other agents who share in the same reality and hence, the same *universal* reasons on which we act.[37] Thusly, one's practical identity – in my argument and in Korsgaard's – amounts to one's ability to act efficaciously, or carry out one's will, with integrity and full knowledge of cause and effect (in both a physical and a moral sense).[38] You cannot climb a tree without some knowledge about gravity and the use of your muscles; you cannot tell a lie without expecting to be lied to in the future. The reasons that we have for acting the way we do – if we are doing it properly – are universal reasons that we all share.[39] This is precisely why I argue Socrates so keenly demonstrated respect for his interlocutors: by engaging another person in their reasons, you respect their personhood. Interpreting SM in this way thus takes us from the abstracted world of instrumental goods in dialogue to a very *present* and tangible intrinsic value: we are ethical, rational agents.

To the extent that we take the 'instructional approach' to education, we disvalue the means by which students must come to check their own belief systems. But to the extent that we treat the SM as a means by which to solicit inherent knowledge, as does the 'instrumental recollection approach,' or as a fertilizer for potential, like the 'instrumental emergence approach,' or as a grounds for humility as does the 'instrumental aporia approach,' we miss out on the true value of the SM.

---

mental matter. To extort from us, outsiders as we are, with our own ideals to look after, the tribute of our grudging recognition, it must back its ideal visions with what the laborers have, the sterner stuff of manly virtue; it must multiply their sentimental surface by the dimension of the active will, if we are to have *depth,* if we are to have anything cubical and solid in the way of character." James 1983, p. 161.

[36] I am making use of Christine M. Korsgaard's notion of practical identity, which she attributes to Kant. Interestingly, Korsgaard uses Plato's idea of the just soul as an explanation of how we must properly order ourselves in order to have a functional, practical identity. See Korsfaard 2009, pp. 134-137.

[37] Ibid., pp. 205-206.

[38] Ibid., pp. 12-4, 37-44.

[39] Ibid., p. 206.

The method is valuable because it best facilitates the means by which each person develops their practical identity and *engages in be*ing; the method is one of *respecting persons*.

I believe that if we interpret the SM as a metaphysical assertion about our interconnectedness – even if it was never an intention of Plato's to do this – this interpretation affords us not only a better understanding of ourselves, but a good reason to introduce the SM into existing schools. If we place a stronger emphasis on a Socratic Interpretation of the Platonic corpus, wherein we assess the dialogue form itself as representing an ontological position, it becomes a method conducive to self knowledge and wisdom; we cannot know anything – even ourselves – without recognizing our interdependent ontology.[40] As Kant puts it:

> Enlightenment is man's emergence from his self-imposed immaturity. Immaturity is the inability to use one's understanding without guidance from another. This immaturity is self-imposed when its cause lies not in lack of understanding, but in lack of resolve and courage to use it without guidance from another … For enlightenment of this kind, all that is needed is freedom. And the freedom in question is the most innocuous form of all – freedom to make public use of one's reason in all matters.[41]

Kant praises the process of deriving knowledge not *from* other people, but through our *relations* with other people. He admonishes the instructional or banking approach to wisdom. We too should realize that thinking for ourselves and behaving philosophically is a way of life which requires our inclusion of other people's experiences and wisdom into our framework of reason(s).[42] Indeed, just as Kant would remind us, we cannot respect ourselves without respecting others.

Conclusion

Love is at the same time the foundation of dialogue and dialogue itself.
Paulo Freire[43]

I have proposed an interpretation of the SM in which the method is valuable as an end in itself because it entails respect for our being *as such*, regardless of performance. This interpretation of the SM dissects the dynamic of inquirer and interlocu-

[40] For an explanation of the Socratic Interpretation, see Corlett 2005, p. 39-66. On the topic of self-knowledge, my view can be seen as akin to Dunson's in that it takes the aporia resulting from the Socratic Method as a means toward self-knowledge, yet Dunson does not take self-knowledge to entail others. Dunson III 2010, p. 205.

[41] Kant 2005, p. 119.

[42] Or in the words of Socrates, "Only the temperate man will know himself and will be able to examine what he knows and does not know, and in the same way will be able to inspect other people to see when a man does in fact know what he thinks he knows." *Charmides*, 167a in *The Complete Works of Plato*.

[43] Freire 2000, p. 89.

tor as suggestive not merely of a protocol or embodied ideal which we ought to pursue, but as a metaphysical truth; we are intimately connected – one's wisdom cannot emerge without a profound humility, respect for one's interdependence, and a desire to be. I hope to have expressed in this essay that respect should not be contingent on performance of certain acts, and yet, the very starting point of an educative journey must begin with a mutual recognition and respect of the rational agents engaged in and capable of such a journey. Respect is the pre-condition.

Students should not have to perform for us in order to earn our respect. Assuming that a student is participating in dialogue to the degree that they are presently comfortable, respect should be granted – if a student is not engaged, I assert that it is our job to make the space conducive for such participation. As it is poetically written in *The Schoolboys of Barbiana*, "It is more honest to say that all children are born equal; if, later, they are not equal, it is our fault and we have to find the remedy."[44] In terms of educating ourselves and others, it seems fitting that we choose pedagogies that respect students equally. There will always be a troubled student, but school should be a place where necessary efforts are made to understand and address the reasons for such troubles, before they become a bigger issue for society at large.

By engaging in dialogue with our students, we acknowledge a student's *right* to an education and indeed their right *to flourish*, rather than impose a condition on their education or on their worth as people. As Jeanne Theoharis writes in *Our School Suck*, "Treating all students as rights-bearing individuals necessitates structuring schools around their concerns."[45] We cannot know the students concerns, however, unless we are in dialogue. Building a community of individuals with rights to an education does not mean that we are promoting individualism. As Lawrence Blum writes in *High Schools, Race, and America's Future*, "the interpersonal and collective dimension of learning has received too little attention in the current insistent focus on individual attainment."[46] Respect in an educational setting means that we appreciate the haeccity of each student, and their right to thrive in our public space, regardless of merit. The pedagogical aim then, beyond respect, should be determined according to the particular subject matter and interest, pursued dialogically, in each particular classroom.

Is this a fairly obvious and simple assertion – that we are connected, that we are social animals, and that no person lives alone? It appears that within Plato studies in education, interpreters tend to side with one of the conclusions presented by interlocutors in the dialogues: either the dialectic process is good because it uncovers our ignorance, or it is good because it points us to intangible truth.[47] My claim is that if we want to elicit in our students the kind of wisdom loved by the philosopher, we must focus our education not so much on the outcome of what our students are *becoming*, but rather, on what it means simply to *be*. We all deserve this much respect. If understood in this way, I believe that the justification for the use of the SM in our schools today can be founded on the intrinsic value of a philosophical way of life,

[44] Hoffman and Milani, 2007, p. 54.
[45] Theoharis, 2009. p. 213.
[46] Blum, 2012, p. 188.
[47] For a description of the 'Mouthpiece Interpretation' see Corlett 2005, pp. 19-38.

rather than on philosophy as a specialization or as a means to some other end.[48] As such, with an interpretation of the SM as an educational approach which models itself off of what it means *to be*, we avoid the pitfalls of taking the SM as a tool to becoming something else. We can view *limitations* in our knowledge as determined not by a metaphysical gap between the 'world of becoming' and 'the world of forms,' but rather as determined by any instances in which we believe ourselves to be privy to epistemic or metaphysical isolation or superiority. Indeed, Plato's character Eros, who is intended to embody the favorable characteristic of *love itself*, is endowed with a genetic make-up which keeps him ever 'in limbo':

> And his nature is neither immortal nor mortal; but sometimes on the same day he flourishes and lives, whenever he has resources; and sometimes he dies, but gets to live again through the nature of his father. And as that which is supplied to him is always gradually flowing out, Eros is never either without resources nor wealthy, but is in between wisdom and lack of understanding.[49]

Perhaps, participating in this kind of limbo is not so bad. Socratic humility, in my view, is based not on our separation from the Form of the Good, but on our ontological status of *participating in reality together*. By interpreting SM as an educational approach modeled on what it means *to be*, as the relational beings that we are, we avoid the pitfalls of taking the SM as a tool to *becoming* something else, and we ground the value of SM as a method irreplaceable in any school that takes respect for all students as a necessary condition of their flourishing.

Reference list

Benson, Hugh H. *Socratic Wisdom: The Model of Knowledge in Plato's Early Dialogue.* Oxford: Oxford University Press, 2000. Print.

Blum, Lawrence. *High Schools, Race, and America's Future: What Students Can Teach Us About Morality, Diversity, and Community.* Cambridge: Harvard Education Press, 2012. Print.

Colebrook, Claire. *Nomadic Education: Variations on a Theme by Deleuze and Guattari*, Inna Semetsky (ed.) Rotterdam: Sense Publishers, 2008. Print.

Corlett, Angelo J. *Interpreting Plato's Dialogues.* Las Vegas: Parmenides Publishers, 2005. Print.

Decker, Kevin. "The Limits of Radical Openness: Gadamer on Socratic Dialectic and Plato's Idea of the Good." *Symposium: Canadian Journal of Continental Philosophy* 2000, vol. 4, no. 1, pp. 5-32. Print.

Dunson III, James A. "Hegel's Revival of Socratic Ignorance." *Idealistic Studies* 2010, vol. 40, pp. 201-214. Print.

Estarellas, Pablo Cevallos. "Teaching Philosophy vs Teaching to Philosophise," *Philosophy Now* 2007, vol. 63, pp. 12-15. Print.

Freire, Paulo. *Pedagogy of the Oppressed.* New York: Continuum, 2000. Print.

[48] Hogan and Smith 2003, pp. 170-172.

[49] Plato 1986, p. 265-266.

Haroutunian-Gordon, Sophie. *Turning the Soul: Teaching through Conversation in High School*. Chicago: The University of Chicago Press, 1991. Print.

Hogan, Padraig and Richard Smith. *The Blackwell Guide to the Philosophy of Education*, Nigel Blake, Paul Smeyers, Richard Smith, and Paul Standish (ed.) Oxford: Blackwell Publishing, 2003. Print.

Kahn, Charles H. *Plato and the Socratic Dialogue: The Philosophical Use of a Literary Form*. New York: Cambridge University Press Syndicate, 1996. Print.

Kant, Immanuel. *Groundwork for the Metaphysics of Morals*, Lara Denis (ed.) Peterborough: Broadview Press, 2005. Print.

Laverty, Megan. "Philosophy for Children and/as Philosophical Practice." *International Journal of Applied Philosophy*, 2004, vol. 18, no. 2, pp. 141-151. Print.

Leonardo, Zeus. "Critical Social Theory and Transformative Knowledge: The Functions of Criticism in Quality Education." *Educational Researcher*, 2004, vol. 33, no. 6, pp. 11-18. Print.

Lipman, Matthew, Frederick S. Oscanyan, and Ann Margaret Sharp, *Philosophy in the Classroom*. Philadelphia: Temple University Press, 1980. Print.

Margonis, Frank." In Pursuit of Respectful Teaching and Intellectually-Dynamic Social Fields." *Studies in Philosophy & Education* 2011, vol. 30, no. 5, pp. 433-439. Print.

Matthews, Gareth. "Whatever Became of the Socratic Elenchus?: Philosophical Analysis in Plato." *Philosophy Compass* 2009, vol. 4, no 3, pp. 439-450. Print.

McCall, Catherine C. "Three Methods of Philosophical Dialogue: Differences and Similarities between Nelson's Socratic Method, Lipman's P4C Method, McCall's CoPI Method," Centre for Phil. and Rel. Studies, accessed October 17, 2011. http://prs.heacademy.ac.uk/projects/elearning/abstracts.html. Website.

Overholser, James C. "Collaborative Empiricism, Guided Discovery, and the Socratic Method: Core Processes for Effective Cognitive Therapy." *Clinical Psychology: Science and Practice* 2011, vol. 18, pp. 62-66. Print.

Pang, Valerie O. *Multicultural Education: A Caring-Centered, Reflective Approach.* Boston: McGraw-Hill, 2005. Print.

Plato, *The Complete Works of Plato,* Edited by John. M. Cooper, translated by G.M.A. Grube. Indianapolis: Hackett Publishing Company, 1997. Print.

————. *The Dialogues of Plato.* Translated by Seth Benardete. New York: Bantam Books, 1986. Print.

Portelli, John P. "The Philosopher as Teacher: The Socratic Method and Philosophy for Children." *Metaphilosophy* 1990, vol. 21, no. 1 and 2, pp. 141-161. Print.

Shah, Mehul. "The Socratic Teaching Method: A Therapeutic Approach to Learning," *Teaching Philosophy* 2008, vol. 31, no. 3, pp. 267-275. Print.

Theoharis, Jeanne, *Our Schools Suck: Students Talk Back to a Segregated Nation on the Failures of Urban Education*. Gaston Alonso, Noel S. Anderson, Celina Su, and Jeanne Theoharis (ed.) New York: New York University Press, 2009.Print.

Vansieleghem, Nancy and David Kennedy. "What is Philosophy *for* Children, What is Philosophy *with* Children – After Matthew Lipman?" *Journal of Philosophy of Education* 2011, vol. 45, no. 2, pp. 171-182. Print.

Wolz, Henry G., *Plato and Heidegger: In Search of Selfhood*. Lewisburg, PA: Bucknell University Press, 1981. Print.

Woodruff, Paul "Socrates and Ontology: The Evidence of the *Hippias Major*." *Phronesis* 1978, vol. 23, no. 2, pp. 101-117. Print.

Nadia Stoyanova Kennedy
(USA)

Community of Inquiry as a Communicative System: Respecting Complexity[1]

Complexity theory has been steadily gaining recognition over the last half a century as a new way of understanding the organization of systems on all levels—whether organisms, social systems, business organizations, or ecosystems. Contrary to a mechanistic, analytic approach to the study of phenomena, the complexity perspective takes into account all interactions between the components of a system, which it understands as in dynamic interplay. In this paper, I will attempt to re-describe the community of inquiry (CI) as a complex system, and draw some implications that follow from taking into account such a description.

By community of inquiry, I mean a relatively small (10-20) group of people engaged in a conversation (or, preferably, an ongoing series of conversations) about an agreed-upon concept or problem or question, which is convened and overseen by a "facilitator" who is committed to certain normative ideals, chief among which is the construction of an "ideal speech situation" (Habermas, 1990)—that is, a discursive setting in which everyone has equal right and opportunity to speak, in which intimidation of any sort is absent, and in which epistemological authority is distributed rather than centralized in one person. The group enters the dialogue with the shared intention of participating in ongoing critical deliberation together about the issues, with the expectation that new meaning will arise from their interaction and the challenging and testing each other's assumptions in the common space of dialogue. In all forms of community of inquiry there is a set of basic discourse rules, implicit or otherwise, that participants abide by, and one or more "facilitators"—who act to clarify and to coordinate the emergent structure of ideas and arguments that the conversation generates.[2]

I will start by spelling out a distinction made by Paul Cilliers[3] between two types of systems: complex and complicated. A food processor is a complicated system—it has intricate sets of mechanisms and automated devices. Because all of those mechanisms have fixed relationships between their elements, the entire food processor can be analyzed by "parsing" it into its different segments, and a thorough description and understanding of the processor can be produced by assembling the descriptions of the different parts that comprise it. On the other hand, an ecosystem

---

[1] The paper was presented at the 2012 conference of the North American Association for Community of Inquiry in Vancouver, Canada.
[2] Kennedy& Kennedy 2010.
[3] Cilliers 1998.

or the brain are complex systems, in that they are characterized by non-linear relationships and feedback loops. Such systems can only yield partial analysis, which can produce partial descriptions. It is not possible to fully understand a complex system, like a cell, an ant colony, human society, or communication among a group of people by taking it apart like a mechanistic device. The traditional analytic method that works well with complicated and simple systems does not fare well with complex systems. The problem is that the traditional analytic approach of taking and studying smaller parts of a system destroys its so-called "emergent properties," which result from the interaction among its components. As we already mentioned, those properties cannot be reduced to the characteristics of the components themselves. An example of an emergent property is consciousness, something that arises from the interactions of single neurons and even mundane phenomena such as walking, which cannot be understood when only parts of the human body are examined.

In community of inquiry, some emergent products are collective arguments or a collectively elaborated concept, and even more ephemeral products like justice, respect, care. Emergent properties are usually the important features of the system that we want to study, and in order to do this, we have to deal with the system as a whole. As the truism associated with complex system goes, "the system is always more than the sum of its parts." Complex systems are typically the ones associated with living organisms or groups of living things like humans, viruses, social systems, language, oceans, or the brain—systems, that shift and change, self-organize and self-produce, of which Community of inquiry (CI) is one example.

CI as a Complex Communicative System

If we accept the social system theorist Niklas Luhmann's[4] argument that social systems are communicative systems, and his useful and compelling definition of complexity, community of inquiry as a communicative system may be understood as complex, in that it contains more communicative possibilities than can be actualized. For example, on the level of group interaction there are always more themes than can be explored, more questions than can be pursued, and more concepts than the group can take up for inquiry. On the individual level, there are always more possible interventions than one can actually make. Community of inquiry shares many important characteristics that Cilliers believes are common to all complex systems: rich, interconnected and nonlinear interactions; recursion, redundancy, feedback, adaptability, and autopoiesis.[5] I provide a brief description of those characteristics below, in the context of the dialogical format community of inquiry (CI hereafter).

Davis and Simmt,[6] in describing the emergence and the functioning of a learning community of preservice teachers as a complex system emphasized eight characteristics of such a community: internal diversity, redundancy, decentralized control,

---

[4] Luhmann 1995.
[5] Chilliers 1998.
[6] Davis and Simmt 2003.

organized randomness, neighboring interactions, regulatory constraints, emergent diversity, and distributed control. I would diverge from Davis & Simmt's description of a learning community in complexity terms, in particular in the interpretation of two characteristics—decentralized control and neighboring interactions. This is due to the difference in the forms of the communities we describe. Davis &Simmt portray the forming of a learning community of preservice teachers who have organized themselves into study groups, thus forming a network of connected study clusters. None of the teachers were in charge of the collective, any more than one individual may be said to be in charge of an ant colony, the growth of a city, an immune system, or the functions of the brain. These are all decentralized systems, without a central authority. The behavior of any element in the system, and thus the system in general, is influenced by the interactions in the systems, and particularly by communication with the most closely located elements, or by the nearest neighbor interactions. Thus, if an ant encounters a high rate of nest-maintenance workers entering and leaving the ant colony, there is a higher probability that it will adopt a nest-maintenance job, and if it encounters ant foragers busy lugging food home, the chances are it will switch to foraging.[7] Similarly, in human learning communities learners are greatly influenced by communications with other learners from the same small cluster. [8]

In comparison, in a community of inquiry every participant is potentially connected to every other, and since all communication has the same range, every communicative intervention is potentially equally influential. Also CI might be better understood as a complex system governed by certain communicative meta-rules from the start, where the facilitator is the central communication organizer, the one who enforces those rules. Thus, the term decentralized control, often used to describe complex systems, does not do justice to the control mechanisms in CI. The facilitator in a CI exercises *control procedurally*—she may act to regulate the distribution of turns or the length of a speaker's intervention, call for paraphrasing, summarization or location of the argument, or insist on a group response to an intervention that has been over-ridden by the next speaker.

Although it may appear that it is the facilitator who is navigating the direction of the group, unilateral navigation is in fact only possible, if at all, in a closed, controlled system, in which the teacher dictates events and meanings, and inhibits any dynamic emergence. Her operative goal is in fact to enable as much as possible communicative diversity and clarity, in the interest of acquiring new meanings, and better participation. In fact we could say that procedural control, because it holds everyone responsible for adhering to the communicative rules, enables a CI to work towards its regulative ideals—*distributed thinking, distributed intelligence, and distributed agency*. The term *ambiguous control*[9] indicates that it is neither centralized nor decentralized control, but a more complex control mechanism that facilitates the organization a complex system of communication.

---

[7] Mitchell 2009.

[8] Davis and Simmt 2003.

[9] Lushyn & Kennedy 2002.

In a collective such as CI, each intervention is understood as potentially important, and it is never exactly clear how much and to what extent an intervention might affect the course of the inquiry, and group dynamics as well. The facilitator may have more perceived authority to steer the group, but other members—those less constrained by the internalized hierarchy of the traditional model—may exercise their distributed authority from the start, which is welcomed by the facilitator, whose long-term goal is the distribution of power within the system, just as she encourages the emergence of distributed thinking and distributed self-expression. In a more mature CI, the facilitator also strives to distribute procedural authority throughout the group—that is, to promote a system-condition in which *all* participants, including herself, share in regulating the distribution of turns, calling for summarization or restatement, and so on, as well as in calling for definitions or examples, encouraging alternative hypotheses, identifying unstated assumptions, and so on.

Neither *distributed control* nor *ambiguous control* imply that control is equally distributed, or that relationships between the members of the group are symmetrical; nor does it mean that those relationships are of domination or exploitation, although this cannot be guaranteed. Non-linearity, asymmetry, power and competition are inevitable to the dynamical nature of complexity, and necessary for maintaining it.[10] If relationships were symmetrical and power was equally distributed throughout, the system would quickly lose energy and stagnate. Asymmetry insures shifts in the "weight" of contributions, and in levels and distributions of communicative control and power.

Ideally, interactions in a community of inquiry are *rich* and *interconnected* in the sense that every interaction influences and is influenced by others. CI deliberations are *nonlinear* in that some interventions are amplified, and have a greater effect than others. This is usually described in complexity theory as the "butterfly effect," in that small causes can have large effects and vise versa. Any member of the group can also intervene and change the direction of the inquiry with new substantive or procedural suggestions. The inquiry itself can shift direction through a series of individual moves within the "conversation plane," and the conversation can shift "vertically" between inquiry, reflection on the inquiry, and feedback. The interactive dynamics are constantly changing—whether in levels of participation or levels of clarity of the "argument." This presents a picture very different from the traditional monological, unidirectional model of classroom conversation, in which, when there is interaction, it is most typically between teacher and individual student.

Complexity thrives on the ambiguous, just-barely-in-control interplay between CI group members, in which the pattern of intervention is *recursive*—new interventions connect with previous ones and may even appear to repeat them, but their measure of difference opens possibilities for future interventions, thus forming patterns of argument that make of the structure of CI an emergent constellation of interactions. In fact, recursion is a primary characteristic of this form of collective dialogue, demonstrated through members' repetition of utterances, or through paraphrase and summary; recursion is thus associated with redundancy, which assures

---

[10] Cilliers 1998.

through repetition that what might not have been well-articulated, or which remains ambiguous, can be communicated again.

Recursion is a sign of redundancy, which means that there are informational overlaps and alternative communicative routes that insure the system's flexibility. Because the system has a memory, and each event informs consecutive events, the system's history is not reversible. Recursion and *redundancy* are carried by the *feedback loops* that are endemic characteristics of complex systems. A *negative feedback* loop has the function of maintaining the system's stability through inhibition and stabilization. For example, a negative loop is initiated when the facilitator or another member suppresses, on the grounds that it is not relevant to the current inquiry, an intervention initiated by a group member that has the potential to open a new direction, or promises to change the current group focus. *Positive feedback* introduces more diversity—for example when a member suggests a new perspective on the issue at hand, thus stimulating reconceptualization or consideration of a new perspective. As a whole, the system operates far-from-equilibrium; equilibrium is in fact an "enemy" to the system, in that it represents stagnation or actual system-death. As such, the system is fed by a flow of new perspectives, new information, and new meanings. Any stability that is achieved is of a dynamic nature, in a communicative zone that is between chaos (too many disconnected interventions, to the point that meaning-making is impossible) and stagnation (no new information at all).[11] It is said that complex systems involve an interplay between chaos and non-chaos, and that they operate at "the edge" of chaos.[12]

All biological and social systems exhibit the two basic characteristics of cooperation and competition. An important insight that comes from a new understanding of living systems is the recognition that networks are basic patterns of their organization, and that a network's complexity involves an interplay between cooperation and competition.[13] Social systems are networks of organisms; organisms are networks of cells, organs and cells are networks of molecules, and they survive because of the intricate coupling between cooperation and competition, where often cooperation on one level underlies competition on another, or the other way around. For example, members of a CI are typically competing for the opportunity to shape the character of the discussion with their own ideas, but do so in the interest of collaborative reconstruction of the concepts in play.

CI as a communicative system is always reproducing itself, in a process that has been termed "autopoiesis" (from "auto" self and "poiesis" production) by the biologist and philosopher Humberto Maturana.[14] Along with the production of utterances that constitute judgments, arguments, and sequences of argumentation, there is the autopoiesis of ideas—new meanings that co-evolve with each individual's thoughts, feelings and expectations. However, all events in the communicative process are discrete and temporal. Thus, the autopiesis of the communicative system as a whole depends on the ongoing dis-integration and re-production of the materials

[11] Kennedy & Kennedy 2010.

[12] Kauffman 1995; Baranger 2000.

[13] Capra 1997; Kauffman 1995.

[14] Varela, Maturana & Uribe 1974.

and the catalysts necessary for the continuation of the process. The autopoietic process constantly increases the complexity in the system, which, in order to survive, struggles to reduce complexity. Out of the necessity for the system to maintain an autopoietic balance in CI, just as among any interconnected elements in any living system, there emerges the necessity for *regulatory constraints*. Constraints are limiting, but are also enabling.

For example, selection is a constraint born from the impossibility of connecting every intervention or communicative event to every other one in the course of the communicative process. If there is no selection, then the proliferation of communicative moves and events will amount to chaos in the system. Selection is both *enabling and constraining* for the production of new ideas and meanings, and therefore must steer its way through the complexity of communication. Any order in a communicative event emerges through a reduction of complexity and through the selective conditioning of this reduction. Without such selections in the communicative process, the CI system would quickly reach incomprehensible complexity.

The emerging communicative structure's self-organizing process is not controlled or predetermined in any way, and is a response to the system's environment, or context. Ashley points out that each dynamic system generates its own form of self-organization in response to its need for survival and for the management of complexity. Only by structuring complexity and imposing constraints can a communication system acquire "internal guidance," and make self-reproduction possible. This is what ensures the quality and connectivity of the communicative events. In that sense, CI develops an organization (structure) of communication that is in unison with the general CI meta-rules that ensure balancing of weight, distribution and good communication "traffic" of all communication moves, but is always unique to the particular system.

Complexity is fed by the diversity in the system, but as Page notes, it's not so much the *fundamental diversity* or the diversity of the members of the group that is important for complexity. Rather, what is essential is the *emergent diversity* in the system, which in CI is manifested at higher levels—that is, in the communicative products of ideas, linguistic expressions, restatements, and summarizations, the recombination of which produces complexity.

Because the elements of the system are interconnected and adaptable, the system as a whole is self-balancing, and although there may be crises and breakdowns, the latter represent—potentially anyway—transitions to a new state of dynamic balance. The autopoietic function finds expression in the idiosyncrasies of the group-as-a-whole and the interactions among its members. Notwithstanding its systemic contingency—for in fact it could always be otherwise, and its path is never completely determined—CI as a communicative system is quite robust, and its emergent structure relatively stable in time and across contexts.

Acknowledgment and respect for complexity

The modern (traditional) way of encountering complexity has resulted, we have discovered, in reductionism and determinism, and in the attempt for a totality of descriptions, truths, and understandings in an attempt to separate, isolate, analyze, predict, and master. Such an approach is equivalent to occupying an epistemological position from which the continuous shifting of relationships in a system are ignored and in fact complexity is avoided. An acknowledgement of complexity requires that we take into account our new understanding of complex systems and their main characteristics and behaviors. But "taking into account" such knowledge will require more than just "knowing about it." Dealing with complex systems requires, I suggest "respecting the complexity" of CI , not only in the dictionary sense of "regard" and "admiration" for the wondrous properties and behaviors of complex systems, but also in the etymological sense of constantly "turning round" and "looking at" (from the Latin "raspicere") the system if we want to understand it better.[15]

What I have tried to provide here is a very general description, which does not pertain to the CI model in a scientific sense. Any models or descriptions that we create will be flawed, and in ways that we cannot completely determine in order to correct them. On the one hand, each member of the system is ignorant of the behavior of the whole system—she cannot "contain" or comprehend the complexity of the entire system.[16] Nor can any model or description predict or control the behavior of a complex system. This is not to say that we don't need theory or description; in fact complexity theory helps us to better understand the dynamics of CI. It also highlights the importance of uncertainty, contingency, local factors, specific context and timing of events. Rather than formulating fixed descriptions or models that portray CI as a fixed and rigid system, we might do better to devote ourselves to a process of describing, in the interest of understanding it, a system that is constantly unfolding and becoming. We can identify no predetermined outcome states, but some states are more possible than others. Such states occupy a space that Stuart Kauffman calls the "adjacent possible"—a space of possible other states that are close to the current state of the system. Kauffman describes it this way: "The *Adjacent Possible* is like a forever expanding house, where passing via a particular door from a room to another room, opens new doors in the *Adjacent Possible* which we explore." [17]

We cannot grasp the essence of the system in some determinate way, since each description provides a limited view, and portrays some aspect of the system from a specific position inside or outside it, and at a specific point in time. In this sense, the description of the system is also distributed.

However, we are bound to "look back or again at," "regard," "consider" (*respicere*, respect) the system constantly, appreciating its complexity; to take different "snapshots" of the system and attempt to make sense of them, acknowledging the fact that they are temporal, locallimited, and unfinished representations, but confi-

---

[15] Partridge 1966.
[16] Cilliers 1998.
[17] Kauffman 2010, para. 14.

dent that they can help us to develop an ever-fuller understanding of the phenomenon called community of inquiry.

Reference List

Ashby, William Ross. "Principles of The Self-Organizing System." Eds. H. Von Foerster and G. W. Zopf, Jr. *Principles of Self-Organization*: *Transactions of the University of Illinois Symposium*, London, UK: Pergamon Press,1962. 255-278. Print.

Baranger, Michel. *Chaos, Complexity, and Entropy: A Physics Talk For Non-Physicists*, 2000. http://www.necsi.edu/projects/baranger/cce.pdf. Web.

Capra, Fritjof. *The Web of Life.* New York: Anchor Books, 1997. Print.

Cilliers, Paul. *Complexity and Postmodernism*. London: Routledge, 1998. Print.

Davis, Brent & Simmt, Elaine. "Understanding Learning Systems: Mathematics Education and Complexity Science." *Journal for Research in Mathematics Education*, 34 (2), 137-167, 2003. Print.

Habermas, Jürgen. *Moral Consciousness and Communicative Action*. Cambridge, MA: MIT Press, 1990. Print.

Kennedy, Nadia & Kennedy, David. "Between Chaos and Entropy: Community Of Inquiry From A Systems Perspective." *Complicity: An International Journal of Complexity and Education*, 7, 2, http://ejournals.library.ualberta.ca/index.php/complicity/index, 2010. Web.

Kauffman, Stuart. *At Home In The Universe: The Search For Laws Of Self-Organization And Complexity*. New York: Oxford University Press, 1995. Print.

Kauffman, Stuart. *Re-Imagining Society: Are We Trapped By Old Ideas?* Retrieved from http://www.npr.org/blogs/13.7/2010/11/01/130976163/, 2010. Web.

Luhmann, Niklas. *Social systems*. Palo Alto, CA: Stanford University Press, 1995. Print.

Lushyn, Pavel & Kennedy, David. Power, Manipulation, and Control in A Community Of Inquiry. *Analytic Teaching* 23, 2: 103-110. 2002. Print.

Mitchell, Michelle. *Complexity: A Guided Tour.* New York: Oxford University Press, 2009. Print.

Page, S. *Diversity and Complexity*. Princeton: Princeton University Press, 2011. Print.

Partridge. Eric. *A Short Etymological Dictionary of Modern English*, 4th edition. NY: Macmillan Publishing, 1996. Print.

Varela, Francisco, Maturana, Humberto & Uribe, Ricardo. "Autopoiesis: The Organization of Living Systems, its Characterization and a Model." *Biosystems*, 5, 187-196, 1974. Print.

Eugene E. Muhammad
(USA)

Taking Interreligious Dialogue to the M.A.T. (Martial Arts Technique): Toward a Rethinking of Respect and Dialogue with the Interreligious Other

Interreligious Dialogue will prove to be one of the most important activities of our time. The globalized modern context has made encountering our interreligious neighbors an almost daily necessity. Unlike those of the past, these encounters are often characterized by terrifying face-to-face intrusions by the religious 'other.' The socio-political barriers that once safe-guarded us from these 'others' have dissolved as a result of the sheer force of economic globalization and the growing diversification of North America. Interestingly, North Americans have had Hindu, Jain, Sikh, Zoroastrian, Jewish and Muslim co-workers and fellow citizens for many decades, but because of western tolerance or "multiculturalism," the *otherness* of our neighbors has practically gone unnoticed and undetected. It took the tragedy of September 11, 2001 for Americans to become more aware of the Islamic 'other' and just how close she had become. Naturally, the reaction was to create safe distances (or space) and to approach this strange creature with a heightened sense of fear and caution. While the historical stage has all the appropriate props and prompts for interreligious dialogue, these simply indicate that there is a genuine need for deep, authentic interreligious dialogue—one that goes beyond tolerance and ritualistic acts of kindness, and facilitates a radical reception and engagement of *the other*.

What is Interreligious dialogue?

What exactly is interreligious dialogue? The word dialogue itself comes from two Greek root words, *dia* and *logos*. *Dia* means "by means of," "through" or "across."[1] *Logos* means a rational discourse, word, speech or account. Dialogue's roots convey a meaning of accomplishing something by means of reason or rational discourse. Furthermore, dialogue connotes a dynamic exchange between people that is carried on via the rational faculties. Dialogue should not be confused with such activities as discussions or negotiations, although these may be an integral part of dialogue. While these and other activities may involve a similar to-and-fro movement that is also characteristic of dialogical flow, usually their parameters are too impersonal and

[1] It should be noted that in Greek mythology Dia meant "heavenly," "divine" or "she who belongs to Zeus."

rigid for the dynamically interpersonal dimension necessary for 'interreligious' dialogue.

Interreligious dialogue places the sort of substantive demand on its participants that pushes them past their internal thresholds to explore an infinite array of outcomes and choices beyond themselves. William Isaacs writes: "Dialogue is a living experience of inquiry *within* and *between* people. A decade and a half of writing about and conducting dialogue around the world has led me to realize that the most important parts of any conversation are those that neither party could have imagined before starting."[2] One such surprise is the degree of personal exchange and sharing that takes place as a result of dialogue.

Central to dialogue is the prospect of learning more about one's dialogue partner(s), as well as more about oneself. Certainly it must be expected that as a result of engaging dialogue, one would increase his/her objective knowledge about their dialogue partner and their respective religious traditions. This learning is actually a two-way exchange and an expansion of one's awareness, which is not only directed at the dialogical partner, but is also reflected back onto ourselves as we surrender to the dialogue.

Interreligious dialogue on the surface appears to be simply a discourse between persons from different religious communities or traditions held in a discourse about religious topics. Leonard Swidler rightly indicates that "in this context, of course, we are speaking about a particular kind of dialogue, namely, interreligious dialogue in the broadest sense, that is, dialogue on a religious subject by persons who understand themselves to be in different religious traditions and communities."[3] Dialogue can simply be dialogue but there is something specific that makes interreligious dialogue unmistakably "religious."

The thing that opens up this dialogue to being truly "religious" goes beyond simply holding a discourse about religious subject matter; instead, it is its propensity to facilitate an encounter with transcendence and alterity in the dialogue partner or *the other*. It must also be noted that the religious dialogue invites the dialogue partner to be fully mysterious and wholly other. Actually, interreligious dialogue has its authenticity rooted in its acceptance of and response to the *otherness* encountered. Paul Knitter insists that within "interreligious dialogue we confront otherness as something we want not only to embrace but also to address."[4] The dialogue participants can arrive fully as themselves, which contributes directly to the previously mentioned open-ended quality of the dialogue.

It would have to be assumed that this sort of contact would not only bring to bear the different contours that one could anticipate, but also those that could not be anticipated. It is the abyss of the unknown that contributes to the confrontational dimension of interreligious dialogue; it is not a mere meeting or conference—it is a confrontation in every sense of the word. John Cobb asks us to consider "the nature of dialogue more closely. It begins with confrontation. Both partners must realize

---

[2] Isaacs 1999, p. 9.

[3] Swidler, *et al.* 1990 p. 57.

[4] Swidler, *et al.* 1990, p. 22.

that there are differences between them and be prepared to take these differences seriously."[5] Furthermore, there is a considerable degree of risk and the possibility of being permanently changed:

> The trusting in the other, considering the other a true source of understanding and knowledge, the listening attitude toward my partner, the common search for truth (without assuming that we already know what words mean to each of us), the acceptance of the risk of being defeated, converted, or simply upset and left without a north—these are not pragmatic devices to enable us to live in peaceful coexistence because the other is already too powerful or vociferous and cannot be silenced.[6]

The encounter of the other within dialogue is experienced as a serious confrontation. The perceived differences serve as a basis for calling into question one's being, truths, myths and identity. One outcome of this is that we begin to see that our perspectives, ideas, viewpoints, axioms, etc. are not absolutes, which destabilizes everything, from the validity of our faith to our very identity constructs.

Responding to the Confrontation

This, of course, seems to demand the sort of openness, on the part of each dialogue partner that almost anticipates displacement or the eviction of one's original position, *Weltanschauung* or ethic.[7] Remember that dialogue calls for each *other* to be fully received and allowed to be fully present in order for the dialogue to function properly. But what if, after much dialogue, discussion, debate and explanation, one discovers that the beliefs that s/he previously thought were just a little outrageous and absurd are actually exceedingly so? Is there room for this conclusion in our present approach? What if this realization was not indicative of a lack of understanding but the opposite—a deeper understanding or recognition of *the other*? What if *the other* is just as much an *other* in reality as they were previously conceptualized to be potentially? What if this other is simply too "other"? The problem is that the degree of change, learning and transformation cannot be calculated due to the ambiguous nature of the other. It is the very nature of the other to elude apprehension from the dialogue machine, and yet the other is to be expected and received.

Instead of making preparation for the coming of *the other* and being receptive to the radical transformation that is likely to result from this event, there is a tendency on our part—quite contrary to everything required of dialogue—to respond in a restrictive manner. This knee-jerk tendency is an attempt to ensure the very safety and certainty that interreligious dialogue resists and is simply unable to guarantee.

---

[5] Ibid., p. 3.

[6] Panikkar 1999, p. 31.

[7] "Thinking together implies that you no longer take your position as final. You relax your grip on certainty and listen to the possibilities that result simply from being in a relationship with others—possibilities that might not otherwise have occurred". (Isaacs 1990, p. 19).

The fact of the matter is that dialogue is dangerous and represents an invitation to a very serious degree of risk, which stems from the unchecked presence of this *other*. To enter into a dialogue disarmed, open and vulnerable to the unknown presents, for many, an unbearable challenge. Panikkar expounds on this potential for danger:

> Yet, to enter the new field of the religious encounter is a challenge and a risk. The religious person enters this arena without prejudices and preconceived solutions, knowing full well that she may in fact have to lose a particular belief or particular religion altogether. She trusts in truth. She enters unarmed and ready to be converted herself. She may lose her life—she may also be born again.[8]

It is the threat of losing one's life, the threat of death, that seems most unacceptable. The death within this context comes in the form of conversion and can be just as frightening and terrifying as physical annihilation. At the very least, we can display the same aversion for the sort of change that involves a whole and complete transformation. It is the likelihood of this radical transformation that causes anxiety and provokes defensive responses, making true dialogue virtually impossible. Cobb demonstrates this tendency in the following:

> Still, there is a deep uneasiness about listening too intently, too expectantly, too openly. Might we not hear ideas that are in conflict with our deepest convictions? How can we be open to those? Do we not need, before entering into a dialogue, to clarify the non-negotiable elements in our own faith, so that we can be clear about that to which we can be open and that which is beyond the pale?[9]

Unfortunately, this search for certainty and security results in two responses: the *exclusion of the other* and *the making of the other in our own likeable likeness*.

The First Strike: Exclusion

The most foundational exclusionary response is rooted in language, which should not come as a surprise since it is language that mediates any dialogue. The language of interreligious dialogue has been determined to be that of unity, peace, collaboration, trust, friendship and love, encompassing all the hopes and expectations that many dialogue proponents bring *a priori*. The establishment of such a "language" is not justified but is based on a violent imposition of an inaugural ethic. This ethic and its violent imposition parallels the Jewish Decalogue, commanding "*Thou shall not convert*" and "*Thou shall not be violent*." It is rather ironic that this established language for interreligious dialogue is used to perpetrate the very violence and conver-

[8] Panikkar 1999, p. 63.
[9] Swidler, *et al.* 1990, p. 2.

sion that it denounces. This mediating language becomes the Master-Signifier, the mother tongue, the rules for determining, managing and responding to the foreigner-other.[10] It is this language of interreligious dialogue that is used as an effective means of maintaining a safe chasm between "us" and "them":

> (L)anguage, not primitive egotistic interest, is the first and greatest divider, it is because of language that we and our neighbours (can) 'live in different worlds' even when we live on the same street. What this means is that verbal violence is not secondary distortion, but the ultimate resort of every specifically human violence.[11]

The very thing that should be the site of hospitality and welcome is used to create and maintain exclusionary borders:

> This simple and all too obvious reflection on the way in which language works renders problematic the prevalent idea of language and the symbolic order as the medium of reconciliation and mediation, of peaceful coexistence, as opposed to a violent medium of immediate and raw confrontation. In language, instead of exerting direct violence on each other, we are meant to debate, to exchange words, and such an exchange, even when it is aggressive, presupposes a minimal recognition of the other party. The entry into language and the renunciation of violence are often understood as two aspects of one and the same gesture.[12]

Those whose language is not guided by the dictates of tolerance, inclusion, unity and peace are judged according to this imposed 'law' of dialogue. This becomes the initiatory site of prejudice, labeling and exclusion prior to knowledge and engagement, especially if *the other* presents a particular degree of intolerable *otherness*.

This tendency is often signaled by the same reasoning as, "I do not dialogue with terrorists because terrorists are not allowed at the dialogue table." More than begging the question, this sort of reasoning makes the very fact of the terrorists' absence confirmation that they are truly terrorists who are unable to be reasonable or open to change. Cobb identifies this tendency as it relates to a particular pariah-group:

> In the case of dialogue with oppressors, there is the danger that sympathetic attention to their needs may lead to acquiescence in structures that continue to oppress. In the case of dialogue with believers in other traditions, there is danger that sympathetic appreciation of their concern may lead to compromise of faith itself.[13]

---

[10] Zizek 2008, pp. 61-62.
[11] Ibid., p. 66.
[12] Ibid., pp. 60-61.
[13] Swidler, *et al.* 1990, pp. 2-3.

This tendency obviously runs counter to the non-prejudiced disposition with which participants are to approach dialogue. It also is antithetical to the open and universal ethic that undergirds true dialogue, but this is only extended to those who belong to the dominant dialogical language group. The very fact that artificial restrictions are interjected and there are delineations of what's "off-limits," betrays the very organic, open, inviting aspect of interreligious dialogue. Such an approach would undermine the very openness that most often claim to be at the very heart of interreligious dialogue. Zizek argues that this is intentional and the resulting violence is to be expected:

> To wonder at this fact is not a proper philosophical attitude. That is to say, what if that which appears as an inconsistency, as the failure to draw all the consequences from one's ethical attitude, is, on the contrary, its positive condition of possibility? What if such an exclusion of some form of otherness from the scope of our ethical concerns is consubstantial with the very founding gesture of ethical universality, so that the more universal our explicit ethics is, the more brutal the underlying exclusion is? What the Christian all-inclusive attitude (recall St. Paul's famous "there are no men or women, no Jews and Greeks") involves is a thorough exclusion of those who do not accept inclusion into the Christian community[14]

A good example of this can be found in something I witness a few years ago. I took a group of students to an interreligious dialogue event that was being held at and hosted by North Park University in Chicago. The majority of the evening was filled by each panelist arguing for greater unity among people of religious communities and the abolition of fundamentalism, xenophobia and exclusivistic dogmatism. Then, during the question-answer period, one student approached the microphone and asked why hadn't the exponents of the radical perspectives been invited to this event. The response from one of the panelists was that these kinds of delicate encounters must be safeguarded from certain dangerous religious perspectives. In the student's retort, she pointed out the obvious value of such an engagement, but was further dismissed and gently reprimanded by the other two panelists.

What the student brought to light was the tendency of some proponents of interreligious dialogue to control the degree of difference or otherness that engages the actual dialogue. A related tendency is to ensure that the otherness of the other is at least palatable, and/or is of such degree that it will not disrupt or disturb the established homeostasis or unity that has been designated as the desired goal. The results of this may be a newly found unity or a surface appreciation of the *other*. This, at its core, turns dialogue into a capacity-building exercise for tolerance at best. Essentially the dialogue participants are kept safe, unchanged, unthreatened, unmoved and oblivious to a radical change or transformation potentially offered by *the other* in all of his/her otherness.

[14] Zizek 2008, pp. 53-54.

The Death Blow: Make the Other in Our Image

> So why, today, this fear of the over-proximity of the Other as the subject of desire? Why the need to decaffeinate the Other, to deprive him or her of their raw substance of *jouissance*? I suspect this is a reaction to the disintegration of the protective symbolic walls that kept others at a proper distance.[15]

Through this means of artificial selection, *the other* who actually is invited to show-up at the table of dialogue looks a lot less threatening and more like our projected image of the "tolerable" *other*. The best example of this can be witnessed in the case of Muslims in the Unites States. Muslims in America, through the various means just mentioned, are adopting more and more the language of peace, unity, tolerance, peace and non-violence. If one looks closely one can see that this is actually an imposition of a Christian ethic—one that Christians do not even think to apologize for failing to embody. Unfortunately, Muslims are becoming the surrogate for representing these Christian values. Muslim leaders all over America are working tirelessly to situate Islam and the Qur'an into the dominant religious language and what is left is an empty shell of a caricatured Muslim. The only Islamic voices that one experiences publicly are those that fit into either the mold of acceptability or the extremist alternative. This helps create the perception of a false dichotomy between the ultra-peaceful Muslim on one side and the radical fundamentalist/ terrorist on the other. It is the responsibility of these "leaders" to subside the anxiety of the dominant society by addressing issues that are not even native to the Islamic community. For instance, when did Jihad (i.e., religious striving) become a sixth pillar of Islam? Who made it so? Why wasn't *zhikr* (i.e., remembrance of Allah) given this position and status instead?

Another indicator of the attempt to make Muslims in the image and likeness of others is the public proclamation: *fighting for the Soul of Islam*. This has been the topic of many editorials, articles, television/radio shows and news broadcasts. The language is intentional and tailored to deal with the *Islamic other* in particular and in a particular manner. How fitting would it be for Muslims to hold forums about fighting for the soul of Christianity or Buddhism? It simply does not fit, no more than the term *Christian terrorist* does; there are some who would even say that this is actually a contradiction in terms.

What all of this amounts to is a situation wherein interreligious dialogue has lost its essence, its soul. In an effort to gain security and safety, we have lost the open-ended platform for dialogical engagement, the open invitation to *the other* and an opportunity to experience radical transformation. Perhaps there needs to be a fight for the soul of interreligious dialogue.

---

[15] Zizek 2008, p. 58.

Saving IRD from the Threat of Becoming an Empty Gesture

There is a serious risk of having Interreligious Dialogue slip into becoming the sort of empty activity that Zizek warned us about:

> The threat today is not passivity, but pseudo-activity, the urge to "be active," to "participate," to mask the nothingness of what goes on. People intervene all the time, "do something"; academics participate in meaningless debates, and so on. Those in power often prefer even a "critical" participation, a dialogue, to silence—just to engage us in "dialogue," to make sure our ominous passivity is broken.[16]

This plastic version of dialogue has the form and formalities of real contact and engagement but an underlying ethic prompts the dialogue participants not to get too close or intrude upon *the other*. The underlying secret of the interreligious dialogue has been its vigilant look-out for *the other*, for the radical impact of *the other's* presence and the gift she bears—a look-out for the other and her gift of death (i.e., conversion). This is perpetuated under the guise of 'respecting' *the other,* but the focus is always on keeping a safe distance and not intruding or causing discomfort. Isaacs echoes this aspect of respect:

> Respect also means honoring people's boundaries to the point of protecting them. If you respect someone, you do not intrude. At the same time, if you respect someone, you do not withhold yourself or distance yourself from them. I have heard many people claim that they were simply distancing themselves from something they did not want to deal with. When we respect someone, we accept that they have things to teach us.[17]

While it may be worth tipping our hats at Isaac's insistence that we not withhold ourselves, we must look upon this idea of *respecting* boundaries with suspicion because boundaries are the very thing that people, wittingly or unwittingly, use to keep *the other* at-bay. This is why, aside from an increase in objective knowledge about a tradition, many interreligious participants leave exactly as they came. By entering into a dialogue, one should be accepting an invitation to encounter, engage, transform and to be transformed in ways beyond anticipation. But here, it seems, this invitation, all in the name of *respecting the other,* is rejected so that neither party is disrupted or harassed by the other's hyper-presence. As a result, dialogue becomes an impotent and sterile civic gesture similar to what Zizek describes: "What we have here is symbolic exchange at its purest: a gesture made to be rejected. The magic of symbolic exchange is that, although at the end we are where we were at the beginning, there is a distinct gain for both parties in their pact of solidarity."[18]

---

[16] Ibid., pp. 216-217.
[17] Isaacs 1990, pp. 114-115.
[18] Zizek 2008, p. 162.

What is gained from this symbolic gesture of dialogue is the feeling of unity and a greater sense of understanding. In reality what has likely occurred is that participants have become a bit more tolerant, less hateful and less fearful of one another. He further highlights the features of this brand of respect and its perverted call to responsibility and duty:

> Today's liberal tolerance towards others, the respect of otherness and openness towards it, is counterpointed by an obsessive fear of harassment. In short, the Other is just fine, but only insofar as his presence is not intrusive, insofar as this Other is not really other.... My duty to be tolerant towards the Other effectively means that I should not get too close to him, intrude on his space. In other words, I should respect his *intolerance* of my over-proximity. What increasingly emerges as the central human right in late-capitalist society is *the right not to be harassed*, which is a right to remain at a safe distance from others.[19]

This is what interreligious dialogues has often become in practice, an empty social gesture, devoid of the opportunity for authentic, deep contact, change and/or conversion. What is needed is an approach that truly *respects* and honors the true natures of both interreligious dialogue and *the other*. This approach would have to be able to facilitate the confrontational aspects of interreligious dialogue, while also allowing *the other* to be authentic, free and dangerous. It seems almost apparent that interreligious dialogue needs to incorporate what would be analogous to a "martial arts philosophy and disposition" in its approach to authentic interreligious dialogue.

Respecting and Receiving the Other - the Martial Arts Way

What would it mean to rethink respect in the context of Interreligious dialogue? What would it mean to truly respect *the other*? The word comes from the Latin *respecere*, which means "to look again." Its most ancient roots mean "to observe." Essentially, it means to look or observe again. Inherently there is a call for a second look. Why isn't the initial look sufficient or whole? This can be taken as an invitation to venture beyond first impressions; where once we saw one aspect of a person, we look again and realize how much of them we had missed. This second look can let us take in more fully the fact that here, before me, is a living, breathing, mysterious being.[20] Respect calls for a deeper look, a full accounting, a holistic recognition of the other without predetermined calculations or outcomes. Respect could also be an acknowledgement that *the other* is an independent "I", over and beyond our it-thou categorizations, so while we look and observe the other, they too are looking and observing. Perhaps this is the source of the second look.

---

[19] Ibid., p. 39.

[20] Isaacs 1990, p. 110-111.

True respect may be the recognition that *the other* is a living mirror who holds our image from a secret place, a place beyond our apprehension. *The other* looks back and observes from a place inaccessible to us and held in secret. This is the basis for receiving *the other* fully, in all of his/her mystery. In its most basic conceptualizations, the idea of respect within interreligious dialogue would have to reflect what Isaacs calls *extraordinary respect*:

> Treating the people around us with extraordinary respect means seeing them from the potential that they carry within them... Treat the person next to you as a teacher. What is it that they have to teach you that you do not now know? Listening to them in this way, you discover things that might surprise you. This does not mean being blind to gaps in what they might say and what they might do, nor does it mean being overly slavish in pointing out their faults. Respect is, in this sense, looking for what is highest and best in a person and treating them as a mystery that you can never fully comprehend. They are a part of the whole, and in a very particular sense, a part of us.[21]

Respect would also have to include the room to allow the other to show up fully as themselves and engaging them as worthy contenders, partners, opponents, allies, enemies, friends, or lovers, but never in a condescending manner that smacks of unfettered ideological supremacy. Zizek makes this point as it relates to the Islamic other discussed earlier:

> Respect for others' beliefs as the highest value can mean only one of two things: either we treat the other in a patronising way and avoid hurting him in order not to ruin his illusions, or we adopt the relativist stance of multiple "regimes of truth," disqualifying as violent imposition any clear insistence on truth. What, however, about submitting Islam-together with all other religions—to a respectful, but for that reason no less ruthless, critical analysis? This, and only this, is the way to show true respect for Muslims: to treat them as serious adults responsible for their beliefs.[22]

In order to achieve this there needs to be an approach that allows *the other* to show up beyond our labels, prejudices, etc. There needs to be an opportunity to face one another and be authentically *respectful*. Most importantly there needs to be an approach that allows dialogue partners to face the one immutable fact of interreligious dialogue: there is real risk and danger involved, and in the face of this, one is called to resist the impulse to evade or run. It is for these reasons that I suggest that interreligious dialogue needs to take on a new paradigmatic approach with a new corresponding metaphor. I would suggest that interreligious dialogue adopt what can be called a *martial arts approach* that would seek to eradicate "impulses caused by

---

[21] Ibid., pp. 116-117.
[22] Slavoj Zizek 2008, p. 139.

the instinct of self-preservation"[23]and remain open to all that dialogue presents. This would add another dimension to our understanding of respect:

> True respect is the essence of the Art of Karate. Respect is the right relationship between teacher and student and between student and student. Respect comes from real affection and not from meaningless tradition. It is not following some code of ethics set down by another. Respect then becomes repetition, blind allegiance. Respect is alive, active. It is not the dead weight of the past, no matter how glorified the past may seem to be.[24]

Instead of mismanaging or repressing our propensity for violence, a *martial arts approach* or model for dialogue would, quite intentionally, force us to deal appropriately with our natural inclinations. A *martial art approach* would "bring our attention to violence," noting that in our everyday lives we have a tendency to "deny our violence or try to act nonviolently by suppressing it in favor of some glorified ideal"; but it is important that interreligious dialogue becomes an arena wherein we "allow ourselves the opportunity to come in direct contact with all of who we are," which includes our predisposition for violence.[25] This should not be taken as a call for indiscriminate, arbitrary, uncontrolled violence. Quite to the contrary, it is being suggested that, not only are dialogue partners invited to put everything on the mat (or the *dojo*), but that there are limits and conditions that establish trust and make authentic confrontation and engagement possible. This is crucial, even though it appears contradictory on the surface. Webster-Doyle explains this approach further:

> It is important to come into direct contact with our violence, to not cover it up with idealistic behavior. The Art of Karate allows us to opportunity to do just this by creating an environment of trust. The word trust here means that nothing is hidden. Also, one needs a controlled environment, with precise limits set on one's behavior in their practice. This controlled environment of trust allows us to act without unnecessary internal restraints, and without giving license to our violence. There is a "middle way," in which we don't move between the polar extremes of repression and expression. In this non-movement there is intelligence, which is understanding the violence and going beyond it.[26]

There seems to be a vigil over death/conversion within interreligious dialogue and this has led us to the death of the very thing that is trying to be preserved. The primary benefit of adopting a *martial arts approach* or disposition in interreligious dialogues is that martial arts build the capacity of people to face death/conversion and to receive the unexpected. The late Bruce Lee commands us, in the face of danger or an opponent, "Do not run away; let go. Do not seek, for it will come when you

[23] Lee 1988, p. 13.
[24] Webster-Doyle 1989, p. 30.
[25] Webster-Doyle 1989, p. 25.
[26] Ibid.

least expected."[27] The key within interreligious dialogue and the martial arts is to be open, hospitable and ready for the unexpected and the incalculable. As previously discussed the drive to convert or radically transform one another is a reality within interreligious dialogue. Instead of trying to avoid this fact, one should seek to accommodate and address it. Paul Knitter identifies this aim within interreligious dialogue:

> And because we speak out of our different religious experiences and convictions, we will seek not only to explain but to *persuade*. If genuinely experienced, religious truth, like all truth, can never be only "for me". . . A quality of "universal relevance" is ingredient to every encounter with or revelation of the Ultimate; what one has seen, felt, been transformed by—can also affect others. All interreligious dialogue, therefore, is animated by a certain missionary élan. We want our partners to see what we have seen; we want their lives to be touched and transformed as ours has been. Yes, let me use the offensive word: we want to *convert* our partners. [28]

Conclusion: The Bow

Instead of being obsessed with creating safe, comfortable meetings of people from different religions and calling them interreligious dialogues, the *martial arts approach* would facilitate tough, deep encounters that would hardly leave the participants unchanged. More than simply tolerating or managing the discomfort of *the other's* proximity, the *martial arts approach* seeks *more*—actually to the point of inviting painful, agonizing contact with *the other*. All of this should have the focused aim of facilitating growth in knowledge and opening up the way for transformation, even unto death or conversion. This is the end to which one becomes committed. The *martial arts approach* "teaches us not to look backward once the course is decided upon. It treats life and death indifferently."[29] This is crucial, especially when the other is expected to maintain all of his/her secrecy and *jouissance*. This approach allows us to recognize that a real face-off with the authentic *interreligious other* and the prospect of death (i.e., deep conversion) dignifies both of us and calls us to a new sense of responsibility:

> Death is very much that which nobody else can undergo or confront in my place. My irreplaceability is therefore conferred, delivered, "given," one can say, by death. It is the same gift, the same source, one could say the same goodness and the same law. It is from the site of death as the place of my irreplaceability, that is, of my singularity, that I feel called to responsibility.[30]

---

[27] Lee 1988, p. 9.

[28] Swidler, *et al.* 1990, p. 22-23.

[29] Ibid.

[30] Derrida 1995, p. 41.

This is the call that challenges and dignifies one as an individual, a challenge that one might have otherwise shirked. What emerges is the sort of dialogue that Panikkar describes as *dialogical dialogue.*[31] It is this sort that "takes you my partner as seriously as myself and by this very fact wakes me up from the slumber of solipsistic speculations, or the dreaming fantasies of a docile partner. We encounter the hard reality of an opposition, another will, another source of opinions, perspectives."[32] This involves the courage to face the other and seeing them as they are. This same raw, respectful view of the other is elaborated by Panikkar:

> The most immediate assumption of the dialogical dialogue is that the other is not just an other (alius) and much less an object of my knowledge (aliud), but another self (alter) who is a source of self-understanding, and also of understanding, not necessarily reducible to my own.[33] The dialectical dialogue is a dialogue about objects, interestingly enough, the English language calls 'subject matters'. The dialogical dialogue, on the other hand, is a dialogue among subjects aiming at being a dialogue about subjects. They want to dialogue not about something, but about themselves: they dialogue themselves.... To dialogue about opinions, doctrines, views, the dialectical dialogue is indispensable. In the dialogical dialogue the partner is not an object or a subject merely putting forth some objective thoughts to be discussed, but a you, a real you and not an it. I must deal with you and not merely with your thought, and of course, vice versa, You yourself are a source of understanding.[34]

What emerges is the kind of dialogue that is authentic and true to its nature and the natures of the interreligious other(s). One central point is that the differences that each brings to the dialogue arena become a source of invitation. As a matter of fact "the very strangeness and difference becomes for us an unthought-of *possibility*. What was foreign, perhaps threatening, now becomes an invitation. The "other" in its otherness becomes a *disclosure* of new possibility, new truth. The other becomes analogical: both dissimilar and similar at the same time."[35] Hopefully, this new construction of respect will allow many new voices and faces to appear at the interreligious table and/or arena. It is my hope that the *martial arts approach* to interreligious dialogue will bring together new dialogue partners and create new bold conversations. It is certainly not in our best interest to repeat the same scripted dialogues.

---

[31] Panikkar 1999, pp. 36-37.
[32] Ibid.
[33] Ibid., pp. 33-34.
[34] Ibid., p. 30.
[35] Swidler, *et al.* 1990, p. 25.

Reference list

Cobb, J.B., Helwig, M., Knitter, P., & Swidler, L. "*Death or Dialogue?* Philadelphia: Trinity Press, 1990. Print.

Derrida, Jacques. *The Gift of Death*. Trans. D. Willis. Chicago: The University of Chicago Press, 1995. Print.

Isaacs, William. *Dialogue and the Art of Thinking Together: A Pioneering Approach to Communicating in Business and in Life*. New York: Currency, 1999. Print.

Lee, Bruce. *Tao of Jeet Kune Do*. Santa Clarita, California: OHara Publications, 1975. Print.

Miller-Keane & O'Toole, Marie *T. Encyclopedia and Dictionary of Medicine, Nursing, and Allied* Health. 7th Ed. Philadelphia, PA: Saunders, 2003. Print.

Panikkar, Raimon. *Intra-Religious Dialogue*. New York: Paulist Press, 1999. Print.

Webster-Doyle, Terrence. *Karate: The Art of the Empty Self.* Middlebury, Vermont: Atrium Society Publications, 1989. Print.

Zizek, Slavoj. *Violence: Six Sideways Reflections.* New York: Picador, 2008. Print.

Eva Marsal
(Germany)

"Who Deserves Respect?" German Children Philosophize about the Conditions for Giving Respect

> "Always having the respect of your fellow men is much more valuable than sometimes having their admiration"[1]

Rousseau philosophized about the importance of *respect.* His recognition that respect plays a fundamental role in human life is still seen as valid today. Etymologically, the concept *respect* derives from Latin *respectus* which can be translated as "looking back," "care," "regard," "consideration."

> The ubiquity and significance of respect and self-respect in everyday life largely explains why philosophers, particularly in moral and political philosophy, have been interested in these two concepts. … Respect for persons is a central concept in many theories of ethical"[2] and political philosophy. One of the main questions about respect that philosophers have addressed in this context is: What category of thing is it? "Philosophers have variously identified it as a mode of behavior, a form of treatment, a kind of valuing, a type of attention, a motive, an attitude, a feeling, a tribute, a principle, a duty, an entitlement, an epistemic and moral virtue.[3]

In this paper I would first like to discuss the categorical classification of the philosophical concept "respect," and then to demonstrate how children work through problems associated with the conceptual field of "respect" in a philosophical community of inquiry.

The philosophical background: The balancing act between one-dimensionality and multi-dimensionality in the concept "respect."

From among the philosophical categories discussed in relation to the construct "respect," I would like to focus on the categories of "epistemic and moral virtue," on

---

[1] See: Rousseau 1712, p. 1.
[2] See: Dillon 2010, p. 2f.
[3] See: Dillon 2010, p. 3.

the one hand, and on the other, "a feeling," to show that the philosophical concept "respect" as "respect for someone or something" alters its requirement profile as the proximity to its object changes. That is, the closer we "zoom in" on the referent, the more concrete the web of conditions becomes which induces us to say "We respect X."

At the same time, greater proximity to a referent alters the inner state of mind: intellectual "epistemic and moral virtue," or virtue as a theoretical position in relation to a broad category such as "human," "person," or "community of moral equals" (also including animals insofar as they fulfill the requirements of personhood) is progressively altered by narrowing the category and singling out a "particular" class or even a single subject or object; it becomes a moral feeling governed by approval or disapproval.

Thus, from a distanced perspective, the condition of belonging to a defined category is the sole requirement for bringing the entire treatment associated with "respect" into play. And so if I acknowledge my counterpart's "humanity," this one condition is sufficient cause for me to grant this referent my respect, that is, to affirm a claim to human rights.

If the defined category refers to "personhood," however, granting or even claiming respect is more difficult, since the construct "person" is an open referent. That is to say, different schools of philosophy assign the designation "person" to differing and distinct entities. But insofar as the respective ascription of "person" is defined as (a) every human being,[4] or (b) only humans capable of consciousness,[5] or (c) all beings within the *circle of moral equals* or at least capable of acting analogously to "*moral agents,*"[6] then here, too, belonging to this category is the only requirement: "personhood" is sufficient to require respect. These ascriptions are highly significant not only in the realm of morality, but also in law and politics, for whoever is respected as "human" or as "a person" has access to a broad spectrum of rights. The right to life counts here as first among these, and not only in the sense of "bios," but also of "eudaimonia," for which the animal ethicists are advocates.[7]

Simultaneously, though, the adult person also has duties that go far beyond the juridical and institutional spectrum. Carrying out these duties, which involve the entire personality structure, cultural adaptation, lifestyle, etc., leads to a categorical change. The human being becomes a concrete person who, in becoming a "you," requires a response from the "I," which, according to David Hume or Adam Smith, evokes moral feelings. In this sense, Smith takes up Hume's empiricist moral philosophy and uses it in his first major work "The Theory of Moral Sentiments" (1759) to underpin the ethical concepts "approbation and disapprobation," "merit and demerit," "justice and benevolence," "duty," "conscience," and so on, which were developed from an analysis of human feelings.

[4] Baumgartner, Honnefelder, Wickler, and Wildfeuer 1997.

[5] Dennett 1997.

[6] Birnbacher 2001; Rollin 1994.

[7] Singer 1944, 2011; Regan 1982.

From this, Smith posits a theory of objective value judgment which influenced Kant. Today Kant's moral philosophy is still the most influential in discussions of respect for persons and their autonomy.

> Central to Kant's ethical theory is the claim that all persons are owed respect just because they are persons, that is, free rational beings. To be a person is to have a status and worth that is unlike that of any other kind of being: it is to be an end in itself with dignity. And the only response that is appropriate to such a being is respect. Respect (that is, moral recognition respect) is the acknowledgment in attitude and conduct of the dignity of persons as ends in themselves. Respect for such beings is not only appropriate but also morally and unconditionally required: the status and worth of persons is such that they must always be respected. Because we are all too often inclined not to respect persons, not to value them as they ought to be valued, one formulation of the Categorical Imperative, which is the supreme principle of morality, commands that our actions express due respect for the worth of persons: 'Act in such a way that you treat humanity, whether in your own person or the person of any other, never simply as a means but always at the same time as an end'.[8] Our fundamental moral obligation, then, is to respect persons; morally right actions are thus those that express respect for persons as ends in themselves, while morally wrong actions are those that express disrespect or contempt for persons by not valuing them as ends in themselves.[9] In addition to this general commandment, Kant argues that there are also more specific duties of respect for other persons and self-respect. But now, we must address the question: What is it to be an end in itself and to possess dignity?[10]

Men and women carry out the duties implied by their humanity or personhood in various ways, thereby evoking in the spectator various evaluative judgments accompanied by corresponding feelings covering the entire spectrum from horror, disgust, rejection, and disapproval all the way to admiration. The subjective feeling that arises leads to the formulation: "I don't respect X because...," or "I respect X because...;" in other words, we specify the reasons that cause us to feel respect. The sole condition that "the other is a human being, a person" seems insufficient to call forth deep emotional acceptance. Respect is now tied to a many-faceted conditional web of qualities.

Because of these feelings, the previous premise that respect is owed to every human being and every person as such is mitigated by questions such as: Must persons *always* be respected? Can one respect everyone? Who merits respect? Which actions merit respect? Can one earn respect? Can one buy respect? Must you respect yourself in order to be respected by others? Is there a false respect? These questions

---

[8] Kant, *Grundlegung zur Metaphysik der Sitten* (*Groundwork of the Metaphysics of Morals* 1785/1996, 4: 429).

[9] Wood 1999.

[10] Dillon 2010, p. 13f.

demonstrate that, depending on the context and category to which the referent belongs, "respect" has different connotations. The philosophical challenge is to bring this field of connotations into a logically and also emotionally satisfactory equilibrium.

Multi-dimensional respect is philosophically divided into different forms: the most important distinction here is the one suggested by Darwall[11] between "recognition respect" and "appraisal respect." With his construct "recognition respect," Darwall wants to indicate that one's own actions and behavior can only be guided properly if the factual situation has been clarified by comprehensive consideration of the object: that is, if the object's value has been realistically understood. But in addition to assessing value, one must clarify one's interest in the object or relevant part of the object by weighing one's own practical intentions.[12]

A great many things can be objects of *recognition respect* such as, for example, laws, dangerous objects or situations, the feelings of others, social institutions, nature, individual identities in various contexts, or persons as such. From this "recognition respect" Darwall separates off "appraisal respect," which presents an attitude of positive valuation toward a person and honors that person's accomplishments. Here evaluation is always based on qualitative standards.

Since it is a matter of the degree to which the object fulfills expectations, *appraisal respect* is assigned by degrees. Thus, we can appreciate a person more or less according to the perspective adopted. Hudson's "evaluative respect" represents a similar category. In our context the three further kinds of respect elaborated by Hudson[13] are likewise significant: "obstacle respect," "directive respect," and "institutional respect."[14]

Obstacle respect can be described using the example of a mountain climber confronting the elements. One regards the object as something that could hinder the attainment of one's goals. This kind of respect calls for compensatory measures, developing counter-strategies, or taking special care.[15]

With *directive respect*, on the other hand, the objects of respect count as directives: objects such as requirements, rules, laws, etc. are used as guides for action. Someone respects a directive when the practiced behavior deliberately conforms to it.[16]

A courtroom full of people rising to show respect for the judge can serve as an example for the fourth form, *institutional respect*. The objects of *institutional respect*, then, are social institutions, procedures, persons or things that represent institutions. Institutional respect is demonstrated by behaviors holding to certain rules that define or decree which behaviors are respectful.[17] "To Hudson's four-fold classi-

[11] Darwell 1977 /2004.
[12] See Dillon 2010, p. 8.
[13] Hudson 1980.
[14] See Dillon 2010, p. 8.
[15] Ibid.
[16] See Dillon 2010, p. 7.
[17] Ibid.

fication, Dillon adds a fifth form, *care respect*, which is exemplified in an environmentalist's deep respect for nature."[18]

By contrast, the element of danger dominates in Feinberg's "reverential respect." According to Feinberg,[19] *respect* expresses an uneasy and vigilant attitude that includes the element "fear." Thus, according to Feinberg, the objects of respect are dangerous things or also things having power over the subject.[20] Even though children whose statements reflect a multi-dimensional respect concept cannot verbalize these forms of respect on a meta-level, they express them on a phenomenal level.

Students at the University for Children in Bretten (Germany) reflect on the concept "respect."

Academic philosophers are not the only ones called upon to consider the philosophical balancing act between one-dimensionality and multi-dimensionality in the concept "respect"; anyone with the gift of reason is, as well, so I would now like to present and comment on a philosophical conversation, carried out in a community of inquiry, with children who considered these questions at the University for Children in Bretten, Germany. Nine boys (B) and four girls (G) aged 6-14 participated in the community of inquiry. The boys were: Finn (6), Loris (7), Philipp (8), Robin (9), Paul (9), Andre (9), Philipp (10), Marvin (11), Nikolas (14); the girls were: Laura (8), Laura 2 (Robins Sister) (9), Alisia (9), Luisa (11). For identification of the transcribed and numbered dialogue the following abbreviations were used: B=Boy G=Girl T=Teacher.

The definition and elements of respect

First the children listened to three stories dealing in different ways with the theme of respect and then considered what they themselves think of as respect.

Marvin distinguishes first between the forms of respectful vs. disrespectful behavior based on the symmetrical vs. asymmetrical relationships between the subjects.

B9 Marvin (11): So there are actually four kinds of respect. Um, the respect you see in this picture here, of children for grownups and also grandmothers and also parents, and once, like from child to child, no respect, then between grown-ups, and from grown-ups to children, with the teacher.

Marvin is the only child who distinguishes at all between different forms of respect, even though these differences are being presented on a very concrete de-

[18] Dillon 2010, p. 8.
[19] Feinberg 1975.
[20] See Dillon 2010, p. 7.

scriptive level. The children don't succeed in classifying by analysis different kinds of respect, such as for example "directive respect" or "institutional respect." But in spite of this their clarifying examples show that they do indeed have the idea that there is an *appraisal respect*[21] that is clearly distinct from other kinds of respect, such as *obstacle respect,*[22] even if they are unable to name these forms. It quickly became clear to them that "respect" is not only an attitude, a feeling, an epistemic and moral virtue, but also an attitude giving rise to a mode of behavior, a form of treatment.

For this reason the children offer operational definitions. An important category here is "helping." Respect is shown by acknowledging the other in his or her circumstances and responding appropriately: that is, acting in the sense of Darwall's "recognition respect" by monitoring the appropriateness of one's own behavior through understanding the situation realistically. Though the children cannot yet formulate this meta-level it is implicitly contained in their statements.

B54 Marvin (11):	So respect is probably when you honor others and when you don't ignore them, as Nikolas said, but when you help them get up, so to speak.
G55 Laura (8):	For example, respect is when my little sister can't reach a cup and I help her. That's respect.
B57 Philipp (10):	You can show respect by helping when someone needs help.
B59 Finn (6):	Or when you help an old woman cross the street.

Philipp also substantiates his operational definition with an example from the adult world; he formulates a definition that is even more concrete by creating a *care-scenario*:

B84 Philipp (10):	It's also respect when you help, like for example, now when we are in Libya: there was hardly anything to eat there, and then they showed respect, like sending food and other things people could use.

Just helping through surrogates is not decisive for Philipp; it is important to him to find his own opportunities to help:

B174 Philipp (10):	That you give people something – we are also members of "Plan": we donate for children in Africa – like we pay a little money every month and then we can also send things, like pencils and so on, together with other people....

For Philipp, just as for many other children, "helping" is an important category of his operational definitions. Respect is shown by acknowledging the other in his

[21] Darwell 1977.
[22] Hudson 1980.

or her situation and responding in an appropriate way. Respect is defined here, then, in the sense of Darwall's "recognition respect." The subject adjusts behavior to a realistic understanding of the situation.

Nikolas, just like Cicero and Kant, begins with human dignity, which he relates to the concept of honor, as a basis for respecting a person:

B52 Nikolas (14): Well, the German Basic Law also says that "a person's honor is inviolable" and no one should violate it, no one should put people down or talk down to them, but should regard them as equals, so to speak. It doesn't matter if you are the head of a big company, for example. From a human standpoint the employees are the boss's equals.

According to Nikolas's operational definition, showing respect, which always occurs in a relational structure (*a responsive relation)*, is defined by the fact that one person sees the other "from a human standpoint" "as an equal," and thus encounters the other on the same plane. Here the emphasis is placed on the "human." The subject (*the respecter*) respects the object, the respected, solely on the basis of the object's humanity. In other more specific situations, on the other hand, no symmetrical attitude needs to be presumed. Thus in a work context subject and object could be employer and employee. In his argumentation, Nikolas does not limit himself to the abstract plane; with his formulations to not "put people down, or talk down to others" he arrives very quickly at a level of concrete action that is emotionally laden. The example chosen by the 14-year-old comes from the adult world and thus, just as with the quotation from the German Basic Law, reinforces the serious and significant nature of the phenomenon under discussion.

As the second category of the operational definition Philipp adopts the "equal value" of persons, which Nikolas had brought into play, and thereby gives his own answer to the question "What is respect?"

B61 Philipp (10): That's why in other countries they also have school uniforms, so you don't see who is not so rich or who is very rich, so that everyone is dressed the same and no one can see, ok, that one is not rich or that one is very rich, because they all are wearing the same clothes.

For the children, then, "respect" means that everyone is treated with equal open-mindedness and everyone has the same chances, for example in education. By choosing school uniforms as an example of "equal valuation," Philipp shows his understanding that people are not "equal," but rather that their factual inequality should be obscured to allow for an equality in the moment that could later lead to a more just alignment of relative status.

This discourse led to the question: "Can one feel respect?" That is, can one feel if one is respected or not? Then is respect something, whose operational definition includes the aspect that it is something one can feel? The answers show that the children think being respected creates a good feeling.

B63 Marvin (11): Well yes, probably if you are noticed by others or if you get help from them, for example, and if you don't get bullied or pestered then you probably can feel it.

B64 Finn (6): Or if someone says "thanks" once in awhile, then you are happy, and if someone says "no" then you aren't so happy.

B69 Nikolas (14): Well I also think that you can feel both respect and disrespect, especially inside. If someone praises you – praise is also part of respect, if someone has done something well, praising that person for something, then you do feel good. But if you are treated disrespectfully, like here, for example, I'm thinking of the opponents, so if that was not on purpose, as you see in the photo, and they are then given that gesture for the bad word I'm not going to say now, they won't feel so great.

Respectful interactions convey positive judgments. That is, the children feel an "appraisal respect" that strengthens them in their sense of self-worth and emotionally stabilizes them ("makes them happy"). Thus they feel the effects of respect on their own well-being, and so for them their definition of respect includes the idea that respect is something that creates a feeling, that one can feel.

In this context they themselves are the "objects" of respect, and they command respect by their actions or by the way they are. In this sense this category corresponds to Darwall's "appraisal respect," which is based on a positive attitude toward a person or that person's accomplishments, derived from the characteristics and merits of the person's character. Here the judgment is always based on qualitative standards. Since these standards are common cultural property, the children are familiar with them. They judge themselves by these standards, and likewise judge the feedback or reactions of others. Thus they can assess whether they are appreciated and evaluated correctly, which calls forth positive feelings, or whether they are dismissed, which leads to negative feelings.

Respect for object areas other than the human, such as "respect for an earthquake," or "respect for the spread of an epidemic," for example, was not thematized by the children.

The question "Who deserves respect?" which is interesting for our approach to the problem, was already implicitly answered in Nikolas's definition of the concept, in the sense that the only decisive factor was being human. In the following, he once again made his statement more precise:

B121 Nikolas (14): As I already said, a respectful basic attitude toward everyone.

Paul also subscribes to this thesis:

B181 Paul (9): You should really respect everyone, even people you don't like the way you like your best friend.

Philipp's example also supports the assertion that everyone should be respected. He tries to express this opinion by converging the extremes of the widest arc he can imagine, namely, by showing simultaneous respect for his best friend and his enemy, though both are engaged in conflict.

B95 Philipp (10): You shouldn't always, I tell my best friend, if for example my friend is having a fight with my enemy, you shouldn't join in right away against your enemy, just for your friend. You should respect them both, so that you also help your enemy and not just your friend. Not always just the ones you like, also sometimes your enemies.

Loris takes up this thought again later in the discussion:

B172 Loris (7): That you shouldn't just help your friends, but your enemies, too.

These statements reveal that the children also rapidly transport the one-dimensional "each person / everyone" from the abstract to the emotional level, especially Paul and Philipp, who refers to his best friend as a background referent.

The other children, by contrast, operate more on the multi-dimensional level; they presume that people to whom respect is owed must also fulfill other conditions, such as, for example, ethical behavior or high achievement. In this case, however, the basis of the feeling is not symmetry, but rather asymmetry. This asymmetry can express itself in the upward gaze, either in the form of high regard:

G105 Alisia (9): Toward…older people and toward teachers or children.
G106 Laura (8): I respect my family, I respect my best friend, I respect my teacher, I respect everyone who also treats me well.
G109 Laura 2 (9): Or for example soon when we have our school presentation and the mayor comes, then I'll feel a whole lot of respect.
B121 Nikolas (14): Well I actually have a respectful attitude toward everyone in principle. And then a special respect for people who have achieved something.

Or in the form of cautious deference toward persons who might represent a threat:

B112 Marvin (11): You show respect toward other kids, say, like when you are walking down the street at night and run into a gang of teenagers who are getting drunk or something like that. Then you show respect and cross to the other side of the street or something.

T113 Teacher:	Would you say then that respect also has something to do with being afraid, or is it the same as fear, since you said you would go away then?
B114 Marvin (11):	Well, probably, so to speak, because I'm not wrong about them, you probably would be a little afraid.
B115 Nikolas (14):	Well now I think, too, that it has a little to do with fear. As we heard in the third story, the one girl is for sure not afraid of her friend because she can take care the housework alone; I think she is afraid she couldn't do the same thing herself.

Marvin's statement fits Darwall's category *recognition respect* well, since Marvin recognizes the danger emanating from the object. But it also fits well with Hudson's category *obstacle respect*, whereby one sees the object as something that could stand in the way of reaching one's goals. This kind of respect calls for taking compensatory measures, developing counter-strategies, or being especially careful. Accordingly, in his *obstacle respect* for the band of drunken teen-agers standing in his way, Marvin comes up with a possible strategy to master the situation.

Since Marvin reflects on respect in connection with the danger factor, he comes close to Feinberg's conception that *respect* expresses an uneasy and vigilant attitude that contains the element "fear." Thus according to Feinberg the objects of respect are dangerous things or things having power over the subject.

For Nikolas, too, "respect" is associated with "fear," but another form of fear than Feinberg or Marvin refer to. For Nikolas, it is about fear of inadequacy. That is, this fear is related to achievement and corresponds to the fear of failure, a significant variable in motivational research. Its effect is comparable to the fear of dangerous things, since this fear also has power over the subject and measurably lowers self-confidence and self-respect.

On the other hand, the attitude of the girls Alisia, Laura, and Laura 2 toward older people, teachers, children, their families or their best friends can be understood as *directive respect*, for which Laura posits the rule: "I respect everyone who treats me well, too." Or Nikolas: "I make it a point to be respectful of everyone and especially to respect people who are successful."

Respect for teachers or for the mayor, as mentioned by Laura 2, can also be interpreted as *institutional respect*. Before the children examine the logical contradiction underlying this use of language, they first look more intensively into the phenomenon "respect." Nikolas points out that expressions of respect are culturally conditioned, so that ignorance can cause something that was meant as a sign of respect to be understood by its object as disrespectful.

B15 Nikolas (14):	I just think that in other cultures respect looks different. For example, in Japan, it's the custom to greet people by bowing, and that can lead to misunderstandings. If I go to Japan and haven't informed myself and greet people as we do here with a handshake, then it seems to them that we aren't showing re-

spect, even though from our point of view we haven't done anything wrong.

This viewpoint brings up the question, "How do we actually express respect?" "Which speech acts and gestures are used or not used?" Here the children begin with their own life praxis:

B20 Marvin (11): Well, by … students not just getting up and running around the classroom.

B31 Finn (6): If you don't curse at people or do this (demonstrates giving the finger) you are also somehow … respectful.

G33 Laura (8): Sometimes, in my school, they give the finger and I always say stop it, that is not respectful toward others.

B70 Marvin (11): If you respect someone, it shows in the way you speak to them; we saw it before, for example, in how you respected Frau Keller and called her Frau Director Keller. …

G137 Laura (8): If....I have respect, then for example I....sometimes the woman in the butcher shop gives me some sausage and then I have to say "thanks a lot" and I'm sure it makes her feel good, and I'm happy about it if she's happy.

B97 André (9): Well sometimes it also happens that the people who actually should be very respectful, teachers, they also can sometimes disrespect you. For example my math teacher always says to me "Keep your trap shut," and things like that.

B139 Paul (9): If someone insults me I wouldn't respect him as much as I would respect someone who was nice to me.

B144 Andrè (9): So also if someone does something by accident, if they say excuse me afterward, that's respectful. You show respect for the other person… for example, if you hit someone by accident, you show respect by saying excuse me, that you are sorry. So if someone gets punched by mistake I say excuse me, I'm sorry. That's respectful, too.

An action is only respectful when it represents an adequate response to the signals coming from the other person, as for example saying thank you for a gift.

The speech acts and gestures that are used are dependent on the context, and based on the exact perception of the situation in which the relationship between subject (*the respecter*) and object (*the one who is respected)* is embedded. Thus the activity of "running around the classroom" is not in itself disrespectful, but is only so if the object of respect is thereby disregarded in terms of his or her expectations and standards.

Especially with physical encounters, the motivation behind the action determines whether disrespect was shown. A disregard for the other person occurs only in cases of deliberate, intentional harm. The feeling accompanying basically respectful actions such as, for example, apologies, also determines whether respect is actually being shown for the other party. Thus an apology is only respectful if it is connected with the feeling, "I'm sorry I did x to you".

This attentiveness to the object is, according to Dillon, a central and salient element of respect:

> Respect is a responsive relation, and ordinary discourse about respect identifies several key elements of the response, including attention, deference, judgment, acknowledgment, valuing, and behavior. First, as suggested by its derivation from the Latin *respicere*, which means "to look back at" or "to look again," respect is a particular mode of apprehending the object: the person who respects something pays attention to it and perceives it differently from someone who does not, and responds to it in light of that perception. This perceptual element is common also to synonyms such as regard (from "to watch out for") and consideration ("examine (the stars) carefully"). The idea of paying heed or giving proper attention to the object which is central to respect often means trying to see the object clearly, as it really is in its own right, and not seeing it solely through the filter of one's own desires and fears or likes and dislikes. Thus, respecting something contrasts with being oblivious or indifferent to it, ignoring or quickly dismissing it, neglecting or disregarding it, or carelessly or intentionally misidentifying it.[23]

The meaning of respect

This intuitive, respectful approach to the other based on precise attention and observation is, in the children's view, not limited in its effects only to the relationship between the two thematized persons, but rather, like waves in a pond, has far-reaching significance.

G79 Luisa (11): So, respect is important because …if nobody respected anyone else there would be total chaos.

B90 Marvin (11): Probably people would…if people didn't respect others, first there would be conflict in the family, and if it went on from there, then probably with all the relatives, then the neighborhood or something, until at some point war would break out, or something like that.

B92 Philipp (10): People improve the world with respect, too, because then you show other people what is better, and then they learn it, too, and develop it further and further, then there's more and more, and you improve the world, too

The children argue that respectful relationships continue to proliferate until the entire world community is included, and thus they lead to improving the world

[23] Dillon 2010, p. 4.

Is it possible to buy respect?

Through a change in perspective looking to the world of commodification, where social and emotional entities also have exchange value, the children discover a novel way to access the essence of "respect." The teacher begins the discussion by asking whether respect can be bought:

T149 Teacher:	Do you think you can buy respect?
B150 Paul (9):	Not really.
T151 Teacher:	Not really. Can you get respect at Edeka, in a can?
G152 Luisa (11):	You can't buy respect with money.
T153 Teacher:	What if I bought a fabulous car, for example, and drove it really fast. Wouldn't you respect me then? If I could drive really fast?
B154 Nikolas (14):	Well, I think it is possible to buy respect (unfortunately) because, as you just said, with the fast car, respect through material things.
G155 Laura (8):	For example when I see someone who has such really nice and expensive things and then thinks "Wow, she looks good, I have to communicate with her," and then I feel that they do it on purpose because they want to be with a girl, with a really super girl. Then the person says "oh, what nice clothes you have. Where did you buy them? I want to get something like that." And I think that's strange, somehow. This or that person only wants to play with me or do something else because they see that I look that way.
T156 Teacher:	I think Laura is saying something very important here. Does buying something very special really earn respect?
G158 Luisa (11):	Well with something like that I could maybe get something like false respect. But you can't buy real genuine respect with material things or money.
B159 Nikolas (14):	Good. Same thing, slightly different formulation: you get respect by having things, sure, but you didn't earn it.
B160 Philipp (10):	So I think you can't buy respect in that sense. You can buy fancy things, and then you will probably get respect, but you can't say, here is 100 Euros I have right now, now I will get respect. That doesn't work. I can buy some material things or something like that and everyone will look at me and think "Wow, he looks great, he'll get my respect." But respect alone can't be bought.
T161 Teacher:	I just thought of something else that might buy you respect: when you donate a lot. That is also like buying something; I spend money and donate it for a good cause and maybe I get respect for it.
B162 Marvin (11):	Probably you can buy respect indirectly. For example, if you spend money to study and get a Ph. D. or something like that,

you actually earn respect for yourself indirectly by spending money for the doctor title, and then you earn respect from others with the title.

B164 Philipp (10): Well, first, you can't really buy respect, but what should you buy respect for, which bothers me because really everyone has respect

The children conclude that you can't buy respect directly, but indirectly you can, either by means of material things like cars or clothing, or by being able to finance a good education and achieve a high position, or by donating money.

Philipp objects that you can't buy genuine respect and also don't need to buy it because every person as a human being deserves respect. Philipp clearly represents the position of one-dimensionality and is outraged that other additional considerations are even under discussion.

Conclusion

Even though the children fundamentally agree that every human is worthy of respect, they contrast this basic attitude with the individual valuations that are intuitively adopted on the basis of the respective level of action. Luisa especially formulates the emotional problems that she has with showing respect to someone who treats her disrespectfully:

G124 Luisa (11): If someone treats me with complete disrespect I would find it very hard or it would be impossible to show respect for that person. What you do to me, I will do to you.

In the continuation of the dialogue Philipp presents an alternative to this a gument "whatever you do to me, I will do to you," wanting to experiment with the positive effects of showing respect.

B146 Philipp (10): So, as Luisa said before, you can treat other people the same way they treat you. But you can also try being nice to your enemies and then also showing them respect…it could be that some people who don't like each other all that much might become friends afterward, if each one treated the other with respect.

For most of the children the logical contradiction between the one-dimensionality and multi-dimensionality of the concept "respect" cannot be resolved. Like Marvin, they persist in the philosophical balancing act:

B125 Marvin (11): Yes, well, if you don't respect someone very much, say, you still actually respect him as a human.

T126 Teacher: So do you respect him more as a human or more for what he does?

B127 Marvin (11): You respect him as basic respect for a human, probably. Either you respect him a little more because of his actions or else less.

Thus the children differentiate between the category of "an epistemic and moral virtue," on the basis of which they feel fundamental respect for all humans, and the category of "a feeling" linked to "approval" or "disapproval" and determined by the actions of the referent object, the one who is to be respected. That means that here, too, the affective degree of respect felt or not felt is dependent on the relative proximity to the object and on the anticipated web of conditions of the subject, the respecter, which must be fulfilled in order to evoke the entity "respect."

Translated by Hope Hague

Reference List

Atwell, John E. "Kant's Notion of Respect for Persons." *Respect for Persons*. Vol. 31. Ed. O.H. Green.Tulane Studies in Philosophy. New Orleans: Tulane University Press, 1982. Print.

Bagnoli, Carla. "Respect and Membership in the Moral Community." *Ethical Theory and Moral Pratice* 100 (2007): 113–128. Print.

_____."Respect and Loving Attention." *Canadian Journal of Philosophy* 33 (2003): 483–516. Print.

Baumgartner, Hans Michael et al. „Menschenwürde und Menschenschutz: Philosophische Aspekte." *Beginn, Personalität und Würde des Menschen.* Ed. Baumgartner, Hans-Michael et al. Freiburg/München: Karl Alber, 1997. 183. Print.

Benditt, Theodore M. "Why Respect Matters." *Journal of Value Inquiry* 42 (2008): 487–496. Print.

Berger, Peter. "On the Obsolescence of the Concept of Honor." *Revisions: Changing Perspectives in Moral Philosophy*. Eds. Stanley Hauerwas and Alasdair MacIntyre. Notre Dame, (Indiana): University of Notre Dame Press, 1983. Print.

Birnbacher, Dieter. "Selbstbewusste Tiere und Bewusstseinsfähige Maschinen. Grenzgänge am Rande des Personbegriffs." *Person. Philosophiegeschichte - Theoretische Philosophie – Praktische Philosophie.* Ed. Dieter Sturma. Paderborn: Mentis, 2001. Print.

Broadie, Alexander and Elizabeth M. Pybus, "Kant's Concept of 'Respect.'" *Kant-Studien* 66 (1975): 58–64. Print.

Brody, Baruch A."Towards a Theory of Respect for Persons." *Respect for Persons*. Ed. O.H. Green. New Orleans: Tulane University Press, 1982. Print.

Buss, Sarah. "Respect for Persons." *Canadian Journal of Philosophy* 29 (1999): 517–550. Print.

Dennett, Daniel C. *Darwins' Dangerous Idea. Evolution and Meanings of Life*. London: Penguin Books, 1995. Print.

_____. "Intentionale Systeme." *Analytische Philosophie des Geistes*. Ed. Peter Bieri. Königstein/Ts.: Anton Hain, 1997.162-166. Print.

Dillon, Robin S. "Respect." *Stanford Encyplopedia of Philosophy* (2010). http://plato.stanford.edu/entries/respect/. Web. 2 Jan.2012.

_____. "Arrogance, Self-Respect, and Personhood." *Journal of Consciousness Studies* 14 (2007): 101–126. Print.

_____. "'What's a Woman Worth? What's Life Worth? Without Self-Respect?': On the Value of Evaluative Self-Respect." *Moral Psychology: Feminist Ethics and Social Theory*. Eds. DesAutels, Peggy and Margret Urban Walker. Lanham, MD: Rowman & Littlefield. 2004. Print.

_____. "Kant on Arrogance and Self-Respect." *Setting the Moral Compass: Essays by Women Philosophers*. Ed. John C.Calhoun. Oxford: Oxford University Press, 2003. Print.

_____. "Self-Forgiveness and Self-Respect." *Ethics* 112 (2001): 53–83. Print.

_____. "Self-Respect: Moral, Emotional, Political." *Ethics* 107 (1997): 226–249. Print.

_____, Ed. *Dignity, Character, and Self-Respect*. New York: Routledge, 1995. Print.

_____. "How To Lose Your Self-Respect." *American Philosophical Quarterly* 29 (1992b): 125-139. Print

_____."Toward a Feminist Conception of Self-Respect." *Hypatia* 7 (1992c): 52–69. Reprinted in Ed. Dillon, Robin S. *Dignity, Character, and Self-Respect*. New York: Routledge, 1995. Print.

Cranor, Carl F. "On Respecting Human Beings as Persons." *Journal of Value Inquiry* 17 (1983): 103–117. Print.

_____. "Limitations on Respect-for-Persons Theories." *Respect for Persons*. Vol. 31. Ed. O.H. Green. Tulane Studies in Philosophy. New Orleans: Tulane University Press, 1982. Print.

_____. "Kant's Respect-for-Persons Principle." *International Studies in Philosophy* (1980): 19–40. Print.

_____."Toward a Theory of Respect for Persons." *American Philosophical Quarterly* 12 (1975): 309–320. Print.

Cummiskey, David R. "Dignity, Contractualism, and Consequentialism." *Utilitas* 16 (2008):629–644. Print.

Darwall, Stephen . *The Second Person Standpoint: Morality, Respect, and Accountability*, Cambridge, MA: Harvard University Press, 2006. Print.

_____."Respect and the Second Person Standpoint. Presidential Address, Central Division of the American Philosophical Association." *Proceedings and Addresses of the American Philosophical Association* 78 (2004): 43–59. Print.

Downie, R.S. and Elisabeth Telfer. *Respect for Persons*. London: George Allen and Unwin, 1969. Print.

Feinberg, Joel. "Some Conjectures on the Concept of Respect." *Journal of Social Philosophy* 4 (1975): 1–3. Print.

_____."The Nature and Value of Rights," *Journal of Value Inquiry* 4 (1970): 243–260. Print.

Flury, Andreas. *Der moralische Status der Tiere. Henry Salt, Peter Singer und Tom Regan*. Freiburg/München: Karl Alber, 1999. Print.

Honneth, Axel. "Integrity and Disrespect: Principles of a Conception of Morality Based on the Theory of Recognition." *Political Theory* 20 (1992): 187–201. Print.

Hudson, Stephen D. "The Nature of Respect." *Social Theory and Practice* 6 (1980): 69–90. Print.

Hume, David, "On the Dignity of Human Nature." *Moral, Political and Literary*. Vol 1. Eds. Green, Thomas Hill and Thomas Hodge Grose. London: Longmans, Green and Co, 1875. Print.

Kant, Immanuel. "Grundlegung zur Metaphysik der Sitten." Trans. and Ed. Mary Gregor. Immanuel Kant Practical Philosophy. *New York: Cambridge University Press, 1996. Print.*

_____. "Kritik der praktischen Vernunft." Trans. and Ed. Mary Gregor. *Immanuel Kant Practical Philosophy*. New York: Cambridge University Press, 1996. Print.

Regan, Tom. *All That Dwell Therein. Animal Rights and Environmental Ethics*. Berkley: University of California Press, 1982. Print.

Rollin, Bernard E. "Der Aufstieg der Menschenaffen: Erweiterung der moralischen Gemeinschaft." *Menschenrechte für die großen Menschenaffen. Das Great Ape Project*. Eds. Cavalieri, Paola and Peter Singer. München: Goldmann, 1994. Print.

Singer, Peter. *Expanding Circle: Ethics, Evolution, and Moral Progress*. Princeton: Princeton University Press, 2011. Print.

_____. *Praktische Ethik*. Stuttgart: Reclam, 1994. Print.

Wood, Allen W. *Kant's Ethical Thought*. Cambridge: Cambridge University Press, 1999. Print.

_____. "Kantian Duties Regarding Nonrational Nature." *Proceedings of the Aristotelian Society* 72 (1998): 189–210. Print.

Authors

Jessica Davis, PhD Candidate for Philosophy and Education,
Teachers College, Columbia University, New York, NY, USA.
E-Mail: "Jessica Davis" <jjd2167@tc.columbia.edu>

Dr. Beth A. Dixon, Professor of Philosophy,
State University of New York College at Plattsburgh, Plattsburgh, NY, USA.
E-Mail: "Beth Dixon" <beth.dixon@plattsburgh.edu>

Dr. Susan T. Gardner, Professor of Philosophy,
Capilano University, Vancouver, B.C., Canada.
E-Mail: "Susan Gardner" <sgardner@capilanou.ca>

Dr. Lena Green, Professor of Educational Psychology,
University of the Western Cape, South Africa.
E-Mail: "Lena Green" <LGreen@mweb.co.za>

Dr. Wayne I. Henry, Professor of Philosophy,
University of the Fraser Valley, Abbotsford, B.C., Canada.
E-Mail: "Wayne I. Henry" <wayne.henry@ufv.ca>

Dr. David Kennedy, Professor of Philosophy,
Montclair State University, NJ, USA.
E-Mail: "David Kennedy" <kennedyd9@verizon.net>

Dr. Nadia Stoyanova Kennedy, Assistant Professor of Mathematics Education,
State University of New York at Stony Brook, NY, USA.
E-Mail: "Nadia S. Kennedy" <nadia@math.sunysb.edu>

Dr. Charles J. List, Professor of Philosophy,
State University of New York College at Plattsburgh, Plattsburgh, NY, USA.
E-Mail: "Charles J. List" <listcj@plattsburgh.edu>

Dr. Eva Marsal, Dipl. Psych., Professor of Philosophy (Theology, Psychology),
University of Education Karlsruhe, Germany.
E-Mail: "Eva Marsal" <marsal@ph-karlsruhe.de>

Dr. Richard (Mort) Morehouse, Professor Emeritus, Viterbo University,
Wisconsin, USA. Visiting Professor at Glyndwr University Wrexham, Wales, UK.
E-Mail: "Richard Morehouse" <remorehouse@viterbo.edu>

Eugene Muhammad, PhD Candidate at the Chicago Theological Seminary, Chicago, Illinois, USA.
E-mail: "Eugene Muhammad" <emuhammad119@yahoo.com>

Dr. Wendy C. Turgeon, Associate Professor of Philosophy, St. Joseph's College, Long Island, NY, USA.
E-Mail:"Wendy C. Turgeon" <wturgeon@sjcny.edu>

Dr. Barbara Weber, Professor, Education and Counselling Psychology, and Special Education. University of British Columbia, B. C., Canada.
E-Mail: "Barbara Weber" <dr.barbara.weber@googlemail.com>